THE COMPLETE GUIDE TO
ROCK
CLIMBING

PRACTICAL HANDBOOK

THE COMPLETE GUIDE TO
ROCK
CLIMBING

MALCOLM CREASEY
WITH NIGEL SHEPHERD, NICK BANKS,
NEIL GRESHAM AND RAY WOOD

LORENZ BOOKS

CONTENTS

INTRODUCTION   6–7

This edition published by Lorenz Books in 2001

© Anness Publishing Limited 1999, 2001

Lorenz Books is an imprint of
Anness Publishing Limited
Hermes House, 88–89 Blackfriars Road, London SE1 8HA

Published in the USA by Lorenz Books
Anness Publishing Inc.
27 West 20th Street, New York, NY 10011

www.lorenzbooks.com

This edition distributed in Canada by Raincoast Books
9050 Shaughnessy Street,Vancouver, British Columbia V6P 6E5

A CIP catalogue record for this book is available from
the British Library.

PUBLISHER Joanna Lorenz
SENIOR EDITORIAL MANAGER Judith Simons
CONSULTANT AND PROJECT EDITOR Neil Champion
US CONSULTANT Bob Durand
DESIGNER Lisa Tai
LOCATION PHOTOGRAPHER Ray Wood
STUDIO PHOTOGRAPHER Mark Duncalf
ILLUSTRATOR George Manley
PRODUCTION CONTROLLER Don Campaniello

Previously published as *The Complete Rock Climber*

Printed in China

10 9 8 7 6 5 4 3 2 1

The author and publisher wish to stress that they strongly
advise the use of a helmet in all climbing situations. However,
some of the photogrpahs in this book show people climbing
without one. Similarly, some photographs show instances of
people a long way above the ground without a rope and
harness. There are no laws or regulations governing the sport
(except at indoor walls and on instructional courses); climbing
and mountaineering are all about self-reliance and taking
responsibility for your own decisions and actions.

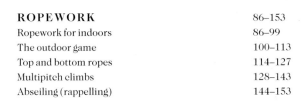

INTRODUCTION

Rock climbing today is a complex sport, complete with its own vocabulary and equipment that have come about over decades of experimentation. It has for many years been one of the fastest growing leisure activities, involving millions of people worldwide. From its relatively simple beginnings in Victorian Britain and Europe, it has evolved into a vast game with many facets, defying easy definition and categorization. Around it there has developed a mass of special terms describing particular aspects of the sport (bouldering, soloing, sport climbing, traditional climbing, competition climbing, and so on); pieces of equipment (harness, karabiner, quickdraws, belay devices, rock shoes); moves (dyno, Egyptian, layback, mantleshelf); and particular holds and how to use them (sloper, off-width, crimp, jam). Even the environment in which the sport takes place has changed and developed – from the original mountain gullies and ridges, to the harder rock walls and faces, the smaller outcrops of rock closer to cities, towns and roads, and finally to the totally modern phenomenon of the indoor climbing wall.

Rock climbing has always been a sport with few rules, and this remains the case today. It has also carried with it from its earliest days the element of risk. Personal safety at an indoor climbing wall is one thing, but out on the crags or in the mountains it is certainly

another. Personal judgement when weighing up the degree of risk involved in doing a particular climb is still an important aspect of being a competent rock climber. To some degree, these things set climbing apart from most other sports, which have set rules, generally carry far less objective risk, and do not exact such a high payment for poor judgement and decision making.

There are many skills to be learned before anyone can claim to be a confident and competent all-round rock climber. These encompass the physical, technical and mental strengths that the sport draws on. The process of gaining new skills in each of these areas never stops. That is one of the great things about the climbing game. Even a highly experienced professional mountain guide cannot claim to know it all! But above all, the sport should bring enjoyment and fulfilment to those who practise it. Each day on the rock should bring a little more fun, an opportunity to learn new skills, and a good reason to explore unknown territory, either close at hand or far away. The challenges that you may choose to accept are always personal ones – they relate to your physical ability and to your own level of risk acceptance. At whatever level you choose to climb, this book will provide you with the essential knowledge to apply safe practice and to gain that all-important experience in this multi-faceted sport.

Above and opposite: These are just two facets of rock climbing today, the indoor environment differing considerably in both physical and mental approach from the outdoor one.

A HISTORY OF CLIMBING

To understand the modern sport of rock climbing, you need first to have some idea of its history and development. Rock climbing has not always existed as an independent pastime – it has grown out of the greater game of mountaineering, which itself has been part of human culture for thousands of years. Early hunters and traders have left evidence of their passage through the mountains and passes all over the world. They developed rudimentary mountaineering skills to cope with the steep ground, the rocky paths and scrambles, and the snow. They even developed special clothing to help them survive the severe cold, wind and rain that are part of mountain travel. A brief history of mountaineering will, therefore, deepen our understanding and appreciation of the sport.

Opposite: *To many rock climbers this is the ultimate challenge, where high alpine terrain has to be climbed quickly before bad weather turns it into a fight for survival. Others, who have no desire for the high mountains, can still enjoy the pleasures that rock climbing brings on less hazardous terrain far from the mountain environment.*

Commercialization

△ *Gravediggers,*
E8 (6c), North Wales
– a route which
symbolizes the
modern trend for
ascending hard,
traditionally
protected routes
using the type of
tactics that are
normally associated
with sport climbing.

While the spirit of fun and fair play that was generated by the early pioneers of rock climbing is still very much alive today, the rapid force of change is re-shaping the cutting edge of the sport. Gone is the light-hearted touch; the modern extreme climber is unashamedly competitive and dedicated. As standards rise and the level of commercialization in climbing increases, it is common practice for those at the top end to take their training and preparation as seriously as any Olympic athlete. The lure of lucrative sponsorship deals and competition prize money now make it possible for a few climbers to make a comfortable living from their sport. Far from being just a hobby, the addictiveness of climbing has a habit of turning into a full-blown obsession, even for those who operate at a more modest level. Heated debates rage over grades and ethical practices, often spilling over on to the pages of the climbing magazines.

SPECIALIZATION

Perhaps the most notable characteristic of modern climbing is the rate at which it has become increasingly specialized. It is now possible for two different people who would categorize themselves as rock climbers to be participating in very different sports. Just as the term "runner" says nothing about whether an individual is a sprinter or runs marathons, the term "rock climber" has become a generalization that is rendered almost obsolete. Whether it is sport climbing, big-wall aiding, free soloing, competitions or bold traditional climbing, the ethics are different, the climbing style is different and the attitudes towards training and preparation could not be more diverse.

WORLD GRADING SYSTEMS

There are now in excess of ten different grading systems used worldwide today to categorize the difficulty of different types of rock climbing. The most popular systems are:

● WORLD GRADING SYSTEM

Britain	USA	Australia	France	UIAA*
Difficult	5.3	11	2	II
Very Difficult	5.4	12	3	III
Severe (4a)**	5.5	12/13	4	IV/IV+
Hard Severe (4b)	5.6	13/14	5	V-
Very Severe (4c)	5.7	15	5/5+	V
Hard Very Severe (5a)	5.8/9	16/17	5+	VI-
E1*** (5b)	5.10a/b	18/19	6a/6a+	VI/VI+
E2 (5c)	5.10c/d	20/21	6b/6b+	VII-/VII
E3 (6a)	5.11a/b/c	22/23/24	6c/6c+/7a	VII+/VIII-

*   UIAA stands for Union Internationale des Associations d'Alpinistes.

**   The British technical grade is given in brackets. This shows how hard the hardest move on a climb will be.

*** E stands for Extreme!

The grades shown above are just a sample selection to illustrate equivalents. Grades in all countries are open-ended; they will continue to increase as long as people attempt harder climbs.

△ Bouldering, while providing a great way to hone your skills for longer rock climbs, has now become a separate sport in its own right.

△ With the aid of bolt protection, sport routes provide the opportunity to focus on the physical and technical challenges of climbing.

△ Top roping on an indoor leading wall: a convenient way of staying in shape during the off-season or an independent sport if you are a competition climber.

(for free climbing) French, British, German, USA, Australian, Norwegian; (for aid climbing) the "A" grades or USA big-wall grades; (for mountaineering-style rock routes) Alpine or UIAA; and (for bouldering) the "B" system, "V" system and Fontainebleau grades.

To the novice climber who is struggling to get to grips with grading in their own country, the thought of travelling abroad and having to tackle all these various systems can be daunting. Fortunately, most guidebooks offer user-friendly conversion tables to help you know what you are letting yourself in for.

As climbing becomes more advanced and specialized, grading systems have adapted and evolved to express the varying nature of the objective difficulties that may be encountered on a particular climb. For example, the early British system used a simple adjectival grade to make an overall assessment of the climb: Moderate (Mod), Difficult (Diff), Severe (S), Very Severe (VS), Extremely Severe (XS). When it was first developed, no climber could possibly have conceived the need for a grade any harder than XS, but it was soon realized that the Extremely Severe grades would need to be extended. They now range from E1 up to E10 at the time of writing. These British

descriptive grades would embrace all aspects of overall climbing difficulty, including strenuousness, seriousness, availability of protection, level of commitment required, presence of hazards such as loose rock, and so on. However, concurrent with the development of the "E" grades was the realization that this system was still incapable of differentiating between the overall difficulty of a climb and the technical difficulty of its hardest move.

◁ Arriving at the crux of a climb – this is the hardest technical move or sequence on the pitch. Modern grading systems use a numerical grade to quantify the technical difficulty of the hardest move.

Grade and ethical debates

By definition, grading is a subjective issue and differences between the heights, builds, climbing styles and opinions of individuals make it impossible to have an entirely standardized system. The main discrepancy that crops up time and again in grading debates is the breadth of each grade and the arbitrary points at which grades seem to overlap. For this reason, climbers are often reluctant to commit themselves and state a definitive grade for a particular route, preferring instead to take the safe option of saying, for example, "Maybe hard French 6c or easy 6c+". Grading first ascents can be especially difficult, as new routers must bear in mind that

most routes clean up (by the removal of dirt, lichen and loose holds) after repeat traffic. In addition, the first ascentionist must cope with the increased psychological pressure from not knowing whether a climb is possible or how hard it will be. A combination of these factors may lead to some new routes being down-graded by as much as two or three grades after repeat ascents.

ETHICAL CONTROVERSIES

Inherently linked with the issue of grading is the complicated and highly contentious issue of the style in which an ascent is made. There is no disputing the fact that when rock climbing evolved as a break-off sport from mountaineering, the idea was to start at the bottom of a cliff and climb it to the top, placing all protection during the ascent and with no prior knowledge of the route. It seems clear and, indeed, if everyone adhered to this simple code there would be no need for ethical debate. The problem comes when individuals reach their own physical and mental limits in climbing using the traditional ethic, but still desire to push things further. At this point it always seems easier to bend the rules rather than spend years of training in an attempt to improve your skills further. Then, with the passage of time, as more and more climbers bend the rules in a similar manner, a new code of practice becomes accepted. It was an inevitable consequence that the use of pre-placed protection (including bolts), pre-inspection of climbs by abseil (rappel), and even top-rope rehearsal prior to the lead would become commonplace if harder routes were to be ascended. The open-minded will embrace both the old (on-sight) style and the new (pre-rehearsed) style.

▷ *Some climbers still bitterly dispute the arrival of so-called modern ethics, arguing that they merely serve to bring the climbs down to the level of the climber.*

▽ *An in situ hanger bolt – the answer to the safe future of climbing or the death of long-standing ethics and traditions?*

△ Free soloing is arguably the purest form of climbing, though with the most serious consequences for failure.

△ A sea-cliff route that can only be reached by abseil (rappel) automatically carries with it a level of seriousness and commitment.

△ A traditional crag where the bolt-free ethic preserves the adventurous character of mountain rock climbing.

● CLIMBING TERMS

Traditional climbing Climbing that puts emphasis on traditional values. This mainly centres on climbing a route using leader-placed protection, which is removed by the second climber, and on climbing without rehearsing or pre-inspecting the route.

Sport climbing A style of climbing that uses bolts as the main form of protection, allowing the climber to concentrate on technique and hard moves.

Big-wall climbing Climbing on big walls that usually take several days to complete. Special techniques, such as aid climbing, sack hauling, and sleeping on portaledges, have all been developed to support this style of climbing.

Aid climbing Climbing that is carried out using pegs (pitons), nuts and other equipment to directly help an ascent, as opposed to being used solely for protection. Equipment can be pulled on or stood in to assist ascent. Aid climbing is usually practised when time is short or where the route is too hard to be climbed in a purer style.

Free climbing Climbing that makes use of natural hand and foot holds only, using the rope and protection only as back-up. Contrast this with aid climbing, in which equipment is used to pull on or stand in to assist ascent.

Free soloing Climbing without ropes or any form of protection. A fall while soloing may be fatal.

Bouldering A form of soloing, but the climber reaches no greater height than they can reasonably safely fall from. It is most often carried out on boulders around 3m–5m (10ft–16ft) high.

Route preparation practices

△ *Extreme,*
traditionally
protected routes are
still made by modern
climbers today.

◁ *With a battery-powered cordless drill,*
expansion bolts can be placed in a matter
of minutes on suitable rock.

The question of which tactics are considered acceptable in the preparation of a new route by a first ascentionist is another highly contentious issue in climbing. If you take the standpoint that all routes should be attempted on-sight, then once again there is no need for discussion. Some incredible new lines have been climbed from the ground up, often with holds being brushed and loose rock being prized off while leading. However, the practicalities of new routing mean that most climbers will settle for a compromise and abseil (rappel) the line first to clean it and make an assessment of available protection. There are, of course, environmental implications to this procedure and excessive "gardening" may present a threat to rare flora or damage softer rocks if a hard brush is over-used. Worse still and now deemed as highly unacceptable is the use of a chisel or drill to improve or manufacture holds. Sadly, chipping has become a widespread practice in certain countries which have failed to appreciate their rock as a non-renewable resource. Climbing is still such a young sport and nobody is entitled to make the assumption that a piece of rock is unclimbable. Future generations of more talented climbers may succeed!

A SPORT WITHOUT RULES

The beauty of climbing has always been that it has no rules and yet it is this very fact that opens the floodgates to an endless list of ethical issues. Of course, it is up to the individual to take their own personal standpoint, provided it does not jeopardize the activities of other climbers. While it is easy to be drawn into debates concerning those practices that are on the borderline of ethical acceptability, hopefully there is no further contention over the biggest ethical crimes.

A more complicated issue is whether glue or epoxy resins should be considered acceptable for the purpose of stabilizing loose rock. Some would argue that this is tolerable, provided that the hold is not improved and that the presence of the glue is highly discrete. Other nations have an almost free-for-all attitude to this type of issue and if a hold breaks off they simply bolt an artificial resin hold on in its place, perhaps smearing glue over it to make it less of an eyesore. If the distinction between indoor and outdoor climbing is to remain, these practices are to be condemned.

USING PEGS (PITONS) AND BOLTS

Another important issue faced by prospective new routers is whether to make use of various forms of fixed or in-situ protection, namely pegs (pitons) or bolts. The argument in favour of pegs is that their placement is still very much governed by the availability of natural cracks and that they cause less damage to the rock than bolts. However, any aid climber knows that the repeated placement and removal of pegs eventually causes hairline seams to be widened into finger cracks. The alternative is for them to be left in place, but here there is the risk that they will corrode away and become highly dangerous. For these reasons many modern free climbers will choose not to place pegs but climb without protection, creating a climb with a higher overall level of seriousness.

With regards to the placement of expansion bolts using either a battery-powered cordless

△ An abseil (rappel) inspection of a climb will provide an abundance of information which may make a subsequent ascent less taxing.

drill or a hand drill, this is perhaps the most over-scrutinized ethical issue in climbing. Countries such as France or Spain accept bolting universally, which means that the use of traditional forms of protection has all but died out, except in high mountainous regions. Countries such as Britain held out against the overwhelming pressure for bolting and then eventually succumbed to the use of bolts in certain designated areas. Other countries, such as the United States and Norway, have a policy of minimal bolting on certain crags, with crack-lines tending to be climbed on natural protection and the blank faces between them often being equipped with bolts. Needless to say it is the type of rock that tends to have the greatest influence on the decision to use bolts. Smoother, less fractured rocks such as limestone offer far less in the way of natural protection and hence become obvious targets for bolting. Any climber who is uncertain of a national policy on fixed protection is advised to consult their governing associations (or relevant guidebooks) before they equip a new line.

● STYLES OF ASCENT

On-sight The purest form of traditional ascent, where the climber starts from the bottom and climbs to the top in one push with no falls, placing all protection on the lead and with no prior knowledge of the intricacies of the climb.

Flash (beta flash) As with on-sight but using prior knowledge of moves, protection or both.

Ground-up (yo-yo) This is essentially a failed on-sight ascent where the climber falls, lowers to the ground and then either pulls the ropes through or, alternatively, top-ropes back up to their high point, either to complete the climb or repeat the same process until eventually the route succumbs.

Pre-inspection This ethic may be applied to traditional or sport climbs by making a prior abseil (rappel) inspection of a climb to clean or examine holds, or assess protection opportunities. If any moves are practised during the abseil then the ascent should be classified as a redpoint.

Redpoint A term developed for sport climbing to describe the process of repeatedly practising the moves of a climb (either by top-rope or repeated leader falls) before eventually completing it in one push, leading, clipping all protection and without falls.

Headpoint A term coined to describe the use of redpointing tactics to ascend bold, naturally protected climbs.

Day ascent The ethical ideal for multipitch free routes. It is common for those routes, which were first climbed with the use of fixed ropes over several days, to be attempted in a day by repeat ascentionists.

◁ Controversy over bolts: these old ring bolts have been chopped, being deemed out of place in an area that maintains a long tradition of adventure climbing.

GETTING STARTED

There are many ways in which you can get started in the sport of rock climbing. Today, one of the most popular is to find an indoor climbing wall. Many towns and cities have climbing clubs, which will welcome new members. This is an ideal way to benefit from the experience of other members. Outdoor centres run courses on climbing and safe practice. Whichever route you choose, you will need to consider the equipment you buy and, once on the rock, your climbing technique. This chapter will help you in these first steps, pointing you in the direction of those all-important early experiences.

Opposite: *Rock climbing is an exciting and demanding sport. Developing good technique early on will stand anyone in good stead for future, harder climbs.*

Choosing clothing

Clothing should be chosen according to the environment in which you intend to climb. What you wear in winter on a heated indoor climbing wall might also be what you wear outside in summer on a hot day – shorts and a t-shirt. However, climbing outside carries an element of uncertainty not found indoors – that of the weather and its changeable nature. It is always wise to carry layers of clothing, providing warmth (fleece or wool), windproof protection and maybe even waterproof protection. Today there is an enormous choice of clothing, covering every conceivable situation and designed to fit all shapes and sizes. Most manufacturers offer key lines in both male and female designs. Consider carefully what you require your clothing for. That way, you will avoid wasting your money.

FABRICS

There are no rights and wrongs about what you should wear to climb in. Personal preference will influence you. However, some fabrics are better than others for different situations. For example, cotton is comfortable and absorbs sweat, but it is not hardwearing, does not dry quickly and does not keep you warm. You might choose it if you are climbing indoors. Man-made fabrics, such as polyester and

◁ It is important to dress for the occasion – and of course with some style! In hot climates, being cool and comfortable will enhance enjoyment.

▷ A breezy day by the sea or on a mountain crag may require full body cover, but be sure that what you wear is light and unrestrictive.

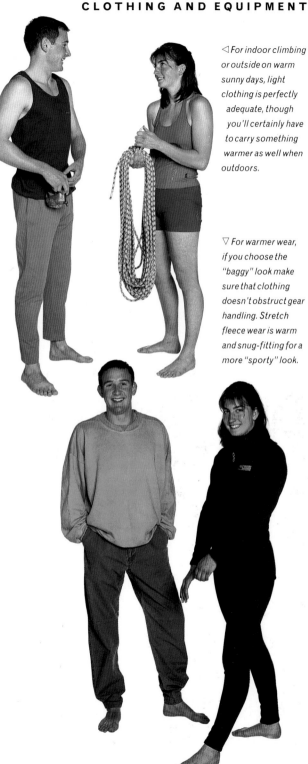

nylon, are hardwearing and dry quickly. Some wick sweat away from your skin. You might choose them when climbing outdoors. Fleece is a fine example of such a fabric and is available in many guises.

If you like tight-fitting clothes, make sure they stretch. Modern fabrics allow manufacturers to be inventive with design, style and variety. Lycra fabrics are perhaps the stretchiest of all; garments fit snugly around the body but do not restrict movement in any way. Lycra in itself is not hardwearing and is usually mixed with other fabrics to provide durability. Out on the crags, walls and boulders, clothing is subject to constant abrasion, which makes this an important consideration.

Close-fitting clothing, particularly fleece, can be quite clammy, especially on hot, sunny days or when you are working hard. It will feel uncomfortable and cause overheating, which saps valuable energy. A great many climbers prefer looser clothing.

◁ *For indoor climbing or outside on warm sunny days, light clothing is perfectly adequate, though you'll certainly have to carry something warmer as well when outdoors.*

▽ *For warmer wear, if you choose the "baggy" look make sure that clothing doesn't obstruct gear handling. Stretch fleece wear is warm and snug-fitting for a more "sporty" look.*

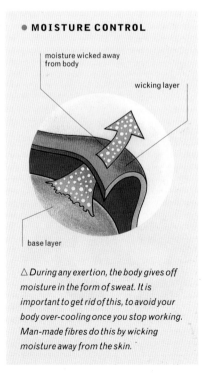

● MOISTURE CONTROL

moisture wicked away from body

wicking layer

base layer

△ *During any exertion, the body gives off moisture in the form of sweat. It is important to get rid of this, to avoid your body over-cooling once you stop working. Man-made fibres do this by wicking moisture away from the skin.*

Choosing equipment

To begin climbing at its most basic level, that of bouldering (either indoors or out), you will need very few pieces of specialist equipment. To get the most out of the activity, you will need a pair of rock shoes and a chalk bag. You might also wish to wear a helmet when you start out on your climbing career. It is highly recommended that you do wear a helmet, but more experienced climbers will often choose not to. At the end of the day, it is a matter of personal preference, but there is no doubt that helmets have saved lives.

▷ *You can have plenty of fun with just a pair of rock shoes and a chalk bag. Equipment is expensive and to begin with you might seek to borrow from friends or to hire from professional outlets.*

ROCK SHOES

The choice of footwear depends entirely on your sphere of activity. If you choose to climb only on indoor walls and to boulder, a light and snug-fitting pair of slipper-style rock shoes is adequate. This type gives a high degree of sensitivity in feeling the holds on which you place your feet. This is advantageous to an experienced climber but the benefits may not be appreciated fully at a beginner level. Slipper-style shoes do not offer much in the way of support and protection for the feet, so if you intend to climb on more adventurous rock you will need to consider this factor and choose something more robust.

The sturdier and more supportive the shoe, the less sensitive it will be to standing on tiny edges or smearing holds. Fortunately, the greatest diversity of shoe design is found in the range of shoes intended for the widest application. As with clothing, not all styles or models will fit all shapes and sizes of feet. It is important to try on as many different shoes as you can. Even so, finding a shoe that is comfortable in the shop does not necessarily mean that it will be comfortable out on the crag. Climbing in hot conditions for hours at a time encourages

● LOOKING AFTER YOUR CLIMBING SHOES

Rock shoes are expensive. They will last longer and give better performance if you take a little time to look after them. Keep the soles clean by wiping them after use. This is especially important after using them outdoors, where grit, mud and sand can all stick to the rubber soles, detracting from their amazing friction properties. Always be sure to wipe them before setting off on a climb.

Rock shoes can be repaired by specialist companies once they start to wear out. This is done by replacing worn-out rands and toe caps, and also the sole, if necessary.

△ *A selection of footwear: two shoe styles, two boots and a slipper.*

feet to swell, and though shoes will stretch a little with use, they might become uncomfortably tight. Very painful feet are not usually conducive to pleasurable climbing experiences.

CHALK AND CHALK BAGS

The use of chalk to increase hand grip is widespread. Chalk absorbs moisture from the fingertips and allows the climber to hold on with greater confidence, which also means the climber endures that little bit longer. Chalk is available in block form and is broken into tiny pieces and carried on a waistband in a small pouch, called a chalk bag. This bag need only be big enough to get the fingers of one hand into at one time. Some indoor walls have banned the use of this type of chalk for reasons of health and cleanliness. Certainly if you fall upside down, a deluge of chalk dust is likely to fall on to your belayer and pollute the air. Chalk balls go some way to alleviating this problem. These are chalk-filled secure muslin (cheesecloth) bags that are simply kept in the chalk bag itself. When squeezed, chalk is released through small holes in the muslin. It is also possible to buy very large chalk bags intended for communal use.

CRASHMATS

If you get really serious about your bouldering you might want to consider acquiring a crashmat. There are a number of types available, some of which fold up into quite small packages and are easy to carry, yet still provide adequate cushioning.

▷ *All you need for sport climbing – shoes, harness, chalk bag, quickdraws and a rope.*

△ *A chalk bag and chalk ball.*

▷ *Bouldering is very much a social activity and though you may find that there will always be someone to "spot" you if you fall off, a crashmat is very reassuring if you are likely to land on your back.*

● HELMETS

There are many different types available commercially. Most are made from plastic or fibreglass, although some new designs have used the cycle helmet model and use very light polystyrene. Things to look out for are weight (most people prefer light helmets), durability (some designs will only take one knock and should then be retired), and fit. They are designed to take an impact from above (in the event of falling stones) and the sides. If a helmet does sustain a major impact, it should be replaced.

△ *A good all-purpose helmet.*

△ *An ill-fitting helmet.*

More equipment

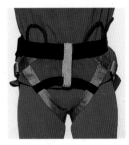

△ *A simple and inexpensive adjustable harness is fine for starting out.*

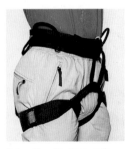

△ *A well-padded harness for rock climbing. This will be comfortable and provide plenty of gear loops for equipment.*

△ *A fully adjustable harness is preferable for all-round climbing use, including winter and alpine mountaineering.*

Climbing beyond bouldering implies the use of more equipment. You will need a rope, harness, belay device, screwgate or locking karabiner, and some quickdraws. This equipment will enable you to start climbing at an indoor wall and on sport routes outside. However, many walls have quickdraws already in place in bolts on the routes for leading and ropes for bottom-roping. You may also be able to hire rock shoes, harnesses and anything else you require.

CHOOSING A HARNESS

More than any other item of gear, harnesses present the widest variety of design and style. This can make it difficult to decide on the most suitable type for your chosen style of climbing. If you climb only on indoor walls and outdoors on sport climbs that are protected by in situ bolts, you will have little need for anything more sophisticated than the simplest and lightest harness available. For comfort, it is better to opt for a harness with a fixed-size waist belt and padded leg loops. You will not need to carry heavy equipment on the harness, nor are you likely to require it to fit over bulky clothing. However, if you plan to climb on high mountain routes, you might like to consider a fully adjustable harness. This will enable you to fit it over whatever clothing you need to wear.

BELAY DEVICES

The belay device and karabiner that you choose are likely to be suitable for almost any climbing situation, either indoors or outdoors, so consider carefully what you buy and you will certainly save money at a later date. However, some climbing walls stipulate the type of device that should be used. In Britain

this is rarely the case, but there are many indoor venues in other countries that insist on a device that has a "fail-safe" mechanism such as the Petzl Gri-Gri. Proper training in the safe operation of whatever device you use is essential and it is quite possible that on a first visit to an indoor wall you will be asked to demonstrate your belaying skills prior to being permitted to climb.

KARABINERS

A belay device needs a screwgate or "locking" karabiner, usually a HMS (or pear-shaped) one. This allows the rope to run smoothly through a belay device and lessens the chance of a tangle occurring or the rope jamming. Snaplink karabiners are used in quickdraws for speedy clipping – the rope goes into the bent gate.

◁ *A belay device with screwgate or locking karabiner.*

◁ *The Gri-Gri is a belay device with a fail-safe mechanism.*

▽ *A few quickdraws will allow you to lead sport climbs.*

ROPES

Ropes come in two main strengths: full (or single) and half (or double). A full rope can be used on its own, whereas a half rope must be used in conjunction with another half rope. Full ropes have traditionally been 11 mm in thickness (although today this has been reduced to 9.8 mm), and half ropes 9 mm in thickness. In terms of length, you can buy standard 45 m (148 ft), 50 m (164 ft), 55 m (180 ft) and even 60 m (197 ft) ropes. Obviously, the thicker and longer a rope, the heavier it will be.

You can also buy ropes that have been treated to repel water. These are useful for climbing outdoors but not necessary if you only climb indoors. This treatment inevitably puts the price of the rope up.

It is important to read the accompanying manufacturer's safety notes when you buy your rope. They will give a recommended lifespan (dependent on how often you use it), and how many heavy falls it could take (see The Fall Factor, page 135).

Ropes are expensive and you may not feel inclined to use your best climbing rope on a climbing wall. The chances are that you will spend a great deal of time at the wall attempting routes that are beyond your ability and consequently might take numerous, though short, falls on to the rope. The longevity of a rope reduces considerably the more frequently it is subjected to a fall. Even short falls will stretch a rope and eventually its ability to

absorb shock will diminish. The ends of the rope will also be subjected to considerably greater wear and tear than the middle part. If you visit climbing walls regularly, say three or four times a week, and you can afford to, it is a good idea to buy a rope that is designed to be used exclusively for this purpose. Manufacturers now produce short ropes specifically to meet this market demand. If you have an old rope that has been retired from more serious use, you could also consider cutting out the worn bits and using that. Be certain though that there is still sufficient life in the rope to justify its continued use.

△ *The accoutred climber. Buy what you need as you gain more experience. The rope is perhaps the single most expensive item of gear you will need but taking care of it will make it last for many years.*

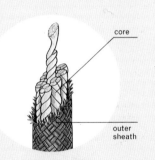

● CROSS-SECTION OF ROPE

core

outer sheath

◁ *Modern ropes are dynamic – they stretch. This property absorbs the energy of a fall. The inner core provides the greatest contribution to strength and elasticity, with the sheath acting as a protective cover.*

△ *A rope bag is useful for keeping the rope clean and for ease of carrying.*

Why warm up?

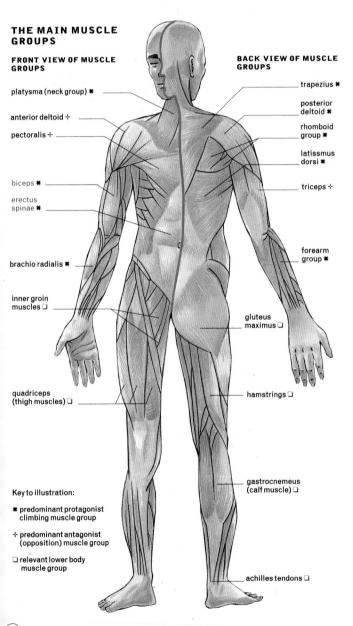

THE MAIN MUSCLE GROUPS

FRONT VIEW OF MUSCLE GROUPS

platysma (neck group) ✱

anterior deltoid ✛

pectoralis ✛

biceps ✱

erectus spinae ✱

brachio radialis ✱

inner groin muscles ❏

quadriceps (thigh muscles) ❏

BACK VIEW OF MUSCLE GROUPS

trapezius ✱

posterior deltoid ✱

rhomboid group ✱

latissmus dorsi ✱

triceps ✛

forearm group ✱

gluteus maximus ❏

hamstrings ❏

gastrocnemeus (calf muscle) ❏

achilles tendons ❏

Key to illustration:

✱ predominant protagonist climbing muscle group

✛ predominant antagonist (opposition) muscle group

❏ relevant lower body muscle group

Whether you are about to attempt your very first climb or compete in the final of a top international competition, the importance of warming up for climbing cannot be stressed enough. Most climbers are notoriously lazy when it comes to correct preparation practices; after all, if you don't take climbing that seriously, then why should you prepare for it as if it were an athletic sport? Climbing is one of the most punishing activities ever invented for joints and connective tissues, and yet many of its participants still seem to hold the belief that injury is something that only happens to other people. Equally surprising are the numbers who have suffered the odd tweaked tendon or muscle and yet completely fail to learn from their previous mistakes. Of course, there are other factors, aside from warming up, that will have some influence on your ability to avoid injury: the amount of rest you take between climbs or climbing days, your sleep patterns and your nutritional intake, to name but a few. But in the short term, the most important variable will be the effectiveness of your pre-climbing preparation routine.

IMPROVE YOUR CLIMBING

If the threat of injury is not a good enough incentive, then the other main reason to warm up is that it helps you to climb better. We all know how it feels to arrive at work having just fallen out of bed – mental and physical attune-ment take their time and you simply cannot expect your muscles to be able to pull their hardest or be smooth and co-ordinated if you

◁ Climbing puts tremendous stress on muscles and joints. It is worth knowing a little about your anatomy to help avoid injury.

△ Build up gradually before launching into steep, dynamic climbing.

△ Even on remote mountain crags, it pays to have a quick boulder around before commencing a longer, more committed climb.

◁ It may help your warm-up routine to have a few practice routes that you know well. Climbing them will indicate how in-tune and warmed-up you really are.

jump from a sedentary state straight into your hardest climb or boulder problem. A warm-up routine also gives you sufficient time to filter out the cluttered chaotic thoughts generated by your work or social schedule, and focus in on the task of climbing.

A SYSTEMATIC APPROACH

How many times at the crag or climbing wall have you seen people arrive looking as if they lack direction? Then while getting changed or chatting to a friend they will go through the motions of a warm-up by performing a few violent helicopter-style arm circles, yank their fingers backwards and forwards and then finish with a half-hearted bouncing touch of the toes? The irony is that some of the bizarre and extreme forms of so-called warm-up that you occasionally witness are potentially more damaging than climbing itself! It is very important to learn safe practices from the very start and to adopt a consistent approach to warming up every time you climb. After all, the warm-up is an ideal time to gauge how good you are feeling, and whether or not you have recovered from your previous climbing session. Climbers who are well in tune with their warm-up will use a series of benchmark exercises as a gauge for how hard they should push themselves throughout the remainder of the session proper. It is also worth taking the time to practise a few standard routine warm-up routes or problems at your regular climbing venues. These will also give clues as to how well you are performing on a particular day.

Progression

▽ Your warm-up will play a vital role in the outcome of a steep strenuous ascent such as this 8a sport climb.

The most important thing about a warm-up is that it must introduce increasing overload to the relevant climbing muscle groups in a gradual and controlled manner over a reasonable time period. To go "too hard too soon" is to ruin your warm-up. You will know when you have done this by the fact that you won't climb anything harder than your so-called warm-up route or boulder problem in the rest of the session. If you are at a crag that has no suitable easy routes and you are forced to warm up on something difficult, make yourself stop intermittently and take rests between individual moves (if a top rope or the protection permits) and treat the exercise as if you were warming up for bouldering. Although less desirable, this is far better than jumping straight on something hard and heading for the inevitable burn-out. If you are pushed for time, then you may be able to cut out certain less relevant parts of your warm-up routine. However, the progressive build-up of effort must always stay if you are to avoid injury, even if it means less climbing time as a result.

SPECIFICITY

Certain core elements of your warm-up must be consistent, while others should vary according to the specific type of climbing that you are about to do. It may sound obvious, but why perform lots of laborious leg stretches if you only plan to go on a steep bouldering wall or fingerboard board? However, if you are about to attempt a leg-contorting slab route you will need to put more time into calf, thigh and groin stretches. It is also vital to make your warm-up intensity-specific. Use easy boulder problems to warm up for bouldering or power-training sessions and use easy traverses, circuits or routes to prepare for longer endurance climbing.

THE FOUR-POINT WARM-UP GUIDE

This covers the core areas of a suggested warm-up routine for climbing. It is laid out in

△ Jogging on the spot provides a good way of raising your pulse at the beginning of your warm-up session.

▷ Some light climbing, where careful attention is paid to form and control, should always precede more strenuous climbing.

the order in which you should do them, to get the most out of your warm-up. The stages are:

① Pulse raiser
② General mobility
③ Specific stretching
④ Progressive climbing build-up

PULSE RAISER

If you are slogging up a steep hill to reach a distant mountain crag, then you can happily forget this first stage. But if you are stepping out of your car to the foot of a roadside sport climbing venue or a climbing wall, then you will need to do something to get your heart and lungs going before you attempt to do any stretching, let alone climbing. By raising your pulse for approximately 3–5 minutes, with a quick jog, skip or some on-the-spot style exercises, you will increase overall blood flow, warm the muscles and generally trigger your body into exercise mode. This vital part of the warm-up also serves to soften joint cartilage in preparation for the impacts of strenuous exercise.

GENERAL MOBILITY

Before you attempt to stretch, it pays to do some controlled circular movements. For example, both the shoulders and hips can be gently rotated to warm the joints up, and to get your muscles, tendons and joints used to working through a full range of motion. To save time, you can combine these with some finger clenches, either with or without the use of a wrist exerciser. Violent swinging movements are definitely out – especially when the spine is involved. Use a smooth "front-crawl"-style swimming action for your arms.

Upper body stretches

As an overall rule your core stretches, which should be common to every climbing session, are the fingers and forearms, elbow tendon insertions, shoulders and neck. For steep rock, pay particular attention to your back and sides, and for lower angled rock, make sure you go through your leg stretches.

FINGER STRETCHES

First perform some finger clenches, either with or without a grip exerciser. Then carefully work through each individual finger and thumb joint, stretching them both ways for approximately 6–8 seconds and up to three times each. Apply even, progressive pressure with no sharp tugging. You can maybe do this on the journey to the crag or wall to save time.

△ Finger clenches with or without a grip exerciser will develop finger and overall hand strength.

△ The thumb stretch.

△ First joint finger stretch.

△ Second joint finger stretch.

△ Third joint finger stretch.

ELBOW AND FOREARM STRETCH

Hold one arm out straight in front of you, clasp the fingers with your spare hand and bend your wrist and fingers back, so as to take up the tension on the flexor tendon insertion to the elbow. Hold for 8–12 seconds and repeat three times for each arm.

SHOULDER STRETCHES

Stand upright, grasp your elbow and bring your upper arm behind your head, applying gentle downward pressure to stretch the deltoid muscles. Then hold your arm out straight in front of you and pull it sideways across your body. Hold each stretch for 8–12 seconds and repeat three times.

◁ *Forearm stretch.*

△ *Shoulder stretch (1).*

△ *Shoulder stretch (2).*

NECK STRETCH

Stand or sit upright, then gently bend your neck to one side, back to the centre and then to the other side, to the front and then to the back, always returning to the centre first each time. Do not rotate your neck.

BACK STRETCHES

For your lats (the large wing-like muscles down your sides), stand legs apart and slightly bent, then lean sideways stretching the leading arm over your head so as to feel the tension in your sides. Place the other hand on your hip or thigh for support. For your upper middle back muscles (rhomboid and teres groups) simply hold both arms out in front with hands clenched together, then curl your arms and shoulders forward.

△ *Side neck stretch.*

△ *Rear neck stretch.*

◁ *Front neck stretch.*

△ *Upper back stretch.*

△ *Side stretch.*

Lower body stretches

For warming-up purposes, lower body stretches can be kept to an absolute minimum. Choose one basic exercise for each muscle group, namely the groin, thighs, hamstrings and calves.

All these exercises can be performed on the rock or wall to help you combine your flexibility work with an element of climbing technique.

This provides a fun way of breaking up the monotony of an extensive pre-climbing stretching routine.

It is worth consulting an elementary yoga or flexibility training manual for more detailed information. However, it is worth prioritizing the following flexibility exercises, which are especially good for the inner thigh.

THIGH AND QUADRICEPS STRETCH
Stand straight, bending one leg up behind you. Hold your ankle to keep it in position. To increase the stretch, gently push hips forward.

◁ A good exercise to prepare you for rock-overs or high step-ups.

▷ This exercise stretches the relevant muscles for standing on small holds.

CALF STRETCH
Place both hands against the wall and stretch one leg out straight behind you. Repeat with the other leg.

HAMSTRING STRETCH
Sit on the ground, stretching one leg out in front of you, and fold the other leg in. Now gently stretch your upper body forwards.

◁ You can also do this hamstring stretch by standing straight-legged and bending forward to touch the toes. Never bounce, but hold the stretch for 8–12 seconds.

FRONT SPLITS

Although ideal for improving your ability for wide bridging moves, this commonly known exercise requires some care and preferably a few easier groin stretches first to help you work up to it. Simply face front with feet pointing forwards and slowly and carefully ease yourself into a bridge position.

▷ *The leg raise and groin stretch.*

▽ *Front splits and bridge stretch.*

FROG STRETCH

This simple exercise can be performed either standing or lying face down on the floor with your feet slightly wider than shoulder-width apart. Lower your hips towards your feet, turning your knees outwards in a ballet dancer's "plié" position. A great stretch for improving your ability to get your weight close in to the rock.

▷ *The inner thigh frog stretch.*

Progressive build-up

Now for the really important part. You are warm, mobile and fully stretched, so the final stage is to subject your muscles and tendons to gradually increasing overload (climbing or climbing-related movements of heightened intensity). As mentioned before, use longer sequences to prepare for endurance climbing and shorter programmes to build up for bouldering. Try, also, to make the moves in your warm-up sequences specific to the crag or wall you are about to use. For example, warm up on steep rock if that's what you are mainly going to be doing. Your first movements should be so easy that you barely notice them; use these to relax, stretch out and to tune in mentally to the sensation of climbing. Then, with the use of intermittent rest, build up until you are almost ready for maximum effort. Once you reach this stage, stop and rest for anything between 6–15 minutes

▽ *After you have warmed up and done some light climbing, it is worthwhile to do some more mobility exercises.*

△ *Even outside you can warm up by doing some easy bouldering, before launching yourself on a hard route.*

● THE WARM-UP SURVIVAL GUIDE

• Always ensure that all the main three finger grip angles are utilized during the warm-up: crimp, half crimp, and open hand. If necessary try to incorporate slopers, pinches or other more specific types of fingerhold if you know they will be required.

• Ensure that all main arm positions are worked through the full range of motion during the warm-up: pull-down, side-pull, reverse side-pull and undercut.

• Try to climb fluidly, smoothly and in control and only attempt faster dynamic moves to recruit your power and timing towards the end of the warm-up.

• For longer endurance climbing, you will always climb better after incorporating a primary pump into your warm-up to open the capillaries and to activate your body's lactic acid transfer systems.

• The different finger grip angles and arm positions are described on pages 54–59. There is in reality an infinite number, but they break down into specific types of holds.

△ Pinching.

△ Using an undercut hold indoors.

▷ Using an undercut hold on a crag.

before you commence with the climbing session proper. It's worth taking a small amount of fluid and having a light secondary stretch during this period.

PUTTING IT ALL TOGETHER

While this chapter proposes an optimum warming-up model for climbing, it is not intended as a comprehensive guide and should be adapted to suit the requirements of individuals. Above all else, you should warm up in a way that suits your own mental and physical conditioning. Remember that it is always better to make the effort to do something, no matter how simple, for your warm-up and if you're going to set the time aside then you may as well do it properly. After all, the purpose here is to give yourself the best chance of climbing well in addition to avoiding a possible injury.

Training and technique

Regardless of your level of fitness or strength, technique is always the deciding factor in climbing. You can incorporate some aspects of technique into your training programme. They will help develop your flexibilty, as well as atune you to more difficult climbing moves. Establishing a repertoire of moves is an important aspect of mental training. These techniques will be looked at again later in the book.

▷ *Frogging –*
a technique that
demands flexibility.

FROGGING

This is a technique that can be used to help bring your centre of gravity in close on vertical or overhanging rock. It is especially relevant where you have either one central foothold or two very close footholds. The idea is to push your hips in as close to the rock as possible by turning your legs out in a sort of ballet dancer's "plié" movement. The more flexible your inner groin, the better you will be at this. Thus, frogging can provide that crucial means of resting when all else is letting you down.

▷ *The Egyptian –*
a good technique for
use on steep or
overhanging rock.

THE EGYPTIAN

So named because of the extreme dropped knee posture that is adopted during these moves, the Egyptian is a useful and cunning method of keeping your centre of gravity as close to the rock as possible when climbing on steep ground. It applies to situations where you have two high footholds either side of you on rock which is usually in excess of 5 degrees overhanging. The idea is to "twist into" the next move by dropping the knee on the same side as the hand that you are about to reach with (the passive side) and turning your body to face the hold that you are currently holding on with (the active side). This brings your hips in close and perpendicular to the rock and creates torque between the footholds which, in turn, will reduce the loading on your arms. The secret is to co-ordinate your Egyptians fluidly between moves and, where the ground dictates, to switch continuously from one Egyptian to the other.

FLAGGING

This is a subtle conterbalancing technique which can be used as a quick and efficient substitute for swapping feet. It applies mainly to situations on steep rock where you only have one central foothold and thus require that fine degree of balance to make the next move. The idea is to pass your free leg either inside you or behind you and hang your body straight down, so as to form a stable "tripod" position with your three points of contact. Then, having completed the move, simply rectify yourself so you are set up to move on.

△ Inner flagging.

△ Outer flagging.

SIDE HEEL-HOOKING

The basic heel-hook is well known and is useful for turning the lips of roofs or for making traverses on very steep ground. However, the side heel-hook can be used far more frequently if the user is sufficiently creative and flexible. In situations where you have a large flat hold just to one side of your waist, simply lift your leg and rotate your foot outwards in such a manner that enables you to get the side of your heel on to the hold. Use it, and then when you're halfway through the move and have gained sufficient height, re-adjust to using your toe. Side heel-hooks can feel weird and insecure the first few times you try them, but like all techniques you will feel comfortable with them the more you practise.

◁ A heel-hook in action at an indoor climbing wall.

● TRAINING TERMS

Overload is the term used to describe the healthy, desirable stresses and strains that are placed on the connective tissues and joints during physical training. It does not necessarily imply the use of excessive or dangerous forces which may cause injury to the climber. See also Chapter 6, Advanced Training.

Intensity in climbing refers to the relationship between the length of climbing and the difficulty of the moves. For example a short boulder problem would be described as high intensity, whereas a long sea cliff climb would be regarded as low intensity. See also Chapter 6, Advanced Training.

Circuits are either random or pre-determined sequences of moves which usually work their way across, diagonally, up and down an indoor or outdoor bouldering wall. See also Chapter 6, Advanced Training.

Timing is the term used to describe the ability of a climber to use neuromuscular co-ordination to pull up and catch a handhold at high speed.

Primary pump is the act of climbing to deliberately induce a light burning cramp into your forearms to prime them for a more severe pump later on in the session.

First steps

Contrary to popular belief, you do not have to be super-muscular with the tenacity of a limpet to be a rock climber. Images in the climbing press do have a tendency to promote this point of view, but there are hundreds of thousands of climbs around the world that require little more than good balance and a head for heights. The first steps on rock can have such a profound influence over subsequent feelings towards this great sport that it is important to take them carefully. A course run by trained and qualified personnel is one of the better ways to be introduced, but many people develop a deep affinity for the sport through friends who are themselves committed climbers. There need be no limitations of age, height or weight for those first steps – whether as a child or pensioner, when you put feet and hands to rock matters little, for there are levels to suit all.

FIRST STEPS

More and more people are introduced to rock climbing through the medium of climbing walls indoors. This is no bad thing, for it does at least allow the beginner to concentrate on

△ Modern instructional techniques allow you to progress to leading easy climbs within a few days of taking your first steps on rock.

◁ An idyllic pose high above a valley. For many climbers, the thrill of an exposed situation spices up the whole experience.

△ Climbing walls are a good medium through which
to learn the basics of movement, but try to avoid
the steep and strenuous climbs when starting out.

◁ As the rock climb gets steeper you will
definitely need muscles and tenacity – and
a great deal of experience.

▽ An ideal angle on which to begin. Concentrate
on precise footwork and learn to trust the
friction properties of your footwear.

movement in a friendly atmosphere that is
always warm and dry. Not all climbing walls
have suitable facilities for beginners. They
are usually too steep and require strength
combined with good technique, normally
acquired over a period of time. The ideal
beginner's venue is a low-angled slab where
much of the body weight is taken over the feet
rather than relying on arm strength to maintain contact with the rock.

An outdoor crag can be more suitable
because of the infinite variety of low-angled
rock that can be found. The major disadvan-
tage is, of course, that you cannot guarantee
finding warm and dry conditions! Wet rock
tends to be very slippery and cold wet rock is
certain to put you off forever. Given that ideal
conditions are available you should try to find
a venue that has a profusion of easy-angled
rock with little or nothing in the way of potential danger. Low boulders are ideal, even more
so if they have lush grassy ground beneath
them or soft sand. Make sure, too, that you are
able to descend from the boulder with ease
either off the back or by climbing down an easy
way. Put on your shoes, and a helmet if there is
a chance of loose rock or a fall, and you're away.
It is always important to ensure that your feet
are dry before you set foot on to the rock. This
can be done by wiping the sole on the inside of a
trouser leg, with your hand or with a rag specifically carried for this purpose.

Feet and friction

Good footwork is one of the main foundations for good climbing. The skill of precise foot placement enables better balance and movement. Your legs are much stronger than your arms, and the more you learn to use them, the farther and longer you will be able to climb. Most beginners concentrate on where to put their hands, ignoring their feet entirely. This approach should be resisted. You must learn to trust your feet, even on the smallest of holds. The use of rock shoes, with their excellent friction properties, makes this much easier to do.

▽ *Spend some time before a climb simply walking around on rock without the need for handholds.*

EASY-ANGLED ROCK

Find a really low-angled piece of rock, say about 25 to 30 degrees, and simply walk around on it. At this angle you will find that it's easily possible to manage without using your hands. Take the opportunity to become acquainted with the superb friction properties of your rock shoes. Try standing on a small ledge of rock with the inside or outside edge of the shoe. Avoid high-stepping movements. Though there are times in rock climbing when you need to make a big step up, a good deal of energy can be saved by utilizing intermediate,

△ *Economy of effort is essential in rock climbing. Try to avoid high stepping movements when taking those first steps.*

perhaps smaller, footholds to reach a more secure one. Keep looking down at your feet and slowly begin to develop precision about where you place them. Each time you put your foot on a hold, it should be placed deliberately and, hardest of all, with confidence that it will stick in place. Try using only the friction between shoe sole and rock to create a foothold. This is known as "smearing".

USING FOOTHOLDS

Having gained some confidence in the stickiness of the shoes, it's time to move on to techniques of standing on specific and obvious holds or ledges. Find a piece of rock that is a little bit steeper and where hands placed against the surface can be used for balance. Balance only, remember! You don't need to use them to pull up on just yet. It was once thought that climbing is more efficient and safer if you maintain three points of contact with the rock at all times, and lean out and away from the rock so that you have a clear view of your feet and the rock in front of you. While this may be useful for easier climbs, in the grand scheme of things it may misdirect you and make later climbing experiences much less efficient.

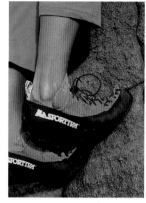

△ The technique of "smearing" the shoes over the rock surface is well illustrated here.

▷ The feet are smeared and the hands are used mainly for balance, though some support may be gained by curling the fingers over the smallest of edges.

● USING SMALL STEPS

It is a good idea to get into the habit of taking small steps up as you climb. This may mean using footholds that are not particularly good. However, it is better to use them and move up for better holds, rather than stretching too high to get to the better holds straight away. Over-reaching immediately puts you off balance and will also put a greater strain on your muscles.

Experiment at your local indoor wall or crag. Choose an easy route (either short, easy bouldering problems or a longer route – but use a rope and be belayed!). Try it first making big reaches with both hands and feet. Now do it again, but taking small steps and making smaller controlled moves. What did you notice?

△ Keep the hands low to avoid over-stretching.

△ Having made the step up, the next handhold is reached.

More footwork

s you gain confidence in your feet, you will come to trust the smaller footholds generally found on harder climbs. Be creative about your approach to footwork, and remember to experiment with your balance, finding out what works and what does not.

▷ *When standing on well-defined ledges, however large or small, try to use the inside of the foot. This will allow you to get your weight closer in to the rock and directly over the foothold.*

▷ *A similar technique is used here, but the outside of one foot is also used to aid upward progress.*

EDGING

Look down towards your feet and try to pick out small or large edges, protrusions and depressions in the rock surface. Each one you find could be a foothold and you should try to use them all, even if it means taking 20 steps to gain a few feet of height. You will quickly discover that by using these features each placement of the foot gains greater security than if it was just smeared on to the hold. If you find an edge that is difficult or uncomfortable to stand on with the front of the shoe, experiment by turning your foot sideways and putting either the inside or the outside edge of the shoe on the hold. This technique will be instantly more comfortable, for the simple reason that you are able to gain more support from the shoe across its width than its length because there is a good deal more rigidity and less leverage

△ *Using the inside and outside of the shoe means you can get more of your foot in contact with the rock, and will ultimately be more comfortable.*

◁ Steeper rock and smaller footholds demand precise footwork and the confidence to stand around while fixing protection or working out the next move.

● CLIMBING BLINDFOLD

At this stage there are lots of little exercises you can do to make learning more fun. One suggestion is to try climbing with a blindfold on and ask a colleague to talk you through the moves. Not only will this help you to gain more awareness of body movement, but the person talking you through the sequence will have to visualize the most efficient sequence for you to follow. Concentrate on being very precise with each foot and handhold. Think about your balance. Being blindfold should help you with this. Be prepared to make lots of small adjustments to your position to find the most efficient body shape to adapt to in the circumstances.

across the sole. When you use the sides of the shoe in this way, it is called "edging". As you venture on to steeper rock, this technique becomes increasingly important.

CROSSING YOUR FEET

Like the often repeated adage regarding three points of contact at all times, ignore those that suggest you should never cross your feet one in front of the other. On a traverse it will be considerably easier if you are able to cross your feet, for it will put you in a good position to transfer body weight over to the next foothold. It is very important that you don't attempt too large a step. Normally your ability to stretch and flex your limbs will dictate the extent to which you can step, so be aware of what your body tells you. If you clearly cannot cope with the stretch, look for alternative and intermediate holds.

△ **1** By crossing one leg inside the other, you are well placed to move comfortably towards the next suitable foothold.

△ **2** The move completed. You are now ready to repeat the sequence and move on to the next holds.

Using handlolds

Handholds are more easily seen, generally speaking, than footholds. They are at eye level, or thereabouts. However, they come in all shapes and sizes and at all angles. You will need to experiment to find the best use of them.

JUGS, FINGERHOLDS AND SIDE-PULLS

Having gained some confidence with your feet, it's time to move on to the hands. We have already experimented a little with the hands for balance. Having an edge to curl your fingers over increases the feeling of security, but we are not yet ready to use holds to pull our body weight up the rock – that has to wait for much steeper occasions. To begin, select a section of rock at a 45–50 degree angle and long enough so that you can make several consecutive

moves horizontally or at a slight rising diagonal across the surface. This sideways movement is called "traversing". The benefits of traversing are that you don't need to climb too high above the ground and that you will also get more continuous movement.

Now you need to look not only at your feet and decide where to put them, but also to consider using your hands to make life easier. You will need to use a variety of handholds. The simplest ones to use are those that you pull on from directly below. No doubt these will sometimes feel large and occasionally so small that they might appear inadequate. Large handholds that you can curl all of the fingers of one hand over are usually called "jugs". Climbers, in their early days on rock, also refer to them as "thank God" holds for

▷ *Holds over which you can comfortably curl your hand are sometimes called "thank God" holds. These are the most welcome holds to find on any climb.*

△ *More large handholds, this time inside and along the edges of a diagonal crack. Use your imagination when looking for holds to grip on to.*

It is always a good idea to remove your watch and any rings or other jewellery. Some types of handholds can be very taxing on your fingers and arms, and may cause damage to anything you happen to be wearing. Apart from scratches to your jewellery, you may also suffer damage to yourself if your jewellery becomes trapped. The forces involved could dent a ring into your finger, for example.

◁ *Small fingerholds are surprisingly secure, particularly if there is an incut lip to the edge of the hold.*

obvious reasons! Holds that you can only get half the length of your fingers on, or your fingertips only, are called "fingerholds".

With these two types of handhold you have enough to be able to climb most moderately graded rock. But other less obvious handholds exist, and to get the best out of them you will need to experiment. For example, a handhold found to lie vertically with the cliff face may at first seem useless. However, if it is pulled on from the side, with your feet positioned to keep you in balance, this type of hold will be found usable. They are called "side-pulls". Side-pulls are great holds to use when traversing, as they help you to pull your body across the rock and to transfer weight from foot to foot. You need to keep a keen eye out for the infinite variety of handholds available. A canny climber will look for, find and use even the most obscure hold to aid progress, so don't dismiss anything lightly.

◁ *Leaning sideways off a hold will allow you to let go with one hand to reach upward and diagonally. In this case, the climber will be able to let go with the right hand and reach up to better holds above.*

Planning your moves

The key to climbing efficiently is to be able to read the rock you are about to climb. This will require some imagination (what will it be like to be up there in that position?) and your past experience, and then planning ahead.

CLIMBING MOVES IN SEQUENCE

To climb a section of rock, whether it is a traverse or straight up, you should try to look upon it as a sequence of interlinked movements. To link the movements successfully, you'll need to look beyond the section of rock immediately in front of you and determine where your sequence will end before beginning the next. Sometimes this will be three or four moves and sometimes considerably more. For example, if you have a clear view of a place where you think you can comfortably stand that is about 3 m (10 ft) above, plan a sequence of moves to reach that point.

READING THE ROCK

To successfully plan a sequence of moves, you'll need to look very carefully at the availability of handholds and footholds over the

△ **1** *The objective is clear – first you need to stand up on the right foot and find suitable holds for the hands.*

△ **2** *Pull your weight over on to the right foot and stand up. Keeping as much weight on your right foot as possible ...*

△ **3** *... reach up with your right hand for the jug. Here, this sequence of three moves will gain you 1 m (3 ft) in height.*

△ **1** *In this sequence, notice how the feet change position but the left hand stays on the same hold.*

△ **2** *The left hand remains in place to aid balance while an intermediate hold is used by the right hand.*

△ **3** *The left hand changes from a pull hold to a push hold and the feet can be comfortably moved higher, now that there is a secure hold for the right hand.*

section of rock. You will need to think ahead in terms of how you might use the available holds and in what order. An interesting insight into this takes place at indoor climbing competitions. A climber taking part in an indoor climbing competition is allowed to see the route they have to climb a little before they actually have to do it. They will stand at the bottom of the route and scrutinize the holds, trying to visualize where they will be when they get to certain points, how their weight may be distributed, where their hands and feet will be and what technique they might use to move up. They will break the route down into manageable sections. To some extent, all climbers with experience will learn to do this to a certain level to help them cope with the climb they are about to do. Quite often there are many different ways to link holds and moves together in a sequence. These variations depend on what you see, what you think you might be able to use, how far you can

reach and your experience or ability to visualize the moves – often referred to as being able to "read the rock". The way one person climbs a sequence is not necessarily the way that another might link it together, though it is quite right to say that having seen someone climb a piece of rock the next climber to attempt it has a distinct advantage.

● VERTICAL CHESS

Some people find it helpful to consider the analogy between climbing and a game of chess. There are an infinite number of moves that you could make but only a few that will lead you into a winning position – and, of course, it is the winning moves that matter most! You might try a bouldering sequence several times, attempting the moves differently each time. Try to gauge which sequence was the most efficient and energy-saving. Try also to analyze what makes a sequence a success or a failure. Climbers often talk about their minds being in tune with what they are trying to do on one day, but out of tune on others. Getting it right is as much a mental achievement as a physical one.

Moving on – a real route

Having spent a few hours practising the basic skills of movement on rock, it is time to move on to something a little more adventurous. The most natural progression is to attempt a short climb on a bottom rope. For advice on how to set up the system, see Chapter 3.

USING A ROPE

When you first climb using a rope, you may feel differently about the whole experience of climbing. There is more to think about than simply making moves. The harness and rope may get in the way, but you will soon get used to them. At this stage try to find a climb that is not too steep, is well endowed with handholds and footholds, and offers a diversity of rock features – by doing so you are assured of success. An ideal height for the climb would be around 10 m (30 ft). Ideals, of course, are rarely

achievable! Before starting out on the climb, stand back and take a good look at the route you think you might take. Look for obvious ledges or breaks in the cliff face, places where you might be able to pause and rest to consider the remainder of the ascent. The knowledge that you gain from this perusal can be used to your advantage in breaking down the climb into short sections that are easier to cope with. You must of course keep the final goal in mind, but don't let it hinder your ability to think calmly.

Remembering the analogy with a game of chess, plan a sequence of moves and put them to the test. If it doesn't quite work out the way you had planned but you still succeed, it matters little. If you find that your calculated sequence doesn't quite work, take a moment to re-think. Do not just look at the rock immediately in front of your nose. Look to the sides of the line you are to take. Quite often there

◁ A short climb, well endowed with holds of all kinds. Here the climber is safeguarded by using a bottom rope safety system.

▷ The same climb being safeguarded with a top rope method. There are advantages and disadvantages to both methods and much will depend on the situation you find yourself in.

△ *Grooves and corners should be straddled for comfort and energy-efficient climbing.*

will be holds off to one side or the other that are not immediately obvious but that you can put a foot or hand on for maintaining balance or resting. They may not be quite the types of big holds you are looking for or expecting to find, but experimentation is quite likely to prove worthwhile.

Grooves and corners in the rock face are usually straddled with both feet and hands for comfort. This is called "bridging" and is a particularly restful and economic way to climb, because much of your body weight is supported by the feet and legs. Find places where you can experiment with taking one hand off, or even both, in order to gain a rest. Climbing on a top rope is totally safe, and though your weight might sag on to the rope, you'll not fall off in the truest sense – it'll only be a slump! Armed with this knowledge, you can forget those worries and concentrate on the task in hand.

Some people find it a useful exercise to climb the same route several times. Each ascent should become more efficient in terms of energy expended and you will learn a great deal about body movement and awareness.

However, rock in all its infinite variety offers so many different combinations of moves that it is as well not to ponder for too long on any particular climb. You need to extend your experience to include widely differing styles of climbing in order to make progress.

△ *An easy-angled slab makes an ideal first climb. Slabs can be surprisingly tiring on the feet and legs, so try to vary the position of your feet frequently.*

◁ *The climbing wall is an ideal place to try things that might be a little too difficult. If you want to attempt something strenuous don't get too demoralized if you find your strength wanes quickly. Your stamina will improve with practice.*

Longer climbs

The next stage is to move on to longer climbs, either single pitch or multi-pitch (see also Chapter 3). Exactly the same principles of movement apply, but bear in mind that you may have to keep energy levels running for longer. It is vitally important to conserve energy and you would do well to

take moments out to deliberately rest during the climb. This means finding a position that is relatively comfortable (by bridging, for example) and allowing yourself time to re-evaluate the situation, to settle yourself into a good frame of mind and to grow accustomed to the situation you find yourself in.

It is in situations like this that your attitude to climbing is important. Your combination of mental and physical resilience will be re-evaluated. A confident approach, tempered with sound judgement and good technique, will stand you in good stead.

COPING WITH EXPOSURE

Many people find sufficient encouragement and motivation to continue from the early steps on low boulders or short single-pitch climbs to attempt longer climbs, but fail to take heed of the fact that longer climbs may have a frightening element that they hadn't bargained for – a big drop below! This is known as "exposure" and it comes in differing degrees and affects individuals in various ways. A small minority of people are so intimidated that they limit themselves ever after to short climbs; but for the majority of others, exposure adds that extra little bit of spice to the outing. Coping with exposure and maintaining concentration on the task of climbing do not always mix well together.

THE FEAR FACTOR

The fear factor has a considerable influence on your ability to climb and the feeling of an airy and forbidding space below your feet tends to

◁ *It is more difficult to find places to rest weary arms on harder climbs, but with imagination and control it is often possible to find something.*

△ *Longer, steeper climbs will inevitably require a certain amount of stamina in equal proportion to strength.*

▷ *The sound of the sea crashing on the rocks below will often add to a feeling of exposure and intimidation.*

preoccupy the mind with all kinds of negative thoughts. Mental preparation for this and taking the time to grow with your surroundings are as important as the actual skills of moving over the rock. Unfortunately it is not so easy to practise in a controlled environment, because the fear factor only kicks in when being scared becomes a reality. Everyone who climbs has their own way of overcoming this factor. There are those who seem oblivious to it but they are few in number. Taking time to mentally stand back and consider your position, and to concentrate on the moves that lie ahead, are important ways to overcome the fear factor.

The way forward

Be selective when you choose climbs to undertake. Pay close attention to the grade and the style of the climb. Those route descriptions found in guidebooks that mention things like "an awkward and strenuous chimney" or "make a bold move up the slightly impending arete" or "a thin and worrying sequence leads to a good jug" or "difficult for the short" or "an airy traverse" – are best avoided. They are coded descriptions for things that might be truly scary!

Enlist the company of a sympathetic friend with whom you can share your experiences. You may have encounters that turn out to be monumental and memorable adventures, which can be recounted years and hundreds of thousands of feet of rock later as happy, innocent moments through which a great deal of experience was gained.

△ *A guidebook will help you to find your way but don't expect it to give you a blow-by-blow account of how to climb.*

STARTING TO LEAD

Progress is not normally a hasty affair. However, quite soon after taking your first steps you may want to begin leading your own climbs. Being on the "sharp" end of the rope is a much riskier proposition, so the first climbs you undertake on the lead should be well within your ability. You will need to learn how to place all the protection equipment you carry, how to arrange your own anchor points and stances, and, above all, choose the way ahead based on what you see and the information given in guidebooks. If you begin climbing on a course staffed by qualified personnel, you are likely to be given the opportunity to lead a very short time after starting out. This is no bad thing, for you will quickly learn to appreciate the finer points of climbing and become more attuned to the rock.

Many people take their first leads alongside an instructor who is attached to a fixed rope by means of a mechanical ascending device. The instructor moves up alongside the student

▷ *Careful choice of the climbs you undertake will help to boost confidence as you gain experience. Don't attempt anything too difficult too soon.*

△ Take a long look at the route before setting off and try to work out in advance where the line goes.

◁ Differing types of rock require particular techniques and are not always suited to all climbers.

▽ Leading with an instructor alongside provides a valuable learning experience.

and, because they don't need to hold on to the rock at all, is able to stop and talk the student through runner placements, selection of line to climb and even ways to make sequences of moves. It is an invaluable method of learning and one in which progress can be made relatively quickly and painlessly. Of course you may discover that leading is not for you. There are thousands of climbers who have absolutely no desire whatsoever to lead, but still get great rewards from rock climbing.

Though there are superstars who shine through within a few years of starting out, for many the road is slower. This has advantages in that by the time you are climbing difficult rock the experience amassed stands you in good stead where safety is concerned. However you begin and however long you

climb, savour those first innocent steps into the vertical world – they are but a tantalizing morsel of the riches beyond.

Defining your terms

Thumb sprags, slopers, crimps and smears are all climbing holds and key words of the rock climber's world. But to the uninitiated they are probably meaningless – this chapter should bring enlightenment! In previous pages we have already mentioned a few holds that are commonly used and simple techniques to employ them to best effect. As you gain more experience, you'll discover that a broader repertoire of holds is required. What follows is a brief look at these types of holds, and where and how they can be used most effectively.

JUG, BUCKET OR "THANK GOD" HOLD

These are huge holds that you can curl all your hand over, rather like holding on to the rungs of a ladder (see also page 44). Jugs instill great confidence for the simple reason that you can hang off them without strength draining away too quickly. Any jug that appears at the end of a particularly harrowing sequence of moves is always very welcome, hence its more descriptive term of "thank God" hold. Large holds are often a good place to linger, taking a well-earned rest (or semi-rest). You can also look ahead to see what's in store.

▷ *The ultimate "thank God" hold. The only worry is whether or not it will bear the full weight of the climber!*

FINGERHOLDS

These are small versions of jugs. The finest fingerhold to use is one that has a small lip to it or is incut at the back. Though you might only be able to curl the ends of your fingers over the edge, it is generally sufficient for a fairly strong pull. Fingerholds are sometimes flat and are fine to pull on from directly below but much harder to hang on to if they are at shoulder level. Normally you'd use a flat fingerhold with fingers bent 90 degrees at the main joint. If, however, you can only get the very tips of your fingers on the hold, you must arch the main joint above the hold and keep the fingers rigid. It helps to place your thumb over the first finger as well so that it can take some of the load. This is sometimes referred to as a "crimp". You might also find some relief from levering your thumb against a protrusion or edge if it's available. By levering inwards or pushing outwards, it makes the fingers feel more securely gripped to the rock.

▽ *A tiny ledge can be crimped (as held by the lower hand) or held with the tips of the fingers.*

△ *A flat edge can be gripped with at least half the length of the fingers to provide a secure hold.*

△ *An incut fingerhold, though small, usually feels very positive.*

Creative handholds

A s we found out on pages 44–45, handholds are not always what they seem. Sometimes, to get the most out of them, you need to be a little creative in your use of them. Here are a few more tips on how to use marginal holds or to create a hold where there doesn't appear to be one!

SLOPER OR ROUNDED HOLD

These types of hold do not generally instill confidence and are particularly worrying the smaller they become. A sloper that you can get your whole hand over can be made to feel fairly secure provided that you can keep your whole arm and body weight directly below it. Basically, what you do is to try to smear the whole hand over the rock and rely on friction and pressure to hold the hand in place.

Sometimes you can slot fingers into tiny depressions in the rock to give valuable extra purchase. Slopers, though they are found on most types of rock, are more prevalent on sandstone and gritstone, and granite that has been worn by water. The classic, if not particularly encouraging, place to come across slopers is at the top of a gritstone crag. Often you can achieve extra pulling power and grip by smearing part of your arm over the rock as well.

PALMING

This is exactly what it says it is – pushing on the inside of the palm. It can be implemented in several ways, each of which is applicable to different types of move. One of the ways it is most usefully employed is where you have a good positive handhold for one hand and need

◁ Sloping handholds may not provide much confidence but you must make the most of what is available.

▷ Imaginative use of a "palming" technique allows the climber to make a high step.

to make a clean, big step up on to a good foothold. Pulling up on the jug with one hand and pushing down on the rock with the palm of the other lightens the weight on each arm, pushes you further away from the cliff face and allows you to make a high step up. Another application for palming is in climbing corners or grooves where there are few handholds. By pressurizing each palm on either side of the corner or groove, you can relieve enough weight from one foot at a time in order to move them higher. There are climbs where this technique, along with smearing for the feet, are the only techniques that will get you up the climb. Needless to say, climbing long sections of rock devoid of any other types of handholds and footholds can be a harrowing experience.

UNDERCLING

Undercling holds are used in many different ways and, when used imaginatively, prove to be one of the most versatile of all for resting between sequences of moves. The most frequently found use for the undercling is in situations where you are confronted with having to make a move over an overlap or

△ *An undercut hold is less tiring on the arms when resting.*

▷ *Undercut holds will also allow you to lean out and look up the rock to see where you are going.*

▽ *Relying wholly on friction for both feet and for both hands requires confidence in the friction properties between boot and rock, and skin and rock.*

overhang. These features on a rock face often have a crack running horizontally beneath which the hands can be slotted in, with the palms facing upwards. Pulling outwards on your arms allows you to arch your back out and pop your head over the obstacle to see what lies ahead. Once you have found suitable handholds over the lip, you can move one hand over while keeping the other firmly gripped in the undercling. Having taken a good grip of the hold over the lip, release the undercling and move the hand up to another hold and pull yourself around or over the overhang. You can use underclings in many other situations. Basically, any hold that you can get your fingers or your whole hand into from underneath is an undercling. Even if there isn't a hole or crack, a small edge might suffice. On steeper rock underclings are used to best advantage to help you rest and recover enough for the next sequence of moves.

More creative handholds

The weakest link in your body climbing machine is in the fingers. Once you have progressed on to steeper, harder climbs, this will become apparent. To use the types of holds described here, you will need to build up your finger strength.

PINCH-GRIP

Whenever you use a hold between fingers and thumb it's called a pinch-grip. They come in many shapes and sizes, from small and rounded to large and square, and can be used sideways, lengthways or on a diagonal. One of the typical features of limestone rock is the tufa, which is a calciferous flow that hardens over time and usually stands proud of the rock surface. Tufa is the ultimate pinch-grip hold as there are quite often little indents into which you can place your fingers for extra grip. You can also pinch sharp edges of rock in a fairly open-handed grip and gain some security for an upward, or sideways pull. Small knobbles

of rock that protrude from the surface are another type of pinch-grip. A good way to train for increasing the power of your pinch-grip is to lift concrete building blocks – it also toughens the ends of your fingers!

POCKETS

Pockets or holes in the rock are most commonly found on limestone crags, but they are by no means exclusive to limestone. They vary in size tremendously from holes that you can only insert one or two fingers into, to great big ones that you can get both hands in at the same time. They are frequently deep enough to get most of the length of the fingers into, and so even though they might be small they offer excellent grip if you have the finger strength to hang on and pull up. Pockets sometimes have a lip on the upper inside and, having used one to pull up on, you may then be able to turn it into an undercling hold when you move above it.

△ An open-handed pinch-grip is useful for maintaining balance.

△ A finger pocket combined with a pinch-grip by the thumb.

△ A one-finger pocket requires strong fingers.

△ *Here, the weight is taken mainly over the left foot with layaway handholds to maintain the climber's position.*

▷ *The left hand has an open-hand pinch-grip held in an undercut position, while the right hand holds an inverted side-pull or layaway.*

SIDE-PULLS OR LAYAWAYS

Side-pulls are commonly used to allow you to lean sideways to reach another hold that would otherwise be difficult to get to. They are also used to pull yourself sideways on to a foothold that is off to one side or the other. The sides of cracks, regardless of size, can be used to pull sideways on, or to layaway off, and so also can any edges that run vertically on the rock surface. They can also be used to gain a rest, provided the rest of the body is in balance. Simply lean away from the hold and try to keep your arm straight. An arm that is straight rests on the bones and joints, and saves the muscles from becoming more fatigued in the process.

Unusual positions

There are usually several ways in which to overcome an obstacle. However, some of these ways will be more efficient in terms of energy expended than others. This is where good technique comes in to play. Here are a few special techniques to try out, experiment with and then make part of your everyday climbing repertoire.

LAYBACKING

Laybacking is a technique that requires the hands and feet to work in unison. The handholds you use are layaways or side-pulls and feet are usually smeared or placed on any available edges. It is a powerful series of moves in which the hands pull in one direction and the feet push in another. Such is the force generated that in a full-on layback if your hands lose their grip you'll almost certainly catapult out and away from the rock! As a series of linked moves, laybacking is very strenuous indeed and it is sometimes very difficult to take one hand off to place or remove protection. When you do take one hand off, the balance of power between feet and hands is altered and there is a tendency to swing outwards towards the direction of your feet. This rather unnerving phenomenon is known by climbers as "barn-dooring". Layback techniques can also be used as an isolated move to gain holds higher up either on the side of a crack or on small edges in the rock surface.

△ **1** The layback position uses opposing forces from feet and hands.

△ **2** As your feet get closer to your hands, the forces increase.

△ **3** Maintain pressure on the feet and one hand, and move the other hand up.

△ **4** Now move your feet up again towards your hands ...

△ **5** ... and keep going for as long as you need to.

MANTLESHELFING

This is a technique rather than a hold, as such. The simplest scenario is one in which you have a ledge to get on to but there are no holds above the ledge that you can reach or use. It requires considerable effort on steep ground, where you might find it difficult to use your feet to help you. You have to reach up to the edge of the ledge and take hold of it with both hands, about shoulder width apart. You then give an almighty heave to bring your shoulders level with the ledge. If you are able, you should try to run your feet up the rock using the smearing technique. Using the momentum you have initiated, keep going upwards until you can turn one hand around into a palming pressure hold on the ledge and lock the arm by bending it at the elbow and throwing your head and shoulders over the top of it. You need to hold that position momentarily while you get the other arm into a similar position, and from there you straighten your arms with another heave and at the same time bring one foot up on to the ledge just on the outside of one arm. Transfer your weight immediately on to this foot and push up on your leg with all your might. As the leg straightens you can bring the other foot up on to the ledge and, in one dynamic movement, stand up.

That is the theory; the practice is considerably different and in the majority of instances you'll end up throwing yourself on to the ledge with a belly roll and then, accompanied by a great deal of leg kicking, nudge the rest of your body on until you are lying sideways on the ledge. Not as graceful but almost as effective!

△ **1** *Get a good grip of the ledge and walk your feet up as high as possible.*

△ **2** *Change the hand grip to a push down and straighten the arms.*

◁ **4** *It is important to keep the arms as straight as is feasibly possible.*

△ **3** *Move one foot up on the ledge by the side of your hands.*

▷ **5** *Finally bring up the second foot and stand up. Mantleshelfing requires a good deal of flexibility in the legs and body.*

Chimneying

This is a technique that you will either love or hate! Chimneys are large fissures in a rock face that will accommodate an entire climber. They can be so tight that there is very little room to manoeuvre, just wide enough to have your back on one side and feet on the other, or so broad that you have to straddle across them with arms and legs spread wide. The techniques for differing widths vary slightly. The classic technique is called back-and-footing. The clearest way to interpret this technique is that you push your back against one wall of the chimney while your feet push against the other and you use these opposing forces to hold you in position.

You don't even need to have handholds and footholds; pressure is sufficient. Although it's easy to hold yourself in, moving up can feel insecure if you take the pressure off. The correct technique for upward progress is vital. Place the palms of both hands on either side of you and just above buttock level. Pressurize them, push your back slightly away from the wall and move up until your buttocks are just above your hands, then immediately lean on to your back. Keeping your palms against the rock, you can then move your feet up, one at a time, until they are on the same level as your bottom. Repeat this process until you reach the end of the chimney. It is helpful if your legs

△ A classic back-and-foot position.

△ The technique of upward progress alternates between these two body positions (left and above).

△ In narrower chimneys it may be possible to utilize the knee for extra security.

◁ *A tight chimney will be awkward but will feel very secure. Note the pressure or palming handhold used to wedge the body more tightly and to help push upwards.*

△ *When a chimney is too wide for back-and-footing you may need to straddle across its width.*

◁ *By squirming with the body and pushing with all your might on feet and hands, it is possible to move upwards.*

don't have to be stretched fully out; a little bend at the knees helps you to exert greater pressure. Make sure that you take only short movements each time in order to maintain the security of the wedge and, if you can, use footholds and handholds to advantage.

Tight chimneys that allow little room for movement are climbed using similar principles but upward progress is achieved more by a wriggling technique in combination with pressure on either side of the chimney. When a chimney is so wide that back-and-footing is impossible, you will need to straddle the gap. Handholds and footholds are more crucial to success, as it is often quite difficult to get a high degree of opposing pressure to keep you in place. By their very nature, chimneys are fairly dark and dingy places and it can be extremely difficult to actually see the rock features in order to find holds – allow your eyes time to accustom to the poor light.

Jamming

Jamming is a technique used in smooth-sided, virtually holdless cracks. If you are adept at using them and a suitable crack exists, you might also jam as an alternative to using normal handholds. The technique is exactly as the term "jamming" suggests;

what it doesn't tell you, though, is how painful it can be if executed incorrectly, damaging the hand in the process.

HAND JAMS

A crack that is suitable for a hand jam is called a "hand crack". Clearly, what might be a hand crack for a person with small hands is likely to be a tight hand crack for someone larger. Assuming that you can get your hand into the crack, place it open-handed. Find a spot where there is about 1–2 cm (½–¾ in) clearance either side of the hand then push the thumb

◁ ▽ *A nearly perfect hand crack will provide very secure jams. On first acquaintance jamming may seem painful, but as you gain more experience a good jam becomes something of a "thank God" type of hold.*

into the palm of the hand. As you do, arch your hand across the crack so that the fingers are pushing against one side and the back of your hand against the other. It is important to stretch the skin as tightly as you can across the back of the hand, as this will prevent the skin from getting too badly damaged. Once you feel the tightening action happen, continue to arch your hand as much as possible. This will tighten the jam and make it much more secure – though it will be difficult to believe it at first! Now you can put some weight on it and see if it works.

FIST JAMS

When a crack is too large for a hand jam, it may be possible to jam your fist into it. The basic theory is very similar in that you need to keep the skin taut across your hand, and you must keep the pressure on as long as you need the jam to grip. There are two ways to jam the fist. One is quite simply to make a fist and the other is with the thumb pressed inside curled fingers.

Fist jams can be used effectively in parallel-sided cracks or in tapered cracks. Normally you would use them with the back of the hand

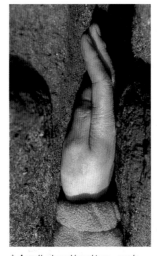

△ *A well-placed hand jam – push the thumb into the palm and arch your hand across the crack to create a sound hold.*

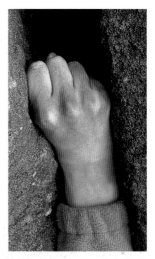

△ *When a crack is too wide for a hand jam, try wedging the fist into the crack. Make sure that the thumb is tucked inside the palm.*

facing out from the crack but in a great many situations you will find them more comfortable to use if the inside of the hand faces outwards. One hand each way is a useful technique to employ for repeated fist-jamming movements.

● FOOT JAMS

Any part of the body can be used to jam with. The toes, or better still, the whole foot, can be utilized in a suitable-sized crack. Toes can be jammed into narrow cracks, about the size you would use for your fingers or hands. The whole foot can be used, either straight in, or placed sideways if the crack is large enough. You must be careful, however, not to jam your foot too deeply into a crack. It is remarkably easy to get a foot well and truly wedged in. This will make moving up impossible! Try to achieve a jam that gives enough security to use successfully, but will not prove a hindrance when moving on.

▷ *This shows a foot jam wedged sideways across a wide crack.*

More jamming

Once you have worked on and perfected the more obvious jamming techniques, you can move on to the more esoteric. Once again, an immunity to pain will help!

FINGER JAMS OR LOCKS

If a crack is obviously too narrow for the whole of your hand, you might need to jam part of it. In an extreme case this might mean just the tips of your fingers, but hopefully the majority of the time it will be at least half the length of your fingers. If you can get your hand in up to the knuckles, the crack is called a tight hand crack. If you can get the fingers in up to the middle joint, it's called a finger crack.

The easiest and least painful way to jam the fingers is to find a constriction in the crack through which your fingers will not slip, regardless of how much pressure is put on them. It is possible to take your body weight on one or two fingers alone, if they are well placed. If the crack is parallel-sided, you must twist the fingers into the crack to create a "camming" action. This is effected by placing the fingers in with the thumb pointing downwards and trying to bend your wrist through 90 degrees. If you are able to lever the thumb against one side of the crack, it helps. It is possible to make a finger jam with the thumb facing upwards, by applying similar principles. It tends to be much more painful though.

KNEE-BARS

The knee-bar is another type of jammed hold. It is particularly useful for gaining a rest or increasing security, and is essential for off-width crack climbing. In its simplest form, it requires a foothold and a constriction in the crack just above knee level against which the knee can be wedged. The other foot must either find a suitable foothold to the side or just

▽ *Long sections of thin finger-crack climbing require a few years' climbing experience.*

△ *A finger jam, where the finger is simply wedged into a constriction in the crack, is secure but sometimes a little painful.*

△ *With this style of finger jam or lock, two fingers are intertwined to form a wider profile for greater security.*

△**1** *This is a strenuous and technical sequence on very steep rock.*

△**2** *A bold laybacking move gains a tiring position where strength may wane rapidly.*

△**3** *Judicious use of a knee-bar allows the climber to release both hands to rest!*

simply be held in place with pressure and friction. You must commit yourself fully to the locking position that can be achieved in order for the technique to be effective. Even on vertical rock faces, it is possible to let go with both hands and hang from a knee-bar.

OFF-WIDTH CRACKS

Quite possibly the most feared of all crack types, off-widths are cracks that are too wide to jam fists and feet into and too narrow to get your whole body into. There are some climbers who are attracted to off-widths, have honed the technique and make any ascent look childishly simple. They are a rare breed, specializing in esoteric arts. Most people avoid any climb with the mention of the word off-width associated with it.

Techniques to cope with an off-width crack are, in theory, straightforward. You basically have to wedge any part of your body into the crack, according to the width. Most of the time you should be able to get a shoulder, one arm and a half a leg in. The rest of your body hangs out of the crack groping around for any kind of

purchase possible. In order to wedge the bits of your body in the crack, you often have to get yourself into some incredibly contorted positions and might even use your head as a wedge! Upward progress is a harrowing experience and at best tenuous.

◁ *Off-width crack climbing is perhaps the most awkward of all styles of climbing. There are, however, a few who delight in the struggle.*

Gymnastic moves

You have already come across some of these techniques in the warm-up section of this chapter. It needs to be stressed that some are difficult, and should only be practised once you are fully warmed up. Needless to say, they may one day prove to be the only way of successfully completing a hard route or sequence of moves.

DYNO

A dyno is a movement rather than a hold. The term is an abridgement of "dynamic leap", and it requires a great deal in the way of confidence, agility, strength and technique. Normally you would only resort to a dyno if the rock between you and the next hold is obviously devoid of anything remotely usable, and the hold you are jumping for is a good one. It goes without saying that should you fail to reach your hold, or if the hold is not as good as you thought, then a fall is the inevitable consequence. You should be prepared for this, placing good runners to protect yourself, and ensuring that the person belaying you is aware of the move you are about to make and is ready for a possible fall. Of course, if you are bouldering, then there should be no problem – you simply fall to the ground if you fail.

THE FIGURE-OF-FOUR

This is a particularly difficult move, though it does enable you to reach holds that may otherwise be out of reach. To carry out a figure-of-four successfully you will need a few very good handholds. Take one leg over your arm, which remains in place on its hold. This leg can now be used by you to move up by pressing down on your arm. You should then be able to reach high with the free hand.

△ The figure-of-four is surprisingly comfortable and effective for making long reaches on steep rock.

△ **1** The climber "psyches up" for a big dyno move – success requires total commitment and belief.

△ **2** Having reached the hold solves only half the problem; there is still a very strenuous move to make.

HEEL-HOOK

A heel-hook is a particularly useful hold for climbing overhangs. A well- positioned heel can take considerable pressure off the arms and can also be used as a lever for pulling yourself over the lip of an overhang. It does require a considerable amount of flexibility and confidence.

△1 *Get a good grip of the handholds over the lip of the roof and hang straight off them. Throw one of your feet up to the hand level and hook the heel of the shoe on to a ledge or protrusion.*

△2 *Pull up on your arms at the same time as levering on your leg. When you get your shoulders to hand level, convert the grip into a downward pressure hold and push your shoulders up.*

△ 3 *Now for the really strenuous bit – lever up on the foot and reach for higher holds with the hands. For a firmer foothold, shift your body weight over the foot as soon as possible.*

ROCK-OVER

A rock-over is a very useful technique to get to grips with. It consists of shifting your balance and weight from a foot on a lower foothold to one on a higher foothold. As this sequence demonstrates, it is another gymnastic move, requiring strong leg muscles and a developed sense of balance.

△1 *Select the foothold to use – the higher the step, the more difficult the rock-over will be.*

△2 *Having placed your foot on the hold, pull your body weight over towards the foot.*

△3 *Transfer all your weight on to the foot and push up with your leg using all your strength.*

Strength and technique

The first few climbs of your newly discovered sport will undoubtedly be fairly low-angled and of an easy grade. As you gain experience and familiarity with movement on rock, your confidence will increase and you'll doubtless have higher aspirations. From here on in the climbs you embark on will become steeper and the holds smaller and fewer. Those less precise techniques that you might have been able to get away with on easier-angled rock will create undesirable difficulties on steeper ground and harder climbs. Shoddy footwork is not forgiven, bad planning may lead you into corners from which there is no escape, and tiring arms lead to waning strength and confidence.

▽ *Low-angled climbs, where you can take most of the weight on your feet, are ideal for developing precise technique.*

BUILDING STRENGTH

There is an enormous amount you can do to improve your strength, which in the long term will help you to climb better. Building up arm and finger strength pays very quick dividends, for example. There are exercises that you can do to help, but at the end of the day climbing is by far the best way to train. This is where the climbing wall comes into its own. Within the confines of the indoor environment you are able to concentrate fully on a well thought-out training programme that will build both strength and ability on a gradual but effective platform. The belief you have in yourself to hang around on small holds for long periods of time contributes massively to success.

TECHNIQUE

Strength in itself is not the answer. Good technique is important – perhaps even more important. Developing good technique is only achieved through many hours on rock. Like many sports there are those who appear to be born rock climbers. To these people movement on rock seems to be second nature, but unfortunately we are not all equal in this respect. Talented climbers display a natural ability and body awareness that allows them to move fluently over the rock in total control of both body and mind. Such movement, like all things done competently, is a pleasure to witness. One of the great things about rock climbing is that this level of performance is within the grasp of almost anybody who perseveres. The lessons we learn on early climbs are the foundation stones for harder ones later on in our career. The basics of good footwork and the ability to work out sequences of moves apply equally, regardless of the grade of the climb.

◁ As your climbs get steeper your strength needs to be developed to enable you to hang on for longer.

▷ A combination of technique and strength in equal proportions makes a good climber.

◁ Bouldering outside in a perfect sun and sea setting. What better way to train for longer climbs?

Finding rests on a route

The ability to find resting positions while in the most unlikely climbing situations pays enormous dividends. On easier climbs there are frequently large ledges to accommodate the whole foot, the rock angle lays back and all the weight can be taken over the feet. On steeper ground it may not be possible to stand in a position where you can take both hands off to rest. You might find yourself standing on a tiny foothold with the edge of one shoe and very little for the other foot. Handholds might be smaller than you would like and the aura of the situation

might be very intimidating. By using your imagination, it is usually possible to find a rest of sorts.

KEEPING CLOSE INTO THE ROCK

On steep rock you must keep your body pushed up against the rock surface and the body weight directly over the feet. To achieve this a fine positioning of the body may be required and the difference of a few centimetres one way or the other can often make a significant difference. To stand efficiently on tiny toeholds, you'll need to use the inside edge of your rock shoe. The reasons for this are simple enough – you need to glean as much support as you can from the shoe and the lateral rigidity offers more than the longitudinal rigidity. It is also possible to stand on the outside edge of the shoe but it is less effective for upward movement unless you are making moves across the rock face. As an aid to resting, however, you'll find it very useful for relieving pressure and tension from cramped feet.

RESTING YOUR ARMS

Try not to hang on too tightly with the hands and arms. Concentrate wholly on placing as much weight as possible over the feet and if your feet tire change position occasionally. The ideal resting handhold is a side-pull or under-cut. The reasons for this are simple enough – the arm is in a fairly low position where blood can flow freely to the muscles. If you are hanging on to a hold above your head, the blood will drain from your arms and the muscles will not be replenished with oxygen.

◁ *Resting between difficult sections of a climb is vitally important and every opportunity should be taken.*

△ By varying the holds that you use, arms and fingers are less likely to cramp up.

△ Arms can be rested most effectively by dangling them at full stretch to allow the blood to flow back into the fingers. Alternate arms for effective rests.

If you are forced to hang on holds above your head, you must try to rest each arm by alternately dangling each down below waist level and shaking the hand loosely to assist blood flow. This is called "shaking out". Try not to rush the process. If you are very tired, it takes a good 5 minutes or more to rest adequately and recover sufficient energy to continue. By moving on before you are properly rested, you'll find that strength wanes very rapidly to the extent that you might not have enough power to complete a sequence. If you have to, don't be afraid to back down to a "no-hands" resting-place, even though it might mean down-climbing a fair distance. It is all about maximizing the remaining power to achieve the next rest or the end of the difficulties.

◁ Sometimes a full rest can be found by climbing down a few feet to a ledge. This is the best possible rest you can have.

Saving your arms

Rests where you are able to use under-cut holds or side-pulls are generally more efficient. You only use strength to hold body weight in to the rock surface rather than hang on. Of course, holds such as these are not always available and some imagination may be required to find the most effective resting position. If you have to hang on to large holds above your head, it's worth trying to open up the hand as much as possible. Big jugs or flat holds can be held with the palm where the wrist is bent over at 90 degrees like a hook – rest with a straight arm to save the precious energy in your muscles. Again, try to alternate hands so that you get a good rest for each arm.

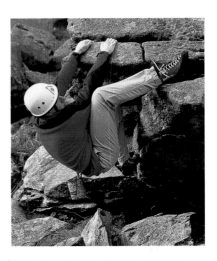

△ A combination of heel-hook with the foot wedged in the crack adds security while also being effective for saving strength.

△ A large jug or ledge can be held in a hook grip for greater comfort.

◁ Experiment with different body positions to find the most comfortable rest.

Crack climbing can be extraordinarily trying and tiring. Feet and hands become cramped from continually being wedged into the crack. If the crack is wide enough, it might be possible to get a hands-off rest by wedging your knee into the crack and levering your foot against one side. This is called a knee-bar. Knee-bars may also be found anywhere where there is a suitable feature and can sometimes even be effected on open features such as below overlaps or overhangs.

The heel-hook is another good way to save energy and it is used to surmount overhangs. It is exactly what it sounds like – by hanging underneath an overhang by your hands, the foot is brought up to the same level and hooked on to a suitable protrusion or ledge. You can take a surprisingly large proportion of the strain from your arms by using the foot and the leg as a lever. The drawback with this is that you do need to be rather gymnastic and flexible, for it is a powerful manoeuvre.

In a similar vein is the toe-hook. Whilst not used as a powerful movement, it is a useful way to maintain balance or equilibrium. Take one example – on a layback sequence you find it difficult to prevent the opposing forces, of feet pushing while hands pull, causing you to swing outwards. This rather alarming effect is known as "barn-dooring" and once it comes into effect it is a struggle to prevent the inevitable flying fall. If you can hook the toe of one boot into a crack or behind a rib of rock, it is possible to use it to hold your body stable while you try to move into a position of more security. Toe-hooks can sometimes be used to help gain a rest in an otherwise seemingly impossible situation.

▷ *A toe-hook in a large hole provides leverage for the move up as well as helping to gain a useful rest.*

▽ *The arms will not tire so quickly if they are used at full stretch or fully bent.*

Energy-saving techniques

By far the most efficient and energy-saving way to climb is to use the technique of bridging. This was, of course, a technique that we introduced right at the very beginning when we took our first steps on rock and it is something that we can apply, with some imagination, to many situations encountered on more difficult climbs. It is possible, for example, to use a bridging technique on a steep, open wall where none of the more recognizable features of grooves and corners are apparent. You might find yourself taking all your weight on the very tip of the inside of the toe of your shoe. This is an incredibly tiring position for the foot to be in for any protracted period of time, but if you are able to reach out and push sideways with the other foot it is possible to alleviate much of the strain.

An "Egyptian" or "drop knee" is a useful technique to conserve energy on very steep rock. It is a comfortable position that allows you to keep the torso very close in to the rock surface and more weight on the feet and legs than would normally be possible. As the illustration (right) shows, however, it is an advantage to be able to contort the body and to retain flexibility. It is such an unconventional technique to employ that many climbers forget its usefulness. Milder forms and shapes than that shown can be achieved in a great many climbing scenarios – all it requires is some imagination.

MORE DYNOS!

Dyno is a shortened term for dynamic motion. A dyno move is one in which the climber utilizes momentum to their advantage. Take

◁ Any feature that can be straddled by bridging across it is likely to be less tiring.

▷ The same feature climbed using the technique of back-and-footing, which is most commonly associated with chimney climbing.

△ On steep, open climbs it is often difficult to engineer a rest position. You will be reliant on good footwork and stamina to get you through.

◁ Here the toe is hooked to a hold to help secure the body in close, thus permitting weight to be borne by the foot and directly below the handgrips. This is sometimes called an Egyptian or "drop knee".

the example of a scenario in which you can see an excellent handhold that is just out of arm's reach or that you can touch but not get enough grip on to pull up your body weight. A little momentum from a small push up from the feet will allow you to make the extra distance needed to curl your hand over the good hold and heave up. An extreme form of dyno is where one might leap for a hold neither knowing whether it is good, bad or indifferent – discovering it to be usable is the only justification for such a technique to be deemed to make life easier for yourself!

"Flagging" is a term applied to describe a technique that is a perfectly natural movement of the body in motion, retaining balance. It is simple enough to use in a huge number of climbing scenarios at any grade – except perhaps the easiest, where it may be frowned upon as unnecessary and energy-wasting. It is often interpreted as a thrashing or leg-kicking movement – the fact that it is useful seems to be overlooked. The leg is used in one of two ways in flagging, either as a counterbalance to maintain equilibrium or as a pendulum action to assist in dynamic motion.

More energy-saving tips

There are other things not directly associated with body movement or holds that will help you conserve energy on steeper climbs. These include the efficiency with which you are able to place protection on the lead and also how you carry or "rack" your gear. There are several ways in which you can do this and every climber will, over time, learn which is the most suitable for their preferences. This does require experimentation and a mind open to change.

Considerable energy can be wasted trying to fiddle a nut into a crack that it clearly will not fit. Sometimes you look at a crack and be so convinced that a particular-sized nut will fit in that you become blind to other possibilities,

▷ Whenever you place runners on steep rock, try to find good holds and a comfortable position from which to operate.

whether of size of nut or even a different part of the crack! You will gain considerable advantage if you carry nuts of a similar size on individual karabiners, say large on one, medium on another and small on a third. If one nut doesn't fit the crack, there will almost certainly be another on the karabiner that will.

PREPARING PROTECTION

Many climbers, when faced with a difficult or crucial nut placement, will prepare themselves while in a comfortable position. If you know, or are fairly positive, that one particular-sized nut is likely to fit into the crack, you could remove it from the rack and if necessary clip in a quickdraw, and then move up to the placement with it held in your teeth. Once you reach the right spot all you need to do is to place it! Obviously you must be certain of the size, because if you're not you will needlessly waste valuable energy.

Some harness manufacturers have developed a special plastic clip for connecting a karabiner to; using the karabiner becomes simply a matter of pulling it rather than unclipping from the gear loop. It is helpful to rack gear in a particular order that you become familiar with. This, too, will save precious energy. Quickdraws, any nuts on rope slings and camming devices also need to be carefully positioned so that they are accessible almost by feel alone. Many items of protection equipment are colour-coded by the manufacturer – long winter evenings can be whiled away learning all the codes for your personal rack. No single method can be said to be categorically the best, so it is important to experiment and adapt a method to suit your needs. You may even find that you come to favour particular pieces of protection. Keep them to hand.

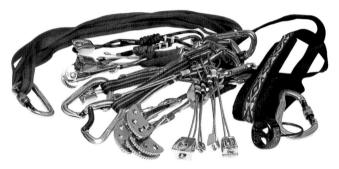

△ *When you rack your gear, make sure you work with a system that you are happy and familiar with.*

▽ *The climber checks out the way ahead. In doing this, he may save precious energy once on the climb.*

△ **1** *A runner gripped between the teeth ready for placement will save valuable energy on steep rock.*

△ **2** *You just have to hope it's the right size!*

Clipping the rope

Efficient clipping of the rope has two main benefits: you save energy the quicker you can perform the task, and there are ways to clip that increase your safety in the event of a fall.

The method by which you clip the rope into protection can also make a tremendous difference to the energy you expend. It is difficult to comprehend perhaps, but a fumbled clip could conceivably lead to dire consequences such as a long fall on the sharp end of the rope.

There are any number of ways to clip the rope into a runner efficiently. Like racking, it is as well to experiment with several before latching on to a method that suits your preferences and dexterity. Regardless of the method adopted, there are two important aspects to remember. Firstly, the gate of the karabiner

◁ *On sustained and steep climbs, energy conservation is crucial to success.*

▽ *Practise clipping the rope into running belays until you can do it blindfold!*

△ *A quickdraw clipped correctly with the straight-gate karabiner clipped to the bolt, and the rope running through the bent-gate karabiner.*

In this situation, the bent-gate karabiner has been clipped to the bolt. This will make it harder to clip the rope. The quickdraw should basically be the other way round (see far left).

◁ *It is not so easy to clip the rope into a straight-gate karabiner.*

into which you are clipping the rope should face away from the immediate direction you are going to be climbing in. This is to ensure that, in the event of a fall, the rope does not unclip itself. Secondly, you must ensure that the quickdraw is not twisted in any way once the rope is clipped in. A twist in the sling of the quickdraw can in rare cases also allow the rope to become unclipped in the event of a fall. It is a simple enough matter of adopting good habits in ensuring both aspects are observed.

One suggested method of clipping the rope into a quickdraw is illustrated. If you are clipping the rope into a runner that is way above your head you might have to pull a short length of rope up, grip it in your teeth and then pull up more so that you have enough slack rope to reach up and make the clip. Once the rope is in the karabiner, you can release the teeth grip and continue climbing. Holding the rope momentarily in the teeth means that you don't have to heave with all your might on the rope to pull it up to make the clip, and thus saves valuable energy resources. If, for whatever reason, you think you might fall off while you are

attempting the clip, don't forget to drop the rope from your teeth as you fall – only circus performers can hold someone in their teeth on the end of a trapeze!

◁ *A well-placed nut, with the quickdraw clipped to it.*

Falling off

Though falling is something that every climber must come to terms with, there are those to whom the idea is complete anathema and there are others to whom it is par for the course. To achieve the utmost purity of style, you should always try to climb without falling. This is called an "on-sight" ascent. Not so many years ago there was a saying amongst climbers that the "leader never falls". In times past this was a good adage to work to because there was little, if any, protection on a pitch. Today the situation has changed significantly. Leading climbs has become less of a risky business as equipment for arranging crack protection has developed and improved. There are still climbs on which it is impossible to arrange adequate protection, but they are fewer in number.

MODERN ATTITUDES

Purity of style and ambition to climb hard are not always good bed partners. Ambition can become headstrong and ignore purity entirely. More commonly, ambition will bring purity around to its way of thinking and a compromise is reached that is acceptable to both. Many climbers will push themselves beyond their "on-sight" grade, knowing full well that they will probably fall off at the crux and may do so several times before successfully completing the sequence. This ethic or compromise approach is better conducted on bolted or "sport" climbs where you know full well that the runners on to which you are falling will be capable of absorbing the shock of repeated falls. Traditional routes, where one places one's own protection, are not always so

△ The old adage, "the leader never falls", was sound advice in the days when climbers tied the rope directly around their waists.

▷ While the modern-day climber with all the safety trappings is more secure, it is still purer to climb without falling. You may find an acute lack of protection on some climbs!

◁ A steep bolt-
protected climb is an
ideal place to practise
falling off!

▷ Make sure that you
push yourself clear of
the rock and look
down to see where
you're heading to.

reliable. It is an accepted method of climbing, but it may not be entirely satisfactory to all climbers. Knowing that it is relatively safe to fall off helps you to keep your composure. At the extreme end of the scale there are climbs of high technical difficulty where the prospect of falling will mean certain death – if you attain those levels one would assume that you have advanced far beyond the scope of this book.

FALLING TECHNIQUE

Taking a fall will come to most leaders at some time. This may be on to bolts at the wall or on a sport climb, or it may be on to gear that the leader has placed. It is important to understand that it is not the act of falling that puts the climber in danger of injury – it is the impact with the rock face, wall, ledge or even the ground itself. Falling into space may be frightening, but provided that is all it is there should be no problem. It will be evident from this that, provided the protection is good and holds, falling off overhanging hard climbs is safer than falling off an easy slab. Falling off a slab means that the climber will come into contact with rock. There some tips for falling more safely. For example, you can push your-

◁ It is easier to
attempt climbs that
are beyond your
current ability on an
indoor wall – here
falling off is much
less serious.

self away from the wall or rock, rather than clinging on and scraping down the surface, doing untold damage. However, this takes a lot of experience and courage to do. The natural instinct is to cling!

Tips for seconding

When discussing techniques and ways to conserve energy, it is easy to forget that seconding a climb can sometimes be as tiring as leading. It may not be as mentally stressful (the fear factor should not be as great as that involved in lead-ing a climb), but stress levels could easily be equal in terms of frustration. Climbing tech-niques apply in the same way, but when it comes to taking out protection, energy loss can be outrageously high.

MENTAL ATTITUDE

Seconding a climb, if you are more used to leading, is generally approached in a rather lackadaisical manner and with the attitude that it'll be a lot easier on the blunt end of the rope. Climbers who set off to follow a pitch in this frame of mind will quite commonly get caught out and surprised by the awkwardness of the climbing. If at the same time they expe-rience difficulties removing runners that the leader has placed, the whole experience could prove quite harrowing.

REMOVING RUNNERS

Sometimes, particularly on the crux of a climb or on sections where it is preferable to keep going, the second might well decide to remove the runners from the crack but leave them on the rope rather than waste valuable energy unclipping them and clipping them on to the harness. When you arrive at a more comfort-able place to rest, the runners can be removed from the rope and placed on the harness. If a piece of protection proves difficult to remove and it is clear that you are going to waste a lot of strength getting it out, it may be better to ask the leader for a tight rope to take your full body weight while you fiddle the offending piece out. It is always a good excuse for a rest!

◁ On serious climbs of great difficulty the role of the second is vital. Having confidence in the second allows the leader to concentrate on the all-absorbing task of leading.

△ *Sometimes you'll find it more difficult to second climbs than you would if you were leading – it's an odd fact of life!*

▷ *Traverses, particularly difficult ones, can be intimidating and very serious for the second.*

● TRAVERSING AND DOWN-CLIMBING

There are certain situations in which seconding a climb can be as risky as leading it. An unprotected traverse is one such situation. Here, if a seconding climber comes off, he or she will swing down and out. If this happens on one of the numerous sea-cliff traverses that can be found around the world, the situation could be particularly exciting! A knowledge of prussiking will come in useful (see Chapters 3 and 5).

Another tricky situation for the second involves down-climbing. If the moves are not protected from above, a fall could be a long one. In these situations, the second needs to be as confident and capable as the leader.

ROPEWORK

Ropework is a fundamental part of modern rock climbing. It is worth practising the techniques described until they become second nature. There are usually several ways of doing things, but the methods shown here are simple and quick to learn. Ropework can be daunting, but taking things one step at a time will help. Do not try to remember everything at once. When learning new skills, it is important to remember the principles behind the instruction. By doing this, it should be easier to remember the steps as progress is made. This step-by-step approach to the ropework required for climbing should provide the tool kit needed to cope with most situations. It is up to the climber to dip into that tool kit and find the necessary tools required.

Opposite: *An exposed, hard route. Although the climbing is relatively straightforward, good judgement, a thorough knowledge of modern ropework and a cool head are necessary for a safe ascent.*

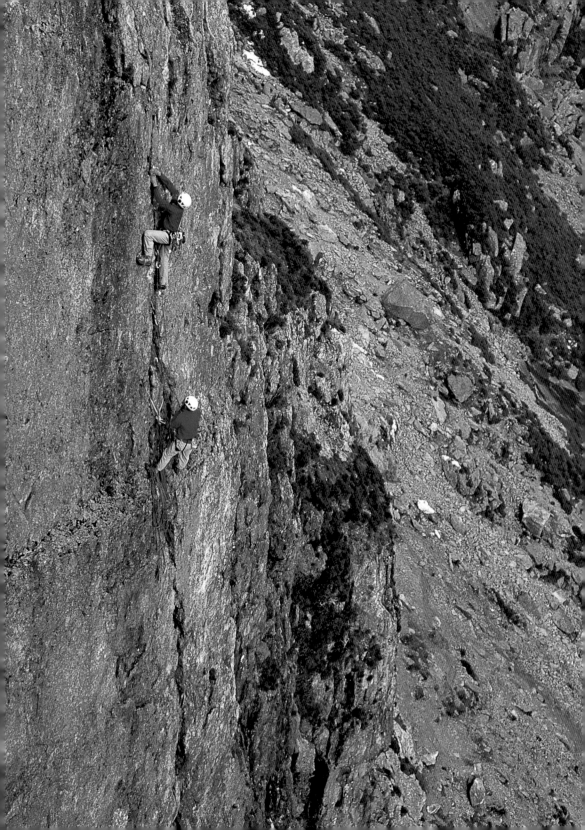

Fitting the harness

Many different designs of harness are available. Most are manufactured in one piece – the leg loops are an integral part of the harness. Some harnesses are "one size fits all", while others are produced in small, medium and large sizes. Some have adjustable leg loops which allow you to wear the harness over several layers of clothing if needed. Those harnesses without adjustable leg loops will require a little more judgement to ensure a good fit.

DOING THE HARNESS UP

Almost all harnesses rely on a double-back system on the buckle. The waistbelt has to be threaded though both parts of the buckle and back through one. This will hide half the buckle and form a "C" for closed and not "O" for open. If the buckle is not doubled back, it can come undone. There are several harness manufactures using different designs, so it must be stressed that in all cases the manufacturer's instructions must be followed to the letter.

△ This is a simple harness designed specifically for beginners. The waist belt cannot be undone completely so a "step-in" system is used. There is minimal provision for equipment-carrying, which makes this this harness more suitable for indoor venues.

◁ Here a climber is being lowered off a modern sport route. The consequences of an uncomfortable or incorrectly fastened harness need only be imagined.

Leg loops may be padded, to a greater or lesser extent, on the inside for comfort. Leg loop buckles should be doubled back like the waist belt, and should be on the outside of the leg. When putting a harness on, ensure the waist belt goes around the waist and not over the hips, and that the leg loops are positioned comfortably at the top of the leg and base of the buttocks.

If the harness has adjustable leg loops, adjust the waist belt part of the harness first and then the leg loops. This should ensure the correct fit. If the leg loops are tightened first, there will be a tendency not to position the waist belt correctly, leaving it too low on the hips. This is particularly important on harnesses that are designed to be put on without having to step into the leg loops, often referred to as a "nappy system" harness.

△ The buckle system is vitally important. Here the strap has not been doubled back, making the harness extremely dangerous because only a small amount of force will be necessary to release the buckle.

△ Here the "C" for closed is clearly visible and although not all harnesses employ the same fastening system, most are very similar. Take the time to look for an obvious way of checking your own and other people's harnesses easily.

● GETTING IT WRONG

There are a number of problems that may occur fitting a harness. The main ones are:

① Not getting the right position around the waist
② Not doing the buckle correctly
③ Getting a twist in the harness or leg loop

There have been many instances where expensive harnesses have been put on incorrectly in the enthusiasm to get on with the climb, but it must be stressed a little care and attention to detail is important at this stage. Spend a couple of minutes doing this job correctly. It is vitally important! Before you climb, make one last check.

△ The leg loops are too tight and the harness is positioned over the hips, making the centre of gravity too low. In the event of a slip, the climber could turn upside down.

△ This picture illustrates how easy it is to see an incorrectly fastened harness when clothing is tucked into the harness – however much or little clothing you happen to be wearing.

△ This is a comedy of errors! The support straps for the leg loops are crossed and the right leg loop is twisted, putting unnecessary strain on the stitching.

Attaching the rope

lthough there are many different designs of harness on the market, the method of tying the rope shown here is almost universal. The rope loop formed around the harness is not only important for the climber but forms an essential part of rope work outdoors, so it is important to get this right from the start.

TYING THE FIGURE-OF-EIGHT KNOT
It is vitally important to do this correctly. The harness and rope are both incredibly strong, but both are useless if they are not joined correctly. Most people use what is called a figure-of-eight knot, although some climbers prefer the bowline. Harnesses will have slight variations on where the rope is threaded and you must refer to the manufacturer's instructions and follow them implicitly.

△ **1** To tie a figure-of-eight knot, form a loop of rope a little over 1 m (3 ft) from the end of the rope.

△ **2** Now twist the loop and pick up the end of the rope. Push this through the loop to form a figure-of-eight knot in the rope.

△ **3** The end of the rope goes through the harness (see also the manufacturer's instructions) and then is re-threaded through the figure-of-eight knot.

△ **4** To do this, simply follow the rope back through the figure-of-eight knot, starting with the part of the knot that is nearest the harness.

△ **5** When the knot is completed there should be a spare tail of about 30 cm (12 in). The rope loop now formed should be fist size and the spare tail tied to form a stopper knot.

MAKING MISTAKES WITH THE FIGURE-OF-EIGHT KNOT

There are several mistakes which are often seen on indoor walls. Although many are not dangerous in themselves, they can lead to situations that can be either painful or dangerous, or both! These include clipping on to the main loop of the harness (if it has one) with a screwgate (locking) karabiner. Although this is still safe (providing it is a screwgate karabiner which is locked), any solid metal object next to the abdomen can cause bruising in the event of a slip. Using a screwgate karabiner also introduces an extra link to the system, which is unnecessary.

Another mistake is tying directly into the belay loop of the harness. Although probably still safe, it is not best practice. The main problem with doing either of the above is the tendency for the karabiner and figure-of-eight to get in the way and not keep everything neat and tidy. If everything is neat and tidy, you can see immediately when things are not right.

△ Tying into the rope using a screwgate (locking) karabiner attached to the belay loop of the harness.

THE STOPPER KNOT

The stopper knot is an important part of the tying-on procedure, ensuring the figure-of-eight cannot come undone while at the same time tidying up any loose ends of rope. Take the spare tail twice around the main rope and then back through itself. The trick is to get the tail the right length in the

△ To tie the stopper knot, take two turns around the main rope, then pass the tail back through the turns. Finally, tighten the knot.

MAKING MISTAKES WITH THE STOPPER KNOT

If the length of the tail of rope is judged correctly in the first place, there should be few problems. If, however, the tail is too long after the stopper is tied, it will not only look untidy but also get in the way and the climber may step on it if it's dangling by the feet. If it is too short, it will not form an effective knot. The only way this will affect security is if the figure-of-eight is allowed to work loose. This is unlikely in an indoor situation because you are only tied on and actually climbing for short periods at a time. The big difference comes when you move outdoors. Here you will use the same system, but in a different environment in which you

first place, about 30 cm (12 in), so that when the knot is finished there are no long ends to get in the way. This is not just for cosmetic reasons but for safety reasons also. A long trailing end of rope dangling down by the feet can be a real problem, especially if it is lying exactly where you don't want it, such as on a hold you are trying to use.

△ The completed "stopper knot" should be tight against the figure-of-eight, and there should still be a short "tail" of about 18–20 cm (7–8 in).

may stay tied into the harness for hours on end. Therefore it's worth taking trouble to get it right! Always ask yourself, what happens if?

△ Doing it wrong: too much rope has been used, and the stopper knot is not snug up against the figure-of-eight knot.

Belaying and belay devices

Until a few years ago climbers were still using the old method of "waist belays". This is where the rope is taken around the waist of the belayer and "paid out" or "taken in" round the waist and through the hands. The traditional waist belay still has a place in the greater game of mountaineering. However, today there are a multitude of belay devices on the market.

USING FRICTION

Although there is a vast range of belay devices on the market, most work on the same principle – that of friction generated by the rope being used to arrest a falling climber. There are, however, some differences which you will need to be aware of. The original metal belay device that uses friction was the sticht plate, which was developed in the early 1970s. There have been many developments in design with this type of belay device, and today there are lots to choose from. These include the Air Traffic Controller (ATC), the Sherriff, Tuba and Bug.

TOO LITTLE FRICTION

Some devices require a particular type of karabiner to give a smooth operation (you should refer to the manufacturer's instructions when purchasing a belay device); but, above all, it

◁ **1** *Here the rope is being "taken in" – the right hand is pulling the rope towards the belay plate while the left hand is pulling through the plate. Note the attention of the belayer to the climber above.*

▷ **2** *The rope is now in the "locked" position ready for the belayer to change hands and be ready for the next time that the climber moves (see also page 94).*

must be a screwgate (locking) karabiner! Devices which are easy and quick to pay the rope through to a lead climber are often referred to as "slick" and require an alert and attentive belayer at all times. This is because in the event of a fall, the rope will start to move very quickly through the belay device. The belayer will need to lock off, and effectively stop the rope running out, as quickly as possible. The slicker the device, the more difficult this will become if you do not act immediately.

PINCHING BELAY DEVICES

There are also devices that operate by pinching the rope to stop a fall. These work automatically – the belayer does not have to actively lock off. Because of this, they have found favour on many climbing walls. An inattentive belayer should, in theory at least, still be able to hold a falling climber. They also allow greater control when the climber is being lowered. However, it is very bad practice to get in the habit of being inattentive. It is a belayer's responsibilty to look after the lead climber, and this should not be taken lightly.

The belayer should always operate the device by keeping both hands on the rope and paying attention to the climber at all times.

Belay devices differ in their operation, but all come supplied with specific instructions, which must be adhered to.

● USING A GRI-GRI

The Gri-Gri has been designed for use at indoor climbing walls and on sport routes that are well equipped with bolts. Because they are less "dynamic" than most other belay devices, they should not be used on traditionally protected climbs – they will put too much force on the protection.

They are deceptively easy to use, but the instructions that come with them must be read and fully understood first. It is, for example, possible to thread the rope incorrectly through the mechanism. Also, when lowering a climber, the brake handle should not be used as a means of controlling speed.

△ The Gri-Gri will give a bigger jolt to the belayer should the climber fall off because it will stop or lock more quickly.

Bottom roping (indoors)

△ *This climber is being belayed from below.*

The most difficult job when starting out is learning how to operate an effective belay system. It is vitally important, because if you can't do this you will soon run out of climbing partners! Many climbing walls will have a section where ropes are permanently anchored at the top using a pulley system. The two ends of the rope will trail down the wall, enabling a climber to tie on to one end, while being protected by the belayer holding the other end. This is called bottom roping, because the belayer is operating from the bottom of the climb.

TAKING IN AND PAYING OUT

A belayer takes in and pays out the rope while the climber goes to the top of the wall and then lowers them back down again. The technique the belayer uses is called belaying and must be done correctly to ensure safety at all times, otherwise all the expensive equipment is of little use. There is a "live", or active, end of rope and a "dead" rope. The active rope goes from the climber to the belay plate via the top anchor, while the dead rope is that which is on the lower side of or below the belay plate. There is therefore a "live hand" and a "dead hand", which can be the left or right hand as occasion and position demands.

Belaying correctly from the start will develop a good technique for any climbing situation. It is important to keep one hand on the dead rope at all times, and in the locked position unless actually taking in, whichever belay device is used. Learn good belay habits from the start and follow the same procedure at all times. Also, remember to practise with your weaker hand.

△ **1** *Take the rope in with the "live" hand and pull through the plate with the "dead" hand. This requires good co-ordination.*

△ **2** *Lock the rope behind the plate with the dead hand and hold it by the hip to leave enough space for the live hand to move on to the dead rope.*

△ **3** *Take over the locking position on the rope with the live hand. You can then take the dead hand off the rope, move it up to take in the rope and repeat the same procedure.*

LOWERING A CLIMBER

When the climber reaches the top of the wall, control their descent with both hands behind the belay device on the dead rope, creating as much friction as possible, and then ease the hands forward as necessary. When lowering a very light climber, it may be necessary to bring the dead rope forward slightly and decrease the friction. Devices like the Gri-Gri and Single Rope Controller (SRC) will need to be released before anyone can be lowered, but keep the hand in the locked position while the brake is released to ensure a controlled descent. You must refer to the manufacturer's instructions before trying out any type of device.

USING BOTTOM ANCHORS

Many walls now provide additional anchors or in situ belays at the bottom of the wall for the belayer to clip on to. This is particularly useful where there may be a big weight difference between the belayer and the climber. In this case, either belay direct from the anchor or clip a sling from the anchor to the main load-bearing loop of your harness to stop you flying into the air in the event of your heavier leader falling off – it does happen!

△ The climber is being lowered under control. The belayer is watching closely from a good braced position against the wall, with both hands controlling the descent on the dead rope.

● GETTING IT WRONG

Common mistakes include loading the rope incorrectly in the belay device, making it impossible to get the "S" shape through the plate. This generates little friction on the belay device. Another mistake often seen is someone holding the "live" and "dead" ropes together in front of the plate. This will also result in little or no friction being generated by the device.

▷ The belay device is clipped to the equipment-carrying loop and will probably rip out in the event of a fall or when lowering.

Learning to lead (indoors)

The natural progression after doing some bottom roping is to lead a route from the bottom of the wall, clipping the bolts (running belays) and the top anchor, and then being lowered back to the ground. Most climbers who are ready to lead will by this time have experienced a good deal of bottom roping.

THAT FIRST LEAD

The first lead should be completed on a climb that you are familiar with. The grade of the climb should be well within your capacity – you don't want to frighten yourself too much on your first lead! There will be a continuous line of bolts (those running belays) placed every few feet on the route to clip as the climber gains height. Each bolt will have a short sling and metal snaplink karabiner on the end which the rope can be clipped in to. If your chosen route does not have these quick-draws already in place, make sure that you carry your own. You will have to place these as you lead the route, so make sure you take enough for each of the bolts. You should ensure that there are no twists in the rope or

△ ▷ Clipping the rope into the quickdraw can be done with either hand. Here the climber demonstrates, using his thumb to hold the karabiner and fingers to work the rope (above, right hand); and fingers to hold the karabiner and thumb to work the rope (right, left hand).

quickdraws as you make the clip, which can cause unnecessary friction or tangles. The best way to avoid tangles is to take one hand off the rock, staying in balance as you do so. Lift the rope from your waist and clip the protection by holding the karabiner steady with the third finger and twisting the rope in with the index finger and thumb. Always warn your belayer (they should be watching anyway) that you require some slack rope to reach up and clip the protection.

THE ORDER OF EVENTS

After checking your harness and the tie-in knot, climb up and clip the first karabiner. With the protection clipped, simply continue up and clip the next bolt with a quickdraw through it, until you reach the top. The belayer pays out the rope to the climber as they gain height and should be alert to their demands, especially when they need to clip a high bolt which requires the belayer to pay the rope out, take in as the climber passes the bolt, and then pay out again! Belay devices that lock automatically (such as the Gri-Gri or SRC) are not so easy to use to pay the rope out, so more warning must be given to the belayer. Lowering with a Gri-Gri employs exactly the same technique as all belay devices, but don't try and control the lower with the handle. The first few leads should be well within the capabilities of the climber, allowing them to familiarize themselves with the technicalities of ropework, rather than be near their technical climbing limit and unable to clip the protection.

Holding a falling leader will create much more of a shock on the belayer and may well lift them off the ground. In this situation you learn the value of using a ground anchor. This may take the form of a metal bolt in the floor or wall, or you may find a belay bag – a heavy bag to which the belayer can attach themselves. When the climber has reached the top, or they fall off (whichever comes first!), take the rope back in to the braking position, hold and control their descent with both hands and release the brake.

△ *The climber has tied the figure-of-eight correctly, but the stopper knot is incorrect and will have to be adjusted before they are ready to lead the climb.*

△ *This is a "slick" device and it is therefore very easy and quick to pay the rope out to a leader, but will be a little more difficult to hold someone. In all indoor situations, the belay device is clipped to the main load-bearing loop of the harness with a karabiner.*

△ *This is similar to the original design of the belay plate. It is simple, relatively inexpensive and very effective. A fairly high degree of friction will be generated with this device so holding falls should be easier.*

Using the climbing wall

There is no need to frighten yourself by jumping into leading when you first start climbing. Use the bottom roping system to get used to ropes, harnesses and belay devices. In this situation, provided the person at the other end of the rope is alert, the rope is positioned correctly and properly attached to your harness, there is very little that should go wrong. As soon as you reach the top of the wall, simply sit back on the rope while your partner lowers you to the ground. Falling off is no problem, because the rope goes from your harness, through the top anchor and down to your anchor person (belayer). You are able to climb in complete safety and this is a very good way to improve your technique, by pushing yourself with minimal risk. Finally, it is important to communicate with your partner. Keep the climbing calls to a minimum. Indoors you should require nothing more than the words "slack" (I want more rope) or "tight" (I want less rope). When the wall is busy it may be important to add your partner's name to avoid confusion. However, a full list of calls is included here with an explanation of what the call means (see opposite). The climbing calls are useful at the indoor wall. However, they become a vital part of the safety system when climbing multipitch routes outside. Communication is essential in this situation, but it is useful to become familiar with the calls early in your climbing career.

CLIMBING WALL PROCEDURES

When you are on a leading wall you will need your own rope, unlike in most bottom roping situations, where the ropes will be in place and it is normal practice to use those. All indoor walls will have their own system for monitoring and checking the ropes periodically. What you must do is establish what the procedures are when you go to an indoor wall, as circumstances will vary enormously. Something else that may vary considerably is the top anchor from which you will lower off. In most cases there will be a screwgate (locking) karabiner which can easily be clipped (and screwed up) before commencing your descent. Other walls may have a system similar to the lower-off points shown on page 104. This should present no problem as long as you are prepared, otherwise things may come as a shock, particularly at the top of your first lead!

▽ The first bolt is often the most difficult to clip but is also the most important. It will stop you hitting the ground in the event of a fall.

● THE CLIMBING CALLS

The call (UK)	The call (US)	Its meaning
Safe!	Off belay!	Leader's call to inform belayer (second) that leader is safe.
Taking in!	Taking in!	Leader's call to second that leader is taking excess rope in.
That's me!	That's me!	Second's call to leader, rope is tight on second.
Climb when ready!	Climb when ready!	Leader's call to second after putting rope through belay plate.
Climbing!	Climbing!	Second informing leader they are ready to climb.
OK!	Climb on!	Leader's affirmative to second, second starts climbing.
Slack!	Slack!	Pay out more rope.
Tight! (Tight rope!)	Take!	Take in any slack rope
Watch me!	Watch me!	Leader's call to belayer to pay attention during sequence of hard moves.

● LIVING DANGEROUSLY

Because of the friendly atmosphere of many indoor climbing venues, and climbers in the main being sociable animals, there is a tendency to be lulled into a false sense of security and to be a little casual. This has to be fought against at all times. One lapse could lead to an accident. Here are some common dangerous situations seen at climbing walls:

• Standing too far away from the wall when belaying. This is especially dangerous if the climber is heavier than the belayer, because it is possible for them to be pulled off their feet and into the wall, letting go of the belay device in the process.

• Allowing the elbow of the "dead" or locking hand to become trapped by standing with it too close to the wall. This could make it very difficult to lock off properly if your climber falls. You need to give your locking-off hand plenty of room to move.

• Talking to people standing around you while you are belaying. This is dangerous because it means you are not concentrating on what your climber is doing.

▷ *These belayers are standing too far away from the wall and are not concentrating on their climbing partners.*

Safety outdoors

Although the techniques used climbing indoors can be used outside on real rock, there are many differences that the novice climber should be aware of. These are not always obvious. Safety and self-reliance become very important in this wider environment, as do considerations such as conservation, first aid, navigation, weather and appropriate clothing and equipment.

● USING A GUIDEBOOK

It is important to have access to a guidebook. This will enable you to find the routes you want. Starting up the wrong route could quickly lead you into trouble if the route is harder than you expected! Remember that guidebooks have different conventions.

▷ Guidebooks often have maps, topographical guides and photographs to help locate your chosen route.

THINKING OF THE ENVIRONMENT

Before looking in detail at climbing outdoors, and particularly the ropework involved, it must be stressed that the natural environment is fragile and easily damaged. All climbers have a responsibility regarding the countryside they enjoy and must ensure a minimal impact and help to preserve it for future generations. Follow the Climbers' Code and be considerate to landowners, property as well as others enjoying the outdoors. As climbers you will come into contact with hikers, backpackers and those just out for a Sunday afternoon stroll.

PERSONAL SAFETY

Even if you are just going bouldering, consider telling someone where you're going and, more important, when you expect to be back. There is a great deal of difference in climbing real rock away from the chalk-laden atmosphere of the indoor wall and many more things to consider, not least of which may be the weather! Remember that rock is a natural material and subject to weathering which will occasionally result in loose hand or footholds; it may be slippery and covered in moss and lichen, so take care, especially in wet conditions. The advice of an experienced person can be invaluable in these situations. The climbing calls are much more important outside, especially on busy crags and on windy days on long pitches. A list of the calls and an explanation of what they mean is given on page 99. Stick to the list to avoid confusion and use your partner's name if the crag is crowded.

◁ This is an example of human erosion, caused by the passage of thousands of feet. It is a serious problem in some areas.

Single-pitch climbs

Ropework in the outdoors follows exactly the same principles as indoors – it's just the environment that's changed! On traditional climbs, anchors must be created using wires, slings, hexes and spring-loaded camming devices (SLCDs) (see pages 108–109), rather than just clipping the bolts, as you would indoors or on sport crags. If the crag is situated at the top of a steep hillside, belays will have to be constructed before starting the climb. The leader will place protection (the wires, hexes, and so on) as they climb, create belays at the top, anchor themselves securely, then take the rope in and belay the second climber. All anchor points and belays require a sound judgement as to how safe or marginal they are. Sport climbs normally have all belays and anchors in place, which makes life much simpler. The following pages deal exclusively with climbs that have only one section of climbing from the bottom to the top. These are called single-pitch climbs. Routes that have two or more pitches are referred to as multipitch routes, and are dealt with later in this chapter (see pages 128–143).

△ *A popular single-pitch climbing venue, offering superb routes at every grade. The rock is gritstone, which provides tremendous friction for the feet.*

● CLIMBERS' CODE

- A climbing party of two is minimum
- Always leave word of where you have gone
- Take care with all rope work and anchors and put the rope on as soon as necessary
- Test each hold, wherever possible, before trusting any weight to it
- Keep the party together at all times
- Don't let desire overrule judgement; never regret a retreat
- Don't climb beyond the limit of your ability and knowledge
- Always carry a first aid kit, whistle and sufficient food and clothing if you intend climbing on outdoor crags
- Check the weather forecast if venturing into the hills

△ *Belaying at the top of a single-pitch climb. But how safe is a belay using snaplink karabiners?*

Sport routes

There are many climbing areas throughout the world consisting entirely of sport climbs. All the anchors will (or should) be in place and fixed lower-off points will be found situated at the top of the climb. This makes life relatively simple for the climber, and certainly cuts down on the amount of climbing equipment that will be needed to deal with a route. You will need your harness, a rope, some slings, and as many quickdraws as there are bolts to clip on the route. You will also need your partner, belay device and some screwgate (locking) karabiners. The clothing you wear (see pages 20–21 and 156–160) will depend upon the weather and your preference. As you are on single pitch climbs, being caught out by the weather may not be as bad as being caught out on a much longer multipitch route. These routes offer an easy transition from indoor climbing.

▽ *Many limestone crags are bolted because they are often difficult to protect in the traditional way. Limestone usually offers steep, exhilarating and gymnastic climbing.*

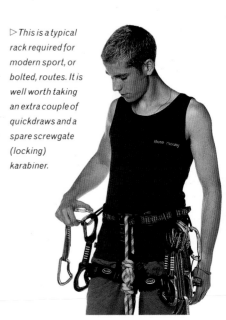

▷ *This is a typical rack required for modern sport, or bolted, routes. It is well worth taking an extra couple of quickdraws and a spare screwgate (locking) karabiner.*

PREPARATION

Before starting, the rope should be run through the hands and laid loosely on the ground. The leader then ties on to the end of rope that is on top of the pile. This is important as it will reduce the risk of unnecessary tangles. If the leader ties on to the end of rope at the bottom of the pile, the rope will run out through the entire length of itself and may at some point create an unwanted knot or tangle. Now check each other's harness and knots. Climbing is about teamwork, and this is where it starts. The leader shoud clean and dry their shoes before starting the climb to remove all traces of dust or dampness – slipping off on the first two or three moves frightens you and doesn't impress your belayer! Do not forget to use the climbing calls either (see page 99).

THE CLIMB

The leader clips the bolts exactly the same as with indoor climbing. This will ensure that, in the event of a fall, they will not hit the ground! The belayer should remain alert at all times, paying out the rope when needed and taking it in when necessary. The bolts are clipped using a short sling, the quickdraw, which has a kara-biner on each end. One karabiner is for clipping the bolt and the other is for clipping the rope. It should be possible to count from the ground the number of quickdraws needed, eliminating the need to carry excess equip-ment (although it's good practice to allow for one or two more quickdraws than seem neces-sary – there's the chance of one bolt being hidden from view, or you may drop a quick-draw in your excitement!). Karabiners with a bent gate should always be used on the rope and not directly clipped to the bolt. This is because there is a possibility of them becoming unclipped in the event of a fall.

△ This is a sport route. The next piece of protection is visible above and to the left of the climber. To reach that point the climber will rely almost exclusively on the superb frictional quality of the rock.

◁ Climbing calls may seem a little pedantic for single-pitch venues, but they are important on windy days and multipitch routes, so develop good habits early in your climbing career.

A fixed lower-off

There should be fixed lower-off anchors in place at the top of sport routes. These will take the form of bolts or rings through which the rope can be threaded. You should always follow a strict procedure when using them, as any mistake could be fatal. You should also keep your belayer informed as to what you are doing, making sure that they know when you want them to start lowering.

◁ *These two anchor points are equally and independently loaded so if one should fail, which is highly unlikely, the other will not be shock-loaded. Having two separate anchors also gives some lateral stability to the system.*

THE STAGES

The stages you should take are as follows. Clip yourself to the lower-off anchor points using the main load-bearing loop of the harness with a quickdraw or sling. Now pull some rope in (you will have to warn the belayer) and thread this through the lower-off anchors. Next, tie a figure-of-eight knot in the rope which is through the lower-off and attach with a screwgate (locking) karabiner to the main load-bearing loop of the harness. The original figure-of-eight knot that you tied to your harness before you started to climb can now be untied. Now remove the quickdraw or sling that you used to attach yourself to the lower-off anchors. Inform your belayer that they can now take in

△ **1** *Clip a quickdraw between the anchor and main load-bearing loop of the harness, pull some rope up from the belayer and pass this through the "lower-off".*

△ **2** *Now tie a figure-of-eight on the length of rope you have passed through the lower-off. Clip this with a screwgate (locking) karabiner into the main load-bearing loop of the harness.*

△ **3** *The original figure-of-eight tied in to the harness can now be untied and taken off, the quickdraw removed and the climber lowered down.*

ROPEWORK

the slack rope and then lower you back down the route in safety. Quickdraws can be retrieved from the bolts on the way down and the rope can be pulled down through the lower-off ready for the next climb. Alternatively, the rope can be left in place and your belayer can bottom rope the route should they decide not to lead it. This is a fairly simple procedure, but must be adhered to step by step. Do not be tempted to take any shortcuts. Good communications should be maintained between the climber and belayer and shouldn't be too complicated. If, however, there are problems in communication (due to a high wind, long pitch or whatever), then you can resort to some form of hand signals or sharp tugs on the rope. It is as well to discuss these other forms of communication before you leave the ground, making sure that both of you know precisely what each gesture or tug will stand for. This goes back to the overall importance of communication when climbing outside.

● SORTING OUT PROBLEMS

Problems can occur when either the sequence of events you should follow to safely carry out a lower-off is forgotten or you don't have a spare quickdraw with which to make yourself safe when you arrive at the lower-off anchors. You can try and retrieve a quickdraw from lower down the climb to use, though this may prove difficult and time-consuming. The important point is clipping the figure-of-eight knot into the main load-bearing loop of the harness. If you were to clip it to the rope loop formed by the original figure-of-eight knot which goes through the harness, you would not be able to untie this original knot, which would at the very least be embarrassing. This is why the quickdraw is used to back the system up in the first place.

The other difficulty occurs when the route is longer than half of the length of the rope (say, over 20 m/65 ft in length), making lowering-off impossible. This is solved by belaying at the top of the route rather than at the bottom. This is called top roping, and is explained in detail on pages 114–127. Take care to keep a good belay directly in line between the anchor and the climber below. If there is a descent route it may be worth taking a pair of shoes suitable for scrambling down steep, slippery paths. Modern rock shoes are wonderful things but useless on wet ground! Alternatively, you could use two ropes to double the length of any lower-off that is required, though this requires a lot of ropework skill and thought.

△ If the climb is longer than half the length of the rope, the true top roping method must be used: that is where the belayer is at the top of the pitch, which is identical to belaying at the top of the first pitch in multipitch routes.

Traditional routes

Traditional climbs do not have any fixed gear in them (in general) to protect the lead climber as they ascend the route. This is why the Victorian climbers had the dictum that the lead climber should never fall. The consequences were too high a price to pay. This may well have restricted many lead climbers of the day to leading routes well within the grade at which they could comfortably climb – although climbing outdoors on traditional routes can, and will, throw up surprises. The picture has changed considerably with the advent of modern leader-placed protection – nuts on wire and spectra, hexes and camming devices. This gear is placed into cracks or pockets by the leader and is removed by the second when they go up the route. What this does mean is that planning a traditional route in terms of the equipment needed is far more complicated than that needed for a bolted sport route.

GETTING TO YOUR ROUTE

Having selected the crag you want to climb on from the guidebook and decided on what route to do, you will need to get to it. This will

△ *A traditional mountain rock climbing venue, where the leader places all the protection they need. The second removes it from the rock as they climb up.*

▷ *This crag is very obvious and only 20 minutes from the road. The difficulty arises when it comes to finding the route.*

involve finding the crag on a map and walking to it (life is a little more adventurous outside!). This may take 2 minutes or 2 hours, but you will need the skills to be able to locate your crag and then the start of your route (see pages 178–191).

ON A TRAD ROUTE

The time has come to get the rope out and uncoil it carefully, leaving the leader's end on top. Put your harness and rock shoes on. Tying on is exactly the same as with indoor or sport routes outside. However, a big difference is that the belay plate is operated from the rope loop formed by the figure-of-eight knot on the harness, and not the main load-bearing loop of the harness. This is particularly important at the top of the pitch where considerably more strain will be applied to the anchor and belayer because the force is directly on to them and not absorbed by any other equipment. On traditional climbs both climbers should tie on to the rope before the leader starts, and if necessary select a good anchor if there is steep and exposed ground below the crag. Although this is not strictly necessary on some single-pitch venues, it will be on others; so if in doubt, follow this procedure.

SORTING OUT A RACK

The leader will need to arrange the rack of hardware on their harness or bandolier (gear sling) so they know where everything is very quickly. Placing protection on traditional climbs can be a precarious and time-consuming operation at the best of times. The last thing a leader will want, when strength and confidence are waning on an overhanging crack, is to be fumbling around searching for the one nut that will fit the crack and provide them with much-needed protection and restore composure! So, the trick here is to become familiar with your lead rack and know where everything is by touch and feel. Stick to the same order of racking each time you come to lead. This will save moments of blind panic when, as your strength fades, you become desperate to place a piece of protection.

◁ *The ground here is safe, so it is not strictly necessary to construct an anchor before leaving. The belayer is in a good position and able to watch the leader closely.*

△ *Here the belayer is still able to watch the leader but is standing in an exposed position and creating slack in the belay. The sideways pull could easily lift the chock out.*

△ *This is a much better position for any exposed belays. The belayer is tight on the anchors and sitting down. Note also the position of the belay plate in the rope loop around the harness.*

Constructing anchors

Protecting yourself and your friends on traditional climbs is an art that requires a creative mind and lots of skill and judgement based on experience. Everything that a rock face or ridge has to offer may be used. This will include cracks and pockets for gear, spikes of rock around which to put the rope or a sling, a thread, a tree (though there are environmental considerations here) and even the friction of the rope running over a rock surface. It is important that you learn the art of protecting a climb and creating safe anchors from which to belay. There are few short cuts to learning this art.

◁ *This is an excellent bollard, on which a full-weight sling sits comfortably. It will take a downwards or sideways pull.*

SPIKES AND BOLLARDS

Tying on to a large spike or bollard of rock was the original way the early climbers anchored themselves to the rock to provide some security for themselves and their colleagues. Spikes are still used but, as with all anchors, any spike should be thoroughly tested to make sure it's part of the crag. If it wobbles like a bad tooth, it should be rejected and something else tried. To test a spike, check it visually for cracks around the base and hit it with one hand whilst keeping the other hand on the spike. Any movement or vibration should be felt instantly. Alternatively, tap the spike with a karabiner and listen to the sound made. It will be obvious to what is good and what isn't. Any spike which produces a hollow sound should be treated with suspicion.

△ *Although this projecting flake is separated from the surrounding rock, it is still an excellent anchor because it is solidly jammed.*

● GETTING IT WRONG

△ *This anchor is poor because the sling is precariously balanced over a poor spike and any lateral movement could lift it off completely.*

△ *This anchor is poor because the sling is too tight around the spike. This will considerably weaken the sling. If a larger sling was used, the anchor would be good.*

△ *Spike belays are always very "directional". In this situation the slightest change in the direction of pull could result in the total failure of the belay.*

HOW TO USE A SPIKE

There are several ways to use a spike:

① Place a sling over the spike and clip the screwgate (locking) karabiner directly to the rope loop of the harness.
② Take the rope from your waist and tie a clove hitch to the screwgate karabiner.
③ If the spike is out of reach, take the rope from your waist, through the screwgate karabiner and clove hitch back to your waist. Alternatively the rope can be taken right around the spike and then clove hitched direct to your rope loop.

It goes without saying that all karabiners on belays should be screwgates (locking). Choose where you want to stand with care directly "in line" between the climber and the anchor. The clove hitch allows easy adjustment, so whenever a belay is constructed keep the rope tight between the anchor and belayer on all occasions, and adopt a good braced position, feet apart and knees bent. Most spike belays

are very "directional", which means they are excellent for a downward pull but can be lifted off easily with an upward pull. Bearing this in mind, they may be much more useful at the top of the crag (downward pull) rather than at the bottom (upward pull) if the leader falls off above some protection (running belay).

THREAD BELAYS

This is where tape slings are threaded in around two immovable objects, either a large boulder which is jammed into a crack or where two large boulders are touching so slings are easily threaded around. As with all belays, check the surrounding rock carefully because the slings are very thin and a boulder will only have to move a couple of millimetres to render the anchor useless. Thread belays do, however, have one great advantage over all others and that is the fact that they are multi-directional so they can be used in any situation irrespective of the pull. When the sling is fixed around the thread, clip the rope into the karabiner and tie in as before, either straight into the rope loop or using one of the methods with the clove hitch. The most important point is the position of the stance (how the belayer stands) and a tight rope between belayer and anchor.

▽ *The sling is taken through a small natural thread and both ends are then clipped together. The result is a belay that will take a "multi-directional" pull.*

● GETTING IT WRONG

◁ *This is a poor thread belay. The boulder is poorly wedged and a good heave on the sling will pull it straight out.*

Using lead-placed protection

Nuts on wires or spectra, camming devices and hexentrics (commonly called "hexes") make up the majority of gear used by climbers around the world to protect themselves on traditional routes. They come in a variety of sizes. There are several names given to some of these items (for example, nuts are sometimes called chocks, rocks or stoppers!). Leader-placed protection is usually placed in cracks. It makes excellent anchors for main belays as well as protection (running belays) for the leader while they are climbing. The function is similar to bolts on indoor walls or sport crags, the big difference being that the leader is using their own judgement about whether the protection is good, marginal or very poor.

PLACING PROTECTION

Each nut or hex (camming devices are dealt with on page 112) is specially designed to provide several options on which way it can be placed. They are also designed to give maximum holding power (using wedged shapes in the case of nuts and an asymmetric shape for hexes). Try and get as much of the metal of the nut or hex as possible in contact with the rock when you are placing it. This comes down to the correct selection of the size of the piece of protection. A general rule is to use the largest size that will fit the crack. Give a sharp down-

△ Slings, wires, quickdraws, cams and karabiners: collectively this equipment makes up a leader's rack.

▷ This is an excellent wired nut: well placed and with a lot of metal-to-rock contact for stability. The placement will even allow a good lateral strain to be applied with no fear of the wire failing.

• GETTING IT WRONG

△ Even though there is a lot of metal to rock contact, this nut is wedged against a loose rock and will take little strain.

△ This is a really poor placement. There is little of the nut in contact with the rock and it is simply resting on minute crystals.

▷ *This large hexentric will offer a range of three different fittings depending on which way it is placed.*

▷▷ *This is an excellent placement and any strain will "cam" this hexentric into the rock.*

▷ *Extend wires with a quickdraw to keep the rope running more freely, particularly where wires are placed under an overhang. This will help prevent rope drag.*

● GETTING IT WRONG

◁ *This is a poor placement because there is little metal-to-rock contact – the corner of the hex can be seen clearly resting against the rock.*

◁ *Don't have wires clipped directly to the rope. This increases friction and may put a lateral strain on the protection and lift it out.*

ward tug to jam or settle the piece of protection into place. Test each one in this manner and be sure to keep a good handhold when doing so, just in case the piece pulls out! Some placements will not be as good as others, but are the best available in the circumstances. As the leader, you will have to be able to cope mentally with this. The best solution is to find another placement as soon as possible that you feel is more reliable – this will calm those nerves and beating heart!

EXTENDING RUNNERS

All wired nuts and hexes must be extended using a quickdraw, otherwise they could be pulled out where any lateral strain is applied. This also applies to any gear placed under an overhang or in a way that the rope is moved out of line with the climb, creating friction in the system.

● RETRIEVING GEAR

The second retrieves all protection when it is their turn to climb. This can be difficult unless you have a nut key – a short steel bar with a hooked end which is used to lever or bash nuts and hexes out of their cracks. There is an art to understanding how best to get gear out, which only comes with time and practice.

▷ *The natural constriction in which this hex is placed makes it extremely secure, so much so that it can take time to remove.*

Camming devices

▷ A selection of camming devices that are designed to work in either parallel-sided or flared cracks where conventional chocks are difficult to use.

△ Place camming devices in the direction they are likely to finish in in the event of a sudden strain being put on them.

▽ This is a large camming device perfectly placed in a parallel-sided crack.

Over the last few years these have made a tremendous difference to the sport, particularly where any cracks are either very wide or parallel-sided and there are few natural constrictions to facilitate the placement of wires or chocks. There are various designs on the market and a variety of names. All have three or four cams that are depressed by pulling the triggers and then placed in a crack. They work well in cracks with parallel sides where conventional chocks would be extremely difficult to place. Some have solid stems and therefore work best in vertical cracks, but care must be taken in horizontal cracks unless the cam is placed with the end of the stem flush with the edge of the crack (see illustrations for more details). Others have flexible stems so they can be placed in either vertical or horizontal cracks with confidence. Try to find a placement where the cams are biting about mid-point, which is the best locking position for the cam. The geometry and direction of pull down the stem should ensure the harder the pull, the stronger the device. The closer the cams are to either fully open or fully closed the less likely they are to hold.

PROBLEMS WITH CAMS

There are several problems with camming devices, working on the principle of the more technical the equipment, the more problems there are, or at least are likely to be! Beware of "over" or "under" camming. The former can create a problem for your second when trying to remove the cam; the latter can be unsafe. If the rope is clipped directly to any camming device, the action of the rope moving backwards and forwards will "walk" the device deep into a crack, much to the annoyance of anyone trying to retrieve it.

● **GETTING IT WRONG**

◁ The camming device shown here is very poor because only a few of the cams are actually working against the rock. The front cam is almost fully open and little force would need to be applied to make it come out. Cams used in "flared" cracks can be good or almost useless, but if there is no other option, they will have to do.

The main belay

For a main belay use at least two pieces of gear which are equally loaded and independently tied off. There are several ways of doing this. Either use a sling to link the two anchors together creating a single point or use the following procedure: clip the rope through both karabiners and then back to a clove hitch on the rope loop of your harness – now clip the other (live) rope into the same karabiner with a second clove hitch. Use a pear-shaped (HMS) karabiner in the rope loop to accommodate both clove hitches and snaplink karabiners back-to-back on main belays if no screwgates are available.

Try never to use poor placements for a main belay. It needs to be able to take a potentially large force from a falling climber. Bolts at the wall or sport crag provide relatively reliable and frequent runners. A fall should not be huge. On traditional crags protection may not be so frequent so longer falls, which exert a greater force on the belayer, are often encountered.

△ This detail of a clove hitch clearly shows the "lay" of the rope (see page 121).

◁ There are many cases where it is not possible to rely just on one anchor, particularly if the anchor is a hex or wire. The answer is to link all the anchors to a single point.

▷ If your anchor is a single point, take the rope, create a clove hitch and fasten the gate.

▷ Any pull on anchors placed at the bottom of a route could be an upward one and is one of the major considerations when selecting an anchor.

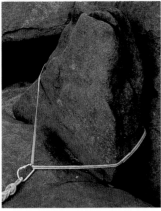

● GETTING IT WRONG

◁ The belayer is not tight on the anchor. If a sudden force is applied to the rope, the belayer will be pulled forward and may let go of the rope or may shock-load the anchor.

The system

rranging top or bottom ropes on outdoor crags has become very popular over the last few years, particularly where several people want to climb together. One reason could be that no one in the group is prepared to take responsibility or is competent enough to lead. Top and bottom ropes require less equipment and follow many techniques discussed in the previous chapter. If there are two or three ropes and two or three competent belayers within the group, it is the ideal way to allow beginners to "have a go" and try rock climbing. The downside to this is that arranging two or three ropes in one area could monopolize the crag and discourage others from attempting

▽ Climbs at this popular venue will be top roped, bottom roped or led from the ground in what many would argue is a purer style of climbing.

the routes. It is important to consider those waiting to climb the routes where the rope is arranged and it costs nothing to push the ropes to one side for a few minutes and allow others their fun, especially if they want to lead the climb. Top or bottom roping can be a little controversial and the complete picture is not here – this is just an insight!

THE TERMINOLOGY

There is often confusion among climbers as to the difference between a top rope and bottom rope, so here is an explanation of the terminology. If the belayer stands at the bottom of the crag or wall, they are bottom roping. They may or may not be attached to a

◁ This is bottom roping and, because of the relative safety, requires nothing other than the belayer to stand close in to the bottom of the crag.

∇ This is top roping where the belayer stands at the top of the climb in a direct line between the anchor and climber, and tight on the anchor. It can be much more difficult to hold someone when top roping.

belay, depending on the exposure of the ground they are standing on and the likelihood of being lifted off their feet in the event of the climber falling. If the belayer is standing or sitting at the top of a climb, they are top roping. Because they are always exposed to being pulled off the crag, they must be anchored to a main belay. Climbs that can be bottom roped must be no higher than half the length of the rope – the rope must go from the climber up to the anchor and back to the belayer, who stands on the ground. If this is not possible, then top roping must be used.

In short, any climb of less than about 20 m (65 ft) should be possible to bottom rope; anything more than that will make it necessary for the belayer to anchor themselves at the top of the climb to belay.

Bottom ropes

We will start by looking at bottom roping, which to add to the confusion relies heavily on the top anchor! In fact the terminology, top and bottom ropes, doesn't relate to the ropes, as we have seen, but to where the belayer is positioned. The belayer is below the climb when bottom roping and above the climb when top roping. These terms only apply for single-pitch, not multipitch, climbs.

TOP ANCHORS

The ideal bottom rope should be established on a route suitable for everyone concerned. The rope goes from the climber's harness, tied on in the usual way, up through the top anchor and down to the belayer in exactly the same way as for indoor climbing. The only difference being the need to create a top belay. If there is easy access to the top of the crag, creating a belay should be relatively safe but do take care if it's slippery or exposed to strong winds. And always warn others before you throw the ropes down. The usual call is a good loud shout of "below" or "rope below". Bottom belays at the base of the crag will also be desirable, especially if the crag is at the top of a steep slope. Failing this, stand close in to the base of the crag just as you would indoors.

SPORT CRAGS

Many sport crags will have two bolts at the top of the routes so it's simply a question of linking these with slings and screwgate (locking) karabiners so the strain is equally divided and each bolt independently tied off. In some cases the bolts will already be linked by a small chain to a central ring and this could not be simpler. Clip a screwgate karabiner to the central point and clip in the middle of the rope. Always ensure any karabiners have the gate away from the rock and the opening end of the gate pointing down. This will ensure any vibration or movement will keep the gate closed. If the bolts are over the top of the crag, extend them with slings to just over the edge to avoid rope abrasion or erosion of the crag. Finally, double-check all screwgate karabiners are securely fastened. The other major consideration to remember is that a failure of the top anchor in any bottom roping situation could be catastrophic. The climbers' weight will also test the anchor when they are lowered so it must be absolutely secure.

◁ *This climber is carefully checking out the top of a single-pitch climb, with a view to setting up a secure anchor for either top or bottom roping.*

CREATING A BELAY

◁ **1** *To create a belay from two bolts is really quite simple. The two ends of a sling are clipped into the bolts with screwgate (locking) karabiners.*

◁ **2** *Gather the sling and tie a simple overhand knot. Keep the double-stitched part of the sling away from the overhand.*

◁ **3** *All the screwgate karabiners should be attached with the gates downwards. Clip the middle of the climbing rope into the bottom karabiner. This method keeps to the principle of equally loaded and independently tied off anchors.*

● POINTS TO REMEMBER

Many crags have "in situ" anchors and bolts, iron stakes or pegs (pitons), which are specially designed steel spikes that can be driven into cracks. If this "in situ" gear looks fairly new and well maintained, it should be okay. There are occasions, though, where some of this equipment may be old and in a poor state of repair, especially on sea cliffs where the salty atmosphere will have affected the metal. Always check carefully and don't trust this equipment implicitly. You don't know how long it's been there, who put it in or how far it goes into the rock. Treat all equipment you find in place on the crag as suspect until it's been thoroughly checked. Finally, if you are bottom roping ensure that the rope is long enough to reach the top of the crag doubled; some ropes have a colour change at the mid-point to assist with this.

◁ *The metal stake here is being used correctly, with a sling wrapped round the bottom next to the ground. This reduces leverage to a minimum.*

● GETTING IT WRONG

△ *In this example, excessive strain will be put on the stake because the sling is well above ground level.*

△ *This sling has not been secured around the stake. This may lead to excessive movement of the sling and consequent wear and tear.*

Using traditional gear

Creating anchors at traditional crags using traditional gear takes sound judgement concerning good placements of nuts, hexes and camming devices. Boulders, spikes and threads are often used as anchors and these too must be checked and deemed to be 100 per cent soundproof before being committed to use. Remember, the anchor you create in this system acts as a pulley and therefore takes around twice the weight of the climber using it. Creating anchors using slings, nuts, hexes and camming devices can be difficult to construct at first because of the inevitable lack of knowledge about what is safe and what is not. Because there will be a considerable strain on the anchor, it's vitally important to make sure it is safe.

Using slings

Slings are used in a variety of ways. For example, they can be placed over spikes, threaded between two immovable boulders or around natural chockstones that are firmly wedged in a crack. They can also be placed around a convenient tree, but this should be discouraged as excessive use will eventually cause severe

◁ Here a sling has been placed over a large spike. The belay would have been improved if the sling had been clipped to the belayer's harness and the belay operated from there.

ANCHOR SELECTION

◁ **1** *An anchor has been created using a nut and a spike.*

▷ **2** *The rope has been attached to the nut with a figure-of-eight and to the spike with a clove hitch. The anchors have been equalized using a figure-of-eight on the bight.*

damage to the tree. If a tree has to be used, place a rucksack under the sling to protect it. Where two anchors are used, slings may be needed to link them to create a central point.

LINKING THE ANCHORS

Nuts and hexes can be placed in cracks and wedged to create an anchor. First look for natural constrictions within the crack and choose a chock or wire of an appropriate size. The trick is to get as much metal to rock contact as possible and settle in with a sharp tug. Never use one nut or hex as a main anchor – two or even three are always preferable. Link the two nuts with a sling (or the rope – see photographs above), gather the middle of the sling together and tie with an overhand knot. This is the simplest knot in the world – just form a loop and pass the end through the loop. Again, the trick here is to "equalize" the sling before tying the overhand. Using this method means that both chocks are equally loaded and independently tied off; in other words, the failure of one will not affect the other. With SLCDs find a placement with the trigger half depressed and the cams at about mid-point

and the direction of pull straight down the stem. Avoid if possible any lateral strain across the stem, although this is not important with "flexible" stems. Another point worth bearing in mind with SLCDs is that they have a tendency to "walk" deeper into cracks if there is any movement in the rope system, so extend them with a quickdraw to minimize the risk of this happening.

◁ *The overhand knot is the simplest knot in the world. Take a section of rope, form a loop and pass the end through the loop. Here it is tied on the bight – a doubled section of rope.*

Constructing a top anchor

There are some special considerations to bear in mind when constructing anchors at the top of a crag. Some of these relate to the fact that if the belayer is at the bottom of the crag, the motion of taking in and paying out rope will inevitably create some friction around the anchor at the top of the crag.

△ Allow enough rope to tie a figure-of-eight below the top anchor. This will reduce abrasion and make for easier rope handling.

▽ Always pad any sharp edges to prevent abrasion on the rope. Use purpose-made rope protectors or empty plastic bottles, thoroughly cleaned, with the top and bottom removed.

EXTENDING THE ANCHOR

All belays should be extended just below the top of the crag to avoid abrasion to the rope from constant rubbing as it is taken in or payed out. This action can also create erosion at the top of the crag, especially in the softer types of rock like sandstone. Where anchors are away from the edge of the crag, a spare rope can be used to extend everything to create a belay just over the top. To do this, tie a

● GETTING IT WRONG

◁ Here, one of the anchors is not taking any strain of the bottom rope. All the weight is on one anchor. It is vitally important to equally load two anchors and tie them off independently. In addition, the belay is not far enough over the edge, and there is a danger that the rope will become jammed in the crack.

TYING AND TIGHTENING A CLOVE HITCH

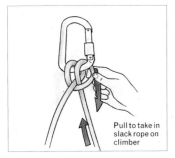

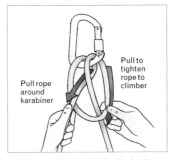

Pull to tighten rope to climber

Pull rope around karabiner

Pull to take in slack rope on climber

Pull to tighten clove hitch

Now tighten on climber

△ **1** To tie a clove hitch, form two identical loops in the rope and pass one in front of the other. Clip on to a karabiner.

△ **2** Tighten the rope to the climber by loosening the knot in the karabiner. Pull on the rope as shown.

△ **3** Once you have the rope tight on the climber, you can pull on the section of rope to tighten the knot safely.

figure-of-eight knot on the bight. Allow a 1 m (3 ft) loop to drape over the edge and tie a clove hitch into the second anchor. To do this, form two loops in the rope, right over left and right over left, and slide the second loop behind the first. Place both loops over the karabiner. The rope loop hanging down the crag is then tied in a figure-of-eight. After the rope protector is put in place, a karabiner is attached to the figure-of-eight and the middle of the climbing rope clipped in the usual way. Check all screwgate (locking) karabiners are locked before descending to the bottom of the climb. The angle formed in the rope leading to each anchor should ideally be between 45 and 60 degrees, but should never exceed 120 degrees as this will increase rather than decrease the strain on each anchor.

● THE COW'S TAIL

Take a long sling and thread it through your harness and then back through itself. Clip a screwgate (locking) karabiner to the end of the sling and attach it to any anchor when you are in an exposed position. This might be at the top of a climb when arranging belays, for example. This method of attaching a sling to a harness (called a lark's foot) is perfectly acceptable for a personal back-up system. It must not be used where a severe strain may be applied.

△ The cow's tail attached to the harness with a lark's foot knot. The karabiner can be used to secure the climber to a belay.

● TYING A FIGURE-OF-EIGHT KNOT ON THE BIGHT

The figure-of-eight knot tied on the bight is a useful knot to know. It is used for securing a climber to the anchors of a belay and for creating a loop in which to put a karabiner on a bottom rope anchor.

△ **1** Take a 1 m (3 ft) loop or bight of rope, and double it back on itself.

△ **2** Take the loop behind the rope, bring it round to the front and pass it through "eye" in the loop.

△ **3** The figure-of-eight knot can now be made more secure by finishing with a stopper knot (see page 91).

ROPEWORK

Creating bottom anchors

Although anchors at the base of the crag are not always necessary or possible to construct, they are worth considering. This is particularly so where the climber is heavier than the belayer, or where there is steep ground beneath the crag and the belayer is not secure. Indeed, in this latter scenario, an anchor of some sort becomes essential.

CREATING THE ANCHOR
Anchors at the base of the crag are created in exactly the same way as they are at the top – using slings, nuts, hexes and camming

▷ In this situation the selection of a good anchor at the bottom of the climb is absolutely essential. Although the anchors here will not take an upward pull, they are the best available.

devices. Remember that the direction of pull from a falling climber in a bottom roping situation will always be upwards and not down. The anchor you make will therefore have to take an upward pulling force. A thread is ideal – it will take a pull in any direction. A spike, which is good for downward-pulling falls, may be useless for an upward pull where a sling might be simply lifted off. Trees also make good anchors, but there is growing evidence that they can be damaged excessively and will eventually die when all the bark is stripped off.

If the ground anchor is not 100 per cent trustworthy, add your own body weight by clipping to the anchor itself and belaying off the main load-bearing loop of your harness. In this way you are doing the best you can to improve the anchor, although you should still question whether it is good enough or not. If unsure, look again and apply some lateral thinking. It is really important to consider what you are trying to achieve when making your anchor. No two situations are ever the same, which makes it difficult to give textbook answers. Look around and get the best anchors you can and use them in the best way you can. If there are no good anchors, either belay from your main load-bearing loop on your harness or abandon the attempt and go elsewhere to create your belay, maybe doing a different route instead.

USING A DIRECT BELAY
If the anchor is absolutely secure, the ideal belaying system to use in this situation is a direct one. Simply attach the belay device to the anchor itself, using a screwgate (locking) karabiner, rather than to your harness. You have remember to keep behind the belay plate, so that you can lock it off successfully in

◁ When the ground anchors are absolutely secure it is common practice to belay "direct" from the anchor.

▷ One problem with bottom anchors is that when standing in front of the belay plate the belayer will have no chance to take the rope into the braking position. There should also be padding between the sling and the tree.

the event of a fall. Alternatively an Italian (or Munter) hitch can be used in the place of a belay device. It is less critical where the dead rope is held when using this. It is also very easy for a more experienced person to "back up" the system by just keeping a hand on the dead rope, thus allowing a beginner to learn how to belay. The Italian (or Munter) hitch is ideal for bottom roping situations, especially if novices are involved.

● TYING THE ITALIAN HITCH

To tie an Italian hitch, form two loops exactly like a clove hitch: right over left, right over left. Fold the loops together and clip both ropes into a HMS (pear-shaped) karabiner. The hitch is fully reversible and ideal for taking in or paying out rope. The friction is increased by taking the dead rope forwards and not backwards. Therefore the locking-off action involves taking the hand holding the dead rope forwards (not backwards, as with a normal belay device). This makes it an ideal knot to use with ground anchors, in that the belayer does not have to

stand behind the anchor – they can stand in front, which is usually an easier position to adopt. Never use a twist lock karabiner when belaying with the Italian hitch – the action of the rope can open this type of

karabiner. Use a screwgate (locking) karabiner.

▷ The Italian (or Munter) hitch can be used in a variety of situations for either belaying or abseiling (rappelling).

△ **1** To tie the Italian hitch, form two loops in the rope and fold them on top of each other ...

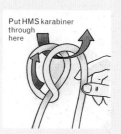

Put HMS karabiner through here

△ **2** ... as shown here. Attach the knot to a HMS or "pear-shaped" karabiner.

Climber ascending

Take in here

△ **3** The Italian hitch in action. The pear-shaped karabiner is essential, as it allows the knot to reverse.

Belaying from the top

There are many situations where it will be necessary to belay from the top of the crag. For example, if the climb is over half the length of the rope you will not be able to belay from the bottom. Instead you will have to create an anchor at the top of the crag and use a top rope.

EXTRA STRAIN

When belaying from above, you should be aware that a top rope will create considerably more strain on you, the belayer, should you have to hold the climber who is coming up from below in the event of a fall. There are two reasons for this:

① There is less energy-absorbing rope in the system.

② The rope does not run through an anchor (where some helpful friction is created) before coming on to the belayer, as it does in a bottom roping situation.

Any force applied will pull directly on the anchor and belayer, so it's vitally important to make sure the belayer is in a direct line between the anchor and the climber. The belay needs to be about 1 m (3 ft) back from the edge of the crag. In situations where there are bolt belays at the top, life is much simpler. Link the two bolts as described earlier (see page 117) and clip into the main load-bearing loop on the harness with a screwgate (locking) karabiner and lock the gate. The belay device or Italian hitch can be operated from the main load-bearing loop in the normal way but be warned: any force will be taken directly through the harness and on to you. This is a major consideration if the climber is heavy! Alternatively you can belay direct from the bolts and consider the use of a cow's tail for your personal safety (see page 121). Either of these methods will work in any situation where the anchors are near, or where you are within a few feet of the top of the climb and the anchors are 100 per cent secure.

If the anchors are 2–3 m (6–10 ft) back from the edge, use the system of clipping a figure-of-eight knot into the main anchor and clove hitching to the second anchor, leaving the loop 1 m (3 ft) back from the edge. The subtle difference here is that a figure-of-eight knot on the bight is now tied by tying a normal figure-of-eight knot, then pushing the end back through and over itself. If done correctly this forms two loops, one to belay off and one for personal safety. In this way the belayer is keeping in position and belaying direct, and if the climber falls off the strain is put on the belay system and not the belayer's waist. Use a belay plate or Italian (Munter) hitch and the climber can either be lowered back down or finish at the top of the crag.

△ When creating a top anchor to belay from, try to find something of a suitable height above waist height. Sitting on the stance, as shown here, can help this situation.

◁ A popular single-pitch venue. There are literally hundreds of climbs at different grades. The rock is gritstone, which is a sedimentary rock similar to, but much coarser than, sandstone. It has excellent frictional qualities and good protection.

△ It is vital that the belayer is correctly positioned. They should be in a direct line between the climber and the anchor.

ROPEWORK

Looking at alternatives

There is very rarely a single correct way to make safe anchors. There are usually lots of ways to make unsafe anchors! The trick is to be able to judge between safe and unsafe anchors. You must always ask yourself what would happen to your overall anchor if one of the pieces of gear failed. Would a big shock-load come on to the remaining anchors? Would the entire anchor fail? In any situation, however you have made your belay, keep asking yourself these "what if?" questions.

THE TOOL BOX APPROACH

If you have understood the basic ideas behind building sound anchors and belays, you should be able to cope with most situations that the crags and mountains will throw at you.

◁ This is an alternative method of creating a single-point belay from separate anchors. The overhand knot is used exclusively to link all the points.

Remember that the skills you learned have to be adapted to these real-life situations. You will have to be inventive in your use of your own personal tool box of acquired skills to cope with the thousands of permutations of anchor creation.

TOP ANCHORS

In situations where several anchor points are needed to create a top belay, the overhand knot can be used in the system. Start as before with a figure-of-eight knot tied on the first anchor. Make sure you create the first loop just over the edge of the crag and then take the rope back through the next anchor, then back to the loop. When all the anchors have been included, tie an overhand knot in all the loops and clove hitch the rope on each anchor point. This will take a little practice to judge the right amount of rope required, but it is very effective and creates several anchor points to work from if necessary.

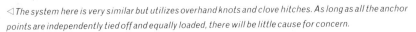

◁ The system here is very similar but utilizes overhand knots and clove hitches. As long as all the anchor points are independently tied off and equally loaded, there will be little cause for concern.

● USING A RIGGING ROPE

▷ Here is a good example of how to set up a bottom rope. A spare – or rigging – rope has been utilized to bring the main load-bearing point over the edge to reduce friction, erosion of the crag and wear and tear on the rope. The anchors are equally loaded and independently tied off so any force applied to the belay will be shared equally between the anchor points. A plastic bottle has also been used to protect the rope from any sharp edges there may be on the crag.

● COILING AND CARRYING THE ROPE

Many ropes are sold with a rope bag which incorporates a sheet on which the rope is laid at the foot of the route and folded around the rope at the end of the day. This is by far the best method not only of storing the rope but also carrying it to the crag. Another good method is to double the rope and feed two arm spans of the doubled ends through the hands.

Now take an arm span at a time and lay each one across one hand. Still holding the rope with one hand, take the two ends and whip them round the main body of coils. Finally a loop can be pulled over the coils and down on to the whipping. The two ends can be used to carry the rope rather like a rucksack, providing the ends are not too short.

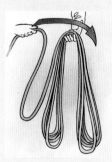

△ **1** *Feed the doubled rope in coils over the hand.*

△ **2** *Leave some rope at the top to secure the coils.*

△ **3** *Feed a bight of rope through the top coil and loop through to secure.*

△ **4** *Sling the rope over the back and tie across the chest and around the waist.*

● THE OVERCROWDED CRAGS

There is evidence that a growing number of large groups are visiting the crags, and the rope systems described here are used extensively by beginners and groups. The main problem is that of monopolizing the crags. The popular areas are under extreme pressure and large, noisy groups can ruin someone else's enjoyment of a peaceful afternoon on the crags. Apart from all the technicalities, tolerance, an appreciation of your surroundings and consideration of others are important to bear in mind when visiting popular areas in a group.

△ *A popular climbing venue on a Sunday afternoon during the summer.*

ROPEWORK

Is this mountaineering?

Multipitch climbing takes us into the mountain or big crag environment. A multipitch route, as the name implies, indicates several rope lengths of climbing at least. All your rope skills and belay judgement, as well as climbing technique, will be called upon to overcome a multipitch route. The rewards are great – you have arrived at one of the culminations of enjoyment that the game of climbing can offer. You will be called upon to lead pitches, create a sound belay on a stance, bring up the second climber and then belay them when their turn to lead comes around. The seriousness of the situation should be stressed. If anything goes wrong high up on a climb, a long way from the road, you will have to draw on your self-reliance.

COMMITMENT

The number of pitches can have little bearing on the difficulty of a particular route, just the commitment required and different skills that will be needed to succeed. The longest rock climbs in the world are often situated in remote areas which could take 2 or 3 weeks just for the approach and several weeks to complete. These require a great deal of commitment, effort and self-reliance because in many cases there would be little chance of rescue if things went wrong. Some of the most difficult climbs, however, will only have a little actual climbing and take only a few minutes to complete but still require hours of preparation and training. These climbs generally have easy access. A good comparison is the difference between a marathon and a 100-metre sprint.

◁ *This climb is steep, exposed and demands a bold approach.*

△ Many mountain routes will demand a full day to complete, starting with a walk of 2–3 hours with a heavy rucksack.

△ High mountain crags such as the one shown here can be very serious places. They may have loose and damp lichenous rock and often provide difficult routes.

▷ This is the other end of the spectrum – a few minutes' stroll from the car and within easy reach of sun, sea and sand. Who said that rock climbing didn't cater for all tastes?

● OUT FOR ADVENTURE

The ultimate ambition for many is to lead their own multipitch climbs and enter the world of mountaineering, and perhaps more important, mountain safety, which a subject in its own right. The old saying, don't try and run before you can walk, is very appropriate, so take time and learn the basic techniques first. Inevitably accidents will occur on the crags, but remember the basic essentials of first aid, airway, breathing and circulation and know how to send for help. Six blasts on a whistle or six flashes on a torch, repeated after 1 minute, should summon help if you can't get to a phone.

Carrying the gear

The problem of how to carry the gear, or "rack", will have become evident on single pitch routes. The problem is particularly obvious when preparing to climb a traditional route, where the amount of gear carried is far greater than that carried on a sport route. On multipitch routes this is more important, particularly if two climbers are alternating leads. Obviously if some of that gear is dropped, it could have serious consequences, not only for the climbers concerned, but others who happen to be below them.

HARNESS OR BANDOLIER (GEAR SLING)

The two choices available are to rack the gear around the harness, which should have adequate facilities, or to use a "bandolier" which is a specially designed padded loop that goes around the shoulders. On steeper routes the bandolier system works very well, and you can simply swap bandoliers at the end of each pitch (at which point it's possible to drop the whole rack). On easier-angled routes, there is a tendency for the bandolier to swing round to the front, making it difficult to see your feet. Using the gear loops on the harness is probably a better option in this situation, and although this may slow you down on the change-overs at the end of each pitch, at least you won't drop the whole rack.

Whichever way, keep the rack organized so everything is in order and always in the same place. Gear will then be quick to retrieve when you're on a long, lonely "run out".

▷ *The system here shows the equipment loops on the harness being used to carry the gear. Many people prefer this method because it allows gear to be arranged so that it is easily accessible.*

▷ *Using a bandolier is a quick and efficient way of carrying gear, especially if two climbers are alternating leads (leading through).*

Problems at the stance

Climbing multipitch routes poses many more questions as to what to do and when to do it. If the chosen climb is in an exposed position above a steep slope, a suitable anchor (belay) will be required. Consider the implications of the leader slipping off the first few moves: if they were to land at your feet it shouldn't be a problem. If, however, they were to fall past you and continue down the steep ground, they could pull you after them. This could, at the least, be an inauspicious start to a day's climbing or at worst lead to a very short climbing partnership! Starting a climb from a steep and exposed position is therefore a much more serious situation, so be aware of potential problems.

If your climb starts from a safe position, it may be okay to stand or sit close to the bottom. There is, however, one complication. If the leader falls with protection placed, they will create a "pulley" effect, lifting the belayer off the ground and possibly into a protruding spike. An upward-pulling anchor, mentioned earlier, becomes much more important here and the biggest problem is making the initial judgement to use one, and then a second judgement as to whether it's good enough! A poor anchor may be worse than no anchor because at least you are aware that there is no belay, whereas if you have one that fails – who knows what will happen? Another way around the problem is to place some good protection (running belay) as soon as possible.

△ *Any multipitch climb is complicated if one climber is leading all the pitches. Care is needed at the stances and the rope will have to be run through so that the leader's end is on top of the pile.*

▷ *Holding a leader fall can be difficult on a multipitch traditional route. The climber (faller) will be climbing past any protection and a fall may result in a greater force being applied to the belayer.*

The safety chain

The safety chain includes everything a climber has in terms of equipment and what to do with it. The harness and rope are probably the most important, but the belay device, nuts, hexes, camming devices, slings and karabiners all play their part. The old adage about a chain only being as strong as its weakest link holds good for climbing, too. Always try to be aware of where the weak links in your safety chain might be. The safety chain is present in single pitch climbing (top or bottom roping and leading), but it is at its most complicated and interesting in multipitch climbing situations.

RUNNING BELAYS

The ultimate challenge is perhaps leading your own multipitch route on natural gear (using nuts, hexes and so on) or on bolted protection. When leading, the question of greatest importance for most climbers is, what is the protection (running belays) going to be like?

△ Clipping that all-important running belay. This may have to be done in a physically tiring position.

◁ To get good protection for a leader on traditional routes relies on good nuts, cams or slings being placed and, as ever, an alert second as belayer.

This is a big question and assumes a greater importance on adventure or traditional routes than on a sport route. Protection on traditional routes relies on the placement of nuts, hexes and camming devices, and the leader may find their position precarious while they fiddle a tiny wire behind a small flake of doubtful security. This is a far cry from sport routes where the protection relies on bolts which are usually bombproof and take only seconds to clip. Another consideration is the steeper the route the safer it is (provided your protection does not fail) because it's not the falling off that damages climbers, it's what they hit on their way down, especially if it happens to be the ground which can be pretty unforgiving. If a route is very steep with lots of protection the climber will bounce gently to a stop in mid-air, with the elasticity of the rope absorbing most of the shock. If, on the other hand, the climber slithers down a granite slab, they will feel sore, at the very least. Always get in what you can, when you can; but remember, the more "runners" you place, the more drag you'll get on the rope and more lateral strain, possibly lifting them out.

DYNAMIC ROPES

By the time any climber is contemplating multipitch routes, it should be fairly evident to them that there is a good deal of stretch in any climbing rope and this is a very important factor. Basically this means that any force or shock in the system is absorbed slowly and with less shock to the climber's body or the belay system. If these forces were stopped with a static, or low-stretch rope, there would be considerably more force, not only on the climbers but also on the belay system, with the distinct possibility of failure of part of that system. This is because of the greater force involved or, put more correctly, same amount of force but over a shorter period of time. Apart from the energy absorbed by the rope, energy is also absorbed by the belay plate, the belayer being lifted off the ground, the knots tightening up or, more drastically, a runner failing. Not to be recommended if it's the only

△ **1** On a sport route clip the bolt with the bent-gate karabiner down and away from you. Now reach down and take the rope between your first and second finger.

△ **2** By hooking the thumb and third finger through the karabiner it will be held steady while the index finger twists the rope into position.

● GETTING IT WRONG

◁ This rope has been clipped the wrong way through the karabiner. If the climber falls there is a distinct possibility that the rope will be taken across the gate and out of the karabiner altogether. Always look ahead to see which way the route is going and clip the quickdraws from behind the gate in the karabiner, with that gate facing away from the direction in which you intend to climb.

---

one you have got in! The whole safety chain is therefore vital and it is only as strong as its weakest link. However, remember that upward-pulling anchors could, if they are too tight, prevent the belayer from being lifted off the ground, which would possibly weaken the belay. So always, always consider the implications and ask your self, "What happens if...?"

Using a single rope

▽ In the situation here there will be so much friction created that either the running belays will pull out or the leader will have great difficulty in making further progress.

You have the choice of climbing on one full rope or two half ropes (see page 25 for an explanation of full and half ropes). Once you have progressed to leading and multipitch routes, you should be aware of the pros and cons of using either. Only in understanding these things can you form your own opinion and come to a decision about what to use on any given route.

△ *Here, the rope is running in a straighter line than in the photograph left. However, the protection could have been extended further with a longer sling.*

ROPE DRAG

In many situations climbers use a single rope and this is adequate on either single pitch or easier multipitch routes. There are, however, some limiting factors, which means that in some situations a compromise must be found to deal with a potential problem. Using a single rope on a complicated traditional route can create a lot of friction as the rope passes through the runners. This is called rope drag. On sport routes the bolts are usually in a straight line, so it isn't generally a problem. On traditional routes the protection has to be placed where it occurs and this presents a problem if the rope zigzags from side to side. If the first piece of protection is to the left of the climber

and the second to the right there will be a great deal of friction on the rope, making it difficult to move and causing a severe lateral strain on the runners which could pull them out. Often it's the amount of friction engendered near the top of a pitch rather than at the start that causes the problem, so there is a need to look carefully which way the route goes and extend any runners that are off to one side. The longer the extender, the more likely it is to stay in place. The other answer may be to place the first two runners, then climb down to remove the first one. The other limiting factors with a single rope are the length of abseil (rappel) possible and the difficulty of arranging suitable protection for the second climber on a traverse.

● THE FALL FACTOR

The fall factor refers to the severity of the forces involved in any fall. These forces vary in severity depending on a number of factors. The fall factor is usually expressed as a number, which is arrived at by dividing the length of the fall by the amount of rope that is involved. The numerical values normally run between 0.1 and 2, with 2 creating the greatest impact of force on climber and belayer. For example, if on the third pitch up a multipitch route a leader climbs 3 m (10 ft) above the belay with no runners in between and falls off, they will fall a total of just over 6 m (20 ft) – they will fall below the belay itself. This is a factor 2 fall. The leader has fallen 6 m (20 ft) with 3 m (10 ft) of rope paid out (6 ÷ 3 = 2; 20 ÷ 10 = 2). If the same leader falls off at 30 m (100 ft) above the stance with a runner at 27 m (90 ft), they still fall 6 m (20 ft) but the elasticity of a climbing rope and the dynamic factors of the safety chain will absorb most of the force. In this situation the belayer may hardly notice the fall. The fall factor in this situation would only be 0.2, although the actual distance fallen is identical. The moral of this is, get a running belay in as soon as you can after leaving the stance.

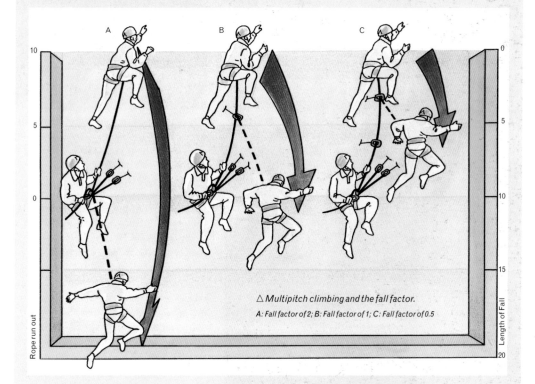

△ Multipitch climbing and the fall factor.
A: Fall factor of 2; B: Fall factor of 1; C: Fall factor of 0.5

Rope run out

Length of Fall

Using double ropes

Double ropes are thinner (usually 9 mm) and lighter than single full ropes. This makes them easier to distribute amongst the climbing party and carry to the crag, mountain or sea cliff. If used properly, they will help reduce or entirely cut out any rope drag. If tied together and used double, they give the potential of a full 50 m (165 ft) abseil (rappel) which can still be retrieved. These advantages are looked at below, and in the following section on abseiling.

TYING ON

This is an easy operation. Simply tie each rope into your harness using the normal figure-of-eight knot re-threaded. It is essential to use two different coloured ropes. This makes life easy when clipping runners. You can let your belayer know that you want slack on red or green or whatever. You should both tie on in the same way and make sure that you have the same coloured rope on the same side (left or right) before setting off on the route. This will help prevent twists in the ropes. Your belayer will thread both ropes through the slots in their belay device. Practice will be needed in paying out separate ropes.

△ It is important to communicate with your belayer when clipping runners to keep them informed as to which rope you need slack on. Keep the instructions short and simple.

ADVANTAGES

Using double ropes can be a tremendous advantage on either harder single pitch or multipitch climbs where the route weaves an intricate path up the crag. Running belays can be clipped either alternately or the ropes can be separated out, one to the left and one to the right. This not only reduces the friction but makes it much easier to arrange protection for the leader and second. Any traverse can be protected for the leader with one rope while the other can be left free to protect the second from directly above. There is also a huge difference in the length of any abseils that can be

▷ Some practice will be needed to overcome the difficulties of handling double ropes, but on longer routes they can be a tremendous advantage.

made. A further point is the ease of tying on to two anchor points at the top of the pitch. Simply take one rope to each anchor, tie on with a clove hitch and adjust each independently so both anchors are equally loaded.

TWIN ROPES

Although not particularly popular, this method of ropework has its devotees, particularly where longer multipitch routes are common. The twin rope method uses both ropes as a single rope when climbing. This means putting both ropes through each point of protection, thereby working on the principle that two are better than one. However, long abseils can be made similar to double ropes, so an effective and rapid retreat can be made if necessary. Because of the different thicknesses of all the various ropes involved in climbing, it is essential that they are used only for the purpose they were designed for and that double or twin ropes are not used singly, even for top roping.

◁ Protecting a climb that has running belays to the left and right of the actual climb is so much easier when double ropes are used, and there is less friction to hinder the leader (see page 134).

△ With doubled ropes, any abseil (rappel) can be increased from half the length of the rope to the full length, in most cases from 25 m – 50 m (80 ft – 160 ft).

△ Using doubled ropes in this situation is a real advantage. The leader can arrange better protection for both leader and second.

● GETTING IT WRONG

◁ Although doubled ropes are being used here, it is not to any great advantage. Both ropes are taken in to the corner, which is going to increase friction and give little support to the second climber in the case of a fall.

Multi-point anchors

▽ Sea cliffs around many coastal areas offer an exciting venue, but the different environment means that specific skills and techniques must be learnt to deal with the hazards of tidal approaches.

On a multipitch route, there are many things to consider when constructing each belay. These will include: the soundness of the anchors; the direction of fall (don't forget that if you are leading through your second will become your leader and will go from climbing below you to climbing above you); your position on the stance; where you will flake the rope (will it be safe from snagging if it simply runs down the rock face?); and how

you will exchange gear when your second arrives at the stance. You will need both hands, so how will you make your second safe while you do this?

DOUBLE ROPES AND ANCHORS

If you are using double ropes, your life is made easier. Where the anchor is a single point and within reach of the belayer, treat both ropes together and tie a clove hitch to the screwgate (locking) karabiner. If there are two anchors, both out of reach, take one rope to each anchor and back to a pear-shaped (HMS) karabiner in the rope loop of the harness and tie with a clove hitch.

By using any of the belay systems described here, any force is transmitted through the belayer and back to the belay, which is a very important point when it comes to dealing with any problems. Any belay anchor or stance will be greatly improved by a good runner being

△ The perfect position, high on a route with steep rock which is warm, dry and comforting.

placed immediately on leaving the stance by the leader (see fall factors, page 135). Of particular importance in multipitch climbing is the need to consider whether to belay left- or right-handed. Any belay device should be on the same side as the belay ropes so that it is much easier to bring the arm back into the locking position; a good deal of dexterity will be required. If the locking hand is on the opposite side of the body to belay it will be much more difficult to create the "s" shape through the belay device because the arm cannot be brought back fast enough. This is important on any rock climb but becomes more of a problem when dealing with a tight, constricted or even hanging stance, where there is little or nothing to stand on. All the belayer can do (after tying on of course) is sit back in their harness.

Any multipitch climbing situation is further complicated if one climber is leading all the pitches. In this situation, great care will have to be taken at the change-overs. The ropes will need to be run back through at each stance so that the leader's end is back on top of the pile when they start on the next pitch. If the climbers are leading through this will be unnecessary because each leader's end of rope will be naturally on top of the pile at each stance. On very small or hanging stances the belayer should drape the rope either across the belay ropes or around their feet to make sure it doesn't hang down the rock face and either get jammed in a crack or annoy other climbers. The belayer should always be able to reach the rope to sort any problems out.

● SAFETY CHECKLIST

A good belay will have all of the following:

① Tight ropes leading to two or three strong anchors.
② Equal tension on each rope.
③ The stance will be stable and adjustable from where the belayer stands.
④ Screwgate (locking) karabiners or snaplinks back-to-back on all the anchors.

USING MULTI-POINT ANCHORS WITH A ROPE

△ **1** Take the rope from your harness to each anchor and back to the harness or rope loop.

△ **2** Tie a large overhand knot or a clove hitch to a pear-shaped (HMS) karabiner and clip to your harness.

USING MULTI-POINT ANCHORS WITH SLINGS

△ **1** To link two nuts or cams to create a single-point anchor, clip a sling to the karabiner and tie an overhand knot loosely in the sling.

△ **2** Clip the other end of the sling to the other karabiner. Adjust the overhand knot to a point where the load is equalized and tighten.

◁ **3** Finally, attach the rope to the sling with a karabiner.

Further knots (2)

U p to now only the minimum number of knots have been described to allow you to get on with the fun and enjoyment of climbing. The time has come, however, to look at some further knots to add to the armoury, because getting into the world of multipitch routes also takes you into the area of learning a little self-reliance and knowing how to deal with everyday problems that may occur.

TYING A DOUBLE FISHERMAN'S KNOT

△ **1** *Take one length of rope back over itself twice and push the end through the hole.*

△ *This chock is threaded on a short length of cord which is then tied with a double fisherman's knot. This is the traditional method of joining two ropes of equal thickness.*

△ **2** *Now push the other length of rope through the same hole, but from the opposite direction. Now do exactly what you did with the first length of rope, that is twice round and back through itself.*

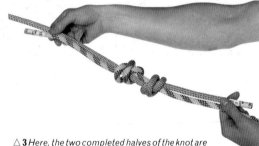

△ **3** *Here, the two completed halves of the knot are being checked. They should be symmetrical and seat well together. If they don't, then try again.*

Double fisherman's knot

The double fisherman's knot has traditionally been used over the years to join two ropes together, often for use in abseiling (rappelling). Although this has now to a certain extent been superseded by the overhand knot, it is still worthwhile knowing how to tie it. The most common use of the double fisherman's knot today is to join the two ends of a short length of rope after threading through nuts and hexes. Take one end of the rope and wrap it twice around itself and then through the hole it has formed. Now push the other end through the loop and wrap this twice around itself and the other rope but in the opposite direction. The two halves of the knot should then slide together and lie side by side. They should look symmetrical. If they are not, then try again. The single fisherman's knot is very similar, almost as strong and uses much less rope. Either will do for joining any two ropes if they are of equal thickness, but be sure to leave adequate lengths of rope after the knot has been tied. The over-

hand knot has being described already but in a different context; here it is used to tie two ropes together so that a longer abseil can be contemplated. The reasons will be discussed in greater detail on pages 144–153. Take the two ends of rope together and tie the simplest knot in the world, always allow 1 m (3 ft) of rope at least on the two trailing ends.

Tying the French prussik (autoblock)

The step-by-step sequence below shows how to tie the French prussik and how to rig it for use as a safety back-up to an abseil (rappel). The French prussik is used in other situations as well, mostly for emergency techniques, such as performing assisted and unassisted hoists and escaping from the belay system (see Chapter 5 for further details).

Advantages: Released under load – amount of friction dependent on turns.

Disadvantages: Can slip without warning. Must be tied with a short sling. Doesn't work with tape (spectra).

TYING THE FRENCH PRUSSIK

△ **1** The best way of giving protection on any abseil (rappel) if you are the first to go down is to use a French prussik. This is a short loop of 6 mm (¼ in) cord wound four or five times round the abseil rope and attached to the leg loop on the harness. This is slid down the rope with your "bottom" hand as you abseil and should "lock" in an emergency.

△ **2** The completed French prussik is shown here.

△ **3** The French prussik attached to the leg loop of the harness. This prussik has many more uses (see Chapter 5).

What is abseiling (rappelling)?

▽ *Having completed a route, this climber is abseiling (rappelling) back to the ground.*

A bseiling (rappelling) is the technique used for descending steep rock either after the climb has been completed, or in certain cases where there is difficult access to the start of the climb. The rope is attached to a safe anchor at the top and a friction device, either a figure-of-eight descender or belay device, placed on the rope and attached to the load-bearing loop of the harness with a screwgate (locking) karabiner. By applying slight pressure with the lower hand below the device, a safe and controlled descent is easily accomplished. Some crags will have abseil descents from the top or in some cases, particularly sea cliffs, an abseil approach. In other situations, such as the onset of bad weather or misjudgement of the difficulty of the route, an abseil may be the only way of getting back down. In the early days of rock climbing, many primitive forms of abseiling were developed. On smaller traditional cliffs it is usually possible to scramble down the easy way. In alpine countries this is not always the case and abseiling is a necessity, particularly on the longer routes. The development of modern equipment makes abseiling far easier than it was but it is important to remember that any abseil is only as safe as the anchor, and that cannot be truly tested until you test it for real.

THE PERFECT POSITION

The perfect position for abseiling is easily achieved on a smooth slab with few ledges or obstructions and it's possible to see all the way down. A high anchor will make life much easier when starting the abseil. This is ideal for a beginner, but with more experience steeper, or even overhanging rock can be descended easily. The anchor must be 100 per cent bombproof. If it isn't, don't abseil! Just as in belaying, there is a live or active hand which is used below the abseil device to control the descent and a dead hand which is usually above the descender, although some beginners will want to use both hands below the device to control their descent at first. Keep the feet shoulder-width

▽ *The perfect abseil (rappel) stance*

Upper hand guiding the rope

Plenty of space between descender and back-up

French prussik or safety rope as a back-up

Looking where going

Body turned towards the leading hand

Lower hand maintaining friction on the dead rope and controlling the descent

Knees slightly flexed, acting as shock absorbers

Feet flat against the rock for a firm stance and shoulder-width apart

apart and turn slightly to the right if right-handed or to the left if left-handed. By turning sideways it becomes much easier to see where you are going and gives more freedom of movement to operate the controlling hand on the descender. The difficult part is committing yourself and going over the edge to start the abseil, but once that is done just feed the rope out and walk backwards down the crag. The feet should be flat against the rock and the closer you are to the horizontal, the less likely your feet are to slip. Flex the knees and control the rope with your bottom hand. There should also be a separate safety rope for beginners or a French prussik (see page 143) as a safety back-up for the more experienced.

△ *This smooth slab is ideal for practising abseiling (rappelling). There are no obstructions or cracks where a boot could get jammed. The ropes can be clearly seen reaching the ground.*

◁ *When beginners practise abseiling (rappelling), there should always be an extra rope used as a safety back-up.*

ROPEWORK

Abseil (rappel) devices

There are several devices that have been developed especially with abseiling (rappelling) in mind. They give a smooth descent and tend to dissipate the heat generated through friction very well. However, it is worth bearing in mind that most devices designed for belaying can be used for abseiling as well. It is a good idea to test a new device in a safe environment (on a short abseil or at the wall) before using it in a more adventurous situation!

THE FIGURE-OF-EIGHT DESCENDER

The figure-of-eight descender is undoubtedly the best device for the job and specifically designed for the purpose, giving a controlled and safe descent. Harnesses which have a central load-bearing loop should present no problems; however, some harnesses require a karabiner to hold the leg loops up or clip the two parts of the harness together. In some cases this can "hold" the karabiner in place and possibly create loading against the gate.

The problem with this type of harness, sometimes referred to as a "Bod" system, is easily overcome by using a "mallion" (designed specifically to take a multi-directional pull) to connect the two parts of the harness together and thus create a central load-bearing loop. It is important to load the rope down through the eye so that it is on top of the descender when it goes over the back bar. If the rope goes up through the "eye" and under the back bar it could catch on a sharp edge of rock and "lock off" around the eye, thus preventing any further descent. (see Chapter 5).

OTHER ALTERNATIVES

As mentioned, most belay devices offer reasonable options for abseiling and a varying degree of friction on either double or single ropes. The biggest problem with most (Tuber excepted) is a relatively small surface area which doesn't dissipate the heat caused by the friction during the abseil. In a series of long multiple abseils it is important to remove the

▽ This is a figure-of-eight descender loaded correctly with the rope over the connecting bar. Get into the habit of doing this automatically and always use a screwgate (locking) karabiner.

▷ With a "diaper" harness system, it is necessary to connect the two halves of the harness together with a "mallion". This is designed to take a three-way pull – karabiners, even screwgates, are not.

△ This is a belay device which works very well as an abseil device. In a learning or practice situation it is possible to abseil on a single rope.

device quickly at the end of each abseil (rappel). Whichever device is used, it is important to always use either a safety rope or French prussik and clip this to the leg loop below the device with a screwgate (locking) karabiner. This is slid down the rope by the control (lower) hand and if this is removed (for whatever reason) the prussik should automatically lock. Where multiple abseils are involved have a "cow's tail" attachment from your harness to clip the anchor on arrival at the next stance before unclipping from the rope.

△ Tie a knot in the end of the rope before setting off. This may prevent you sliding off the end!

● GETTING IT WRONG

It is very easy to make mistakes setting up your abseil (rappel). To guard against this, make sure that you check your harness, abseil device and screwgate (locking) karabiner. A common mistake is to feed the rope up through the main hole of the figure-of-eight descender. If the rope is underneath the main bar of the descender it may turn in to a "lark's foot" if it catches an edge on the way down. This will lock the descender solid and necessitate a rescue, especially if you are on a free abseil and can't reach the rock.

△ A dangerous situation: the abseil (rappel) device is connected to the harness with a snaplink karabiner.

△ The common mistake of allowing clothing to get caught in the descender.

Joining the rope

Traditionally the double fisherman's knot or reef knot with a double fisherman's knot either side have been used to join two ropes, which allows a longer abseil (rappel). A much better method which is becoming common practice is a simple overhand knot. This allows the rope to "roll" outwards away from the rock when it's being retrieved and reduce the chance of the knot jamming on the way down. Always leave a long "tail" (1 m or 3 ft) and use a second overhand to prevent clipping the device in to the "tails". The second overhand can be removed just before leaving the stance after checking everything (twice). Even when using this method of joining two ropes, it is important to check the position of the knot carefully and make certain

that it will run clear of any cracks. When the first climber has abseiled, get them to try pulling the ropes a little to check whether they will run. If not try and reposition them. Finally, clip a quickdraw on to the rope that needs to be pulled – just as a reminder.

ABANDONING EQUIPMENT

This is something which no self-respecting climbers like to do, but in serious situations there may be no option. After all equipment, although it's expensive, can be replaced unlike a life. There are, however, some tricks of the trade which may be of value in the situation where there is a doubtful anchor but with a perfectly reasonable second anchor nearby. Use the doubtful anchor as the main abseil

▽ *The overhand knot has recently found favour as a way of joining two ropes. The knot will "roll" away from the rock when the end is pulled and is therefore less likely to jam in a crack.*

△ *This abseil (rappel) has been rigged so that the rope can be retrieved, but not the karabiner and sling. The karabiner is a snaplink, so it may have been better to thread the rope directly into the sling.*

▷ *A popular way to get down off a crag – but the tree at the top is suffering.*

point and put all the load on to that anchor. Now put a good back-up into the second anchor with a few centimetres (inches) of slack in the system and send the heaviest climber first! If the doubtful anchor holds for the heaviest person, in theory the secondary anchor can be retrieved before the second (lighter) person abseils! If nothing else, this should provoke a few arguments among the party as to who is the lightest! It must be stressed that this is for really serious situations only – in particular where equipment is at a premium and may be needed further down the mountain. In 30 years of mountaineering and rock climbing the author has only used the technique three or four times and anyone who tries this must ask themselves what price is equipment anyway.

△ The ropes have been joined using an overhand knot and placed over a large flake. There will be some friction when the rope is pulled through once the climber is down.

△ The rope has been threaded which may create far too much friction for the rope to be retrieved.

RETRIEVABLE ABSEILING (RAPPELLING)

Do you leave a sling in place to ensure that the rope can be retrieved or do you risk it? In truth there is often no easy solution, unless one person goes down and tries to pull the rope through a few centimetres (inches) first. If at that stage it doesn't run round the anchor, the second person would have to rearrange the rope and try again. As a general rule, if there is any doubt leave a sling. On long multipitch routes many leaders carry a few metres (feet) of cord or tape specifically for rigging abseils and leaving behind, and a penknife for cutting to the required length. It is worth being particularly careful when dealing with a rounded spike – there is a tendency for rope to "roll" off when the rope is loaded. In this situation, a short length of tape would be much less likely to roll.

◁ The perfect retrievable abseil (rappel). However, the screwgate (locking) karabiner and sling will be left behind. The climber has a French prussik for safety and has clipped a quickdraw to the rope that will need to be pulled through once down.

● ABSEILING (RAPPELLING) IN SAFETY – TOP TIPS

- Make sure your ropes reach the ground, or at least to another stance.
- Get a sound anchor, at any price.
- Practise and become familiar with the technique.
- Use a French prussik from your leg loop, and of the right length. This is usually a 1.25 m (4 ft) length of 6 mm (¼ in) cord joined with a double fisherman's knot.
- Keep your anchor as high as possible in relation to the take-off point.
- Don't use trees unless you really have to, and then leave a sling or length of tape.
- Back the anchor up if in doubt.
- Buy yourself a mallion if your harness requires "holding" together at the front, for example a "Bod" system.

The anchor point

On sport crags, the anchor points are invariably good, although don't trust bolts implicitly, especially some of the ancient relics from a bygone age and always abseil (rappel) with care. The steadier you go down, the less strain there will be on the anchor, ropes and harnesses. On traditional climbing areas it can be much more difficult and the perfect anchor, one which allows the rope to be retrieved, is often elusive. In some cases it may be necessary to abandon a sling and abseil off this rather than risk getting the rope jammed in a crack. Trees often make excellent anchors but this causes serious damage when ropes are pulled down. However, if it is absolutely necessary, leave a sling in place and abseil off this rather than placing the rope directly round the tree. Many trees have been killed over the years by continual use, particularly by people abseiling at many climbing venues throughout the world. This is bad enough, but further damage will be caused to the crag when the root systems die, so use them only as a last resort. Choose a high anchor point, at least above waist-height. Having a low anchor not only raises the risk of the rope slipping off but increases strain on the anchor because of the outward directional pull on it. Finally a low anchor will make life difficult, and therefore dangerous, when you are going over the edge. Last but by no means least, choose the place to abseil with care, making sure that no one is climbing up and giving a good warning shout of "rope below" when throwing the ropes down just in case.

◁ *Where there are several pieces of equipment to abseil (rappel) off, try and link all the anchors to ensure all are equally loaded and independently tied off.*

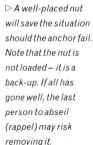

▷ *A well-placed nut will save the situation should the anchor fail. Note that the nut is not loaded – it is a back-up. If all has gone well, the last person to abseil (rappel) may risk removing it.*

△ A high anchor point makes life easy at the start of an abseil (rappel). The anchor is above the belay device and allows the abseiler to get the correct position before going over the edge.

● GETTING IT WRONG

A very poor site has been chosen, especially for someone who is just learning. The abseiler will be unable to see if the ropes reach the bottom because of the extremely steep take-off point and low anchor. This will create difficulties as they go over the edge. They could turn upside down because of the direction of pull on the anchor. There have been a few cases where a hole has been punched in the karabiner gate, causing the system to fail. This is much more likely if an anchor point which is lower than the take-off point has been chosen, allowing the descender to flick over and pull across the gate.

△ Choice of anchors for an abseil (rappel) is crucial for success. Here the anchors are too low.

The popularity of abseiling as the normal means of descent from many crags is due to the dislike of slithering down muddy paths in expensive footwear that is totally unsuited for the purpose. Abseiling is an essential (and inherently dangerous) technique to be learnt. There are many shiny gadgets on the market which are designed to make life easier, but none are of the slightest use unless the anchor point is chosen with care and due regard for the consequences of the abseil. Once you have leant back and weighted the rope and anchor, there is no turning back. The anchor must not fail! When abseiling, all climbers trust the rope without question, but remember the rope is only as good as the anchor.

◁ Never abseil (rappel) above a climber who may be leading a route. The last thing a leader wants is for someone to dislodge stones on to their head.

Security

THE ITALIAN HITCH

Although the Italian hitch is not ideal for abseiling it can be used in a situation where no other device is available, although in double ropes extensive twisting will occur. If the rope is used singly (that is, tied off at one end) the Italian hitch is much easier to use, although it still may twist alarmingly. It is essential to use a large pear-shaped (HMS) screwgate (locking) karabiner (not a twistlock type) to ensure the rope runs smoothly and to increase the heat dissipation. To create an Italian hitch, form two loops, right over left, right over left, fold the loops together and then clip the two ropes into the karabiner. The use of a French prussik as a "back-up" will make it possible to untangle the ropes. In spite of the problems, this method can be used in any situation where the abseil device has been dropped or forgotten. If using this method, ensure that the Italian hitch is operating against the back bar of the karabiner and not anywhere near the gate.

USING A PRUSSIK

This is a length of 6 mm (¼ in) cord about 1.5 m (4½ ft) long. Tie the ends together with a double fisherman's knot to form a loop; the loop should run from the thumb to a point level with the elbow. This is wound at least four or five times round the ropes, taking care to include both ropes if double ropes are being used.

Keep the French prussik short and snug and do not use any other prussik knots in this situation as they are not easily released once they are loaded.

Consider also how each device will be affected if the prussik is too long. In some cases the prussik will simply be released and in others it may be dragged into the abseil device.

△ **1** If you want to stop mid-descent (to retrieve some gear left on a route, for example), you can use the following method to free your hands.

△ **2** Take a length of rope around your leg for three or four turns. Make sure you keep hold of the controlling rope.

△ **3** Now carefully let go of the controlling rope. The wraps around your thigh should stop your descent. Your hands are now free.

Either way it could be disastrous and best not to find out, so keep those prussiks short and snug. There are of course some devices which are designed to lock automatically so a French prussik may be unnecessary, unless of course a malfunction (grit, dirt or inexperience) causes a problem in any way. In that case you'll look foolish if you haven't used one. An alternative way of providing safety back-up once the first person is down (or there is a responsible person already at the bottom) is to get them to pull gently on the bottom end of the rope. This should have the effect of locking off the abseil device and will not only give confidence to beginners but could save a good deal of time if multiple abseils are involved.

● SECURITY FROM BELOW

Today this is the standard way of helping beginners to gain confidence when learning to abseil (rappel). Good communication is important for both parties. Surprisingly little tension is required on the rope and with a little practice the person at the bottom can lower the abseiler (rappeller) a few centimetres (inches) and then lock off again. The same technique can also be used in a situation where a series of abseils is needed to get off a major climb. The first climber should go down protecting themselves with a French prussik and the second climber protected by the first in exactly the same way. This will speed the whole process up for both parties. If the abseil is an emergency one where the Italian hitch is used, the technique will still work although in some cases there will be a little less friction on the rope so more tension will be needed. The amount of tension needed will depend on the amount of friction, and this will depend upon several factors: the thickness of the ropes, whether you are using single or double ropes, the type of belay device, the weight of the abseiler, and so on.

△ **1** An alternative method of providing security for the abseiler (rappeller): the first abseiler down simply holds the abseil rope lightly.

△ **2** Should they need to stop the next abseiler from descending any further, they simply pull on the rope, applying tension to the system. This will lock the abseil device.

4

INTO THE HILLS

Days out on the crags are not always sunny and warm affairs – life would be much less interesting if we didn't get a good soaking from time to time. We have already looked at the basic requirements for rock climbing, which are enough to get you going. By now, though, you'll be hooked and it's time to delve a little deeper into the wallet for that extra equipment you'll need to adventure farther afield in greater safety – but we'll not get too carried away. It is important to think carefully about your equipment in terms of staying warm and dry in the mountains. Any fool can be uncomfortable, after all! It takes careful thought and planning to be able to cope with whatever nature throws at you.

Opposite: *The full outdoor experience – wilderness, solitude and a sense of self-reliance. Rock climbing in this environment requires more skill and judgement than that required on a roadside crag or indoor climbing wall.*

The layer system

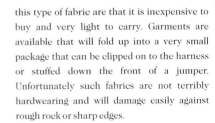

The shell clothing that you choose forms the outer part of the layering system. This begins with a warm comfortable layer next to the skin followed by other thicker and warmer layers on top. The number of layers is entirely dependent on the outside temperature. Regardless of the number of layers you wear, try to ensure that you do not parcel yourself up too tightly for this will only limit the range of movement that you are capable of. Fortunately, modern fabrics perform extremely well and even seemingly thin layers offer effective insulation.

WINDPROOF CLOTHING

Light showerproof and windproof clothing is also worth considering. The advantages with this type of fabric are that it is inexpensive to buy and very light to carry. Garments are available that will fold up into a very small package that can be clipped on to the harness or stuffed down the front of a jumper. Unfortunately such fabrics are not terribly hardwearing and will damage easily against rough rock or sharp edges.

GLOVES AND HATS

Gloves and hat are important additions to the safety gear you'll need to carry in the mountains. Here again, weight and a combination of functionality and good design is important. You may need to wear a hat with a helmet on top. Clearly, Granny's home-knitted hat is unsuitable for this purpose. Some manufacturers offer hats that are

◁ Make sure that the layers of clothing you choose do not restrict movement, and that by adding subsequent outer layers you combine insulation with wind and water repellency.

▷ A basic layering system might begin with thermals and then light fleece or hardwearing fabric on top. A lightweight shell top and leggings would complete the outfit.

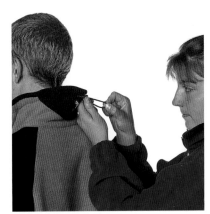

△ The collar of this jacket features a neck warmer that can be adjusted to a snug fit, thus retaining valuable body heat.

▷ These jackets are reversible. On one side they have a windproof material, and on the other a warm fleece layer.

close fitting and specifically designed to fit under a helmet while there are many others that will suffice. Style, colour and fashion are all influences over the choice of hat for personal use, though fleece is possibly the most practical fabric.

Gloves merit closer scrutiny. Light fleece gloves made from a fabric such as Wind-bloc™ or Windstopper™ are worth consideration. Unfortunately fleece is not terribly hardwearing, and for the occasions where you might actually want to climb with gloved hands you'll be better off having gloves with leather fingers. Though such products will be more expensive, the fact that they will last longer is a strong enough reason to sway your choice in that direction. For climbing you'll benefit from finger gloves rather than mittens. Handling gear with mittens is awkward, to say the least.

◁ A light and effective pair of gloves made with leather palms for better grip and windproof and warm fleece.

● FIRST AID KIT

Finally, but certainly not of least importance, is a first aid kit. Wherever you venture, be it 500 m (¼ mile) from the road or 50 km (30 miles) into the mountains, a first aid kit is essential. Having cobbled one together, it is the sort of thing that can remain in the bottom of your pack until it is required. A suitable pack need not be heavy or widely comprehensive – a few plasters, wound dressings and a triangular bandage are all that's needed. Make sure that the pack is kept tightly sealed in a waterproof bag so that nothing is likely to become sodden and ruined and periodically check the condition of the packages. It is also worth putting in a lightweight foil survival blanket and a whistle for dire emergencies.

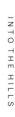

Footwear

I t is important to consider what you want your mountain footwear for – approaching a climb where it will be taken off and exchanged for rock shoes or wearing on an easy long route or scramble?

THE APPROACH SHOE

A simple approach walk to the crag might be undertaken in a pair of ordinary training shoes. In fact climbers have adopted this type of footwear for many years, and in response to this fact manufacturers now produce a range of footwear categorized as "approach shoes" or cross- functional footwear. There are considerable advantages in travelling to the crag in lightweight footwear, not simply because it is more comfortable. Many climbs finish high on a mountainside from which the descent might be a either a moderate walk or a difficult scramble. Clearly, rock shoes are impractical, uncomfortable and potentially lethal on such descents. A lightweight pair of shoes can be clipped on to the back of the harness where they will be barely noticed during the climb but greatly appreciated for the descent.

THE MOUNTAIN BOOT

There was a time, and not so long ago, that fully stiffened rock climbing boots were used quite widely. Whilst the demand for this type of boot has waned considerably, there are occasions where the benefits of a stiffer-soled boot might be advantageous. Examples of such situations include long technically easy climbs or mountaineering routes that might include the occasional

△ Approach walks to the crags might be hot and sweaty affairs or you may feel the need to be warmer.

◁ Approach shoes.

patch of snow or ice to cross. Despite the demise of the fully rigid rock climbing boot, there is still a wide range of boots available that will fulfil these requirements and in recent years one or two manufacturers have re-introduced the specialist stiffened rock boot.

IMPORTANT CRITERIA

The important criteria to consider after comfort are the rigidity and type of sole unit. Boots that are totally rigid are uncomfortable to walk in but excellent for climbing. On the other hand a boot with considerable flex will be comfy to walk in but horrendous for rock climbing. The compromise is one that you can stand on the very tiptoe of and that offers some support to the foot. When trying a boot on in the shop, stand on the toe on a small edge for a couple of minutes without moving. If the boot is sufficiently rigid, your foot will not tire or cramp up during this test. Boots in this category do not include plastic boots or any boot of double construction. They are usually full leather or soft Nubuck.

△ Full-blown mountain wear for those days when you encounter a bit of everything.

Rucksacks

A simple rucksack of rudimentary design is more than adequate for carrying gear for a short distance to the foot of a climb and back home again. However, if you intend to go farther afield, and particularly if you think you might need to carry a pack on your back while climbing, you are certain to need something much more sophisticated.

THE CLIMBING PACK

A pack that will be comfortable for climbing should conform to one or two basic design principles. Firstly it shouldn't be too large for your needs. Avoid the temptation to go for a larger pack in the belief that it will squash down to a smaller size if it isn't full. A pack with a capacity of around 30–40 litres (7–9 gallons) should be large enough for most needs on a daily basis – after all, you only need to carry a little food and water, a light shell and maybe a spare fleece.

The pack should have no internal frame other than a padded back. It should be quite narrow so as not to restrict movement of the arms from side to side and it should be fairly short so that head movement remains unrestricted, particularly when tilting the head backwards. A teardrop-shaped pack with zip closure at the top seems to be the preferred style of day pack for rock climbing. It is also useful to have a large strong loop at the top of the pack, which is used both as a handle and to clip the pack to the belay when it is not being carried.

▷ *A frameless rucksack of between 30–40 litres (7–9 gallons) and a rope bag. In addition to rope, the rope bag can be used to carry any extra bits of gear, as necessary.*

△ *A good pack will barely be noticed on the back. Make sure that you are not over-burdened.*

Climbing among mountains

△ *Beinn Shuas in the Scottish Highlands, a long walk in, isolation and big rewards.*

▷ *The bolt – providing sanitized and safe climbing?*

◁ *A true mountain setting. Self-reliance and all your mountaineering skills will be needed here.*

Rock climbing amongst the mountains is the main reason for climbing for many people. Here, it is not necessarily the technical difficulty of the climb that is important (though many mountain routes are as extreme as they come) but the special atmosphere, the solitude, the self-reliance and the companionship of a few other souls.

ADVENTURE IN THE HILLS

A sweeping sun-touched arete, crisp mountain air, snow-clad hills all around, early morning and already five pitches up. Cragging in a mountain setting is hard to beat. Rock climbing grew out of the alpinism of the Victorian era and soon developed into an entity in its own right. Until the 1960s most climbers felt that rock climbing anywhere but in a mountain setting was a cop-out or a compromise to be made if the weather was bad or you could not get to the mountains because of work or some other diversion. Roadside crags, sun-drenched sea-cliffs and quarries were ok, but it

was the real thing they hankered after. The thought of hurling yourself from bolt to bolt or up and down a bit of artificial rock in a dust-filled shed was definitely beyond the comprehension of the hardy mountaineering types. The arrival of the "rock jock" was still some way off. The idea that rock climbing should be safe, warm and comfortable was beyond the grasp of climbers who had been through one, and in some cases two, world wars. Climbing was dominated by tough characters who enjoyed pitting their mental and physical wits against the mist-shrouded crags. Rain, snow, wind, falling rocks and darkness were all seen as challenges that added to the heroics and the mystique of this eccentric pastime.

SANITIZED CLIMBING?

At some stage climbers realized that it was possible to climb on solid rock using pre-placed equipment that was guaranteed to keep you safe, but most were too embarrassed to let on. It was not until sometime in the early 1980s that some of the old die-hards faltered under the influence of the "new wave" and admitted that climbing didn't have to be cold, wet, miserable and dangerous. It all made so much sense, but climbing had changed forever. It had been sanitized and made to fit in with the changing ideas of the latter part of the twentieth century.

ADVENTURE CLIMBING

What some of today's climbers now want is adrenalin rushes without the risk. Sadly, throughout the mountains of the world climbers are bringing the mountains down to them rather than rising up to meet them. Happily though, adventure climbing still exists and its advocates guard it jealously. The challenge of adventure climbing on big mountain crags or committing sea-cliffs utilizes every physical and psychological skill a climber can cobble together, and as a result provides a level of retrospective satisfaction that can make your toes wriggle with joy for months afterwards. The technical skill may be less (though not always) but the overall experience far greater than that found on a sport climb.

◁ A bolted sport climb will often be desperately hard but relatively safe due to the nature of the protection used.

▽ The climbing may be easier, but the agenda is bigger. Placing your own protection requires planning, strength and mental coolness.

Finding your crag

Big, serious crags do not give of their pleasures easily and can give you a humbling cuff under the ear with the greatest of ease! To sample the pleasures and to avoid the chastisement requires plenty of research, foresight and a combination of boldness and commitment that must be learnt but cannot really be taught.

MAPS AND GUIDEBOOKS

Much of the fun associated with adventure climbing lies in the anticipation and dreaming, which is bolstered by endless reading of guidebooks and climbing literature prior to setting off for the crag. Most writers hype up the accounts of climbs, so your job is to filter out the important information from the

△ Time spent ensuring that you are on the right route and your starting point is correct is time well spent. Study the guidebook well.

◁ Finding your crag and finding the start of your route are often the biggest challenges in the mountains.

▷ *Navigating accurately to your chosen mountain crag can be complex and confusing even with good weather and visibility.*

embellishment. Having settled on your crag and route, the next thing to wrestle with are the mysteries of the map. This will ensure you have a good picture of how best to get to and from the crag and what type of terrain you can expect to encounter. Interpreting maps and spotting the problems before you lurch off is an important skill. Climbers are notorious for being poor navigators but it doesn't have to be like this.

WEATHER – FRIEND AND FOE OF THE CLIMBER

On a committing crag you should always be armed with as much knowledge and information as possible, the more up-to-date the better. Rain can turn the delightful finishing groove into an unclimbable grade III rapid, an electrical storm can fry you on the spot, and nil visibility can turn the gentle descent from the crag into an epic return to the wrong valley or a night out clad only in your rock shoes and T-shirt. Conversely, you can easily spoil a perfect day by running off with your tail between your legs in the early morning cloud and drizzle, only to discover it is an inversion which burns off with the arrival of the sun to give a perfect anti-cyclonic day.

ESCAPING

If you are about to buy a one-way ticket to hell, it is best if you know this and are prepared for the consequences. Having a workable escape plan tucked up your sleeve to deal with exhaustion, changing terrain, time and weather is essential on a big crag. As you become more experienced, this can almost become subconscious; but in your early sorties it needs to be a reasonably formal exercise. Be aware that on many big routes you cannot abseil (rappel) off and your escape plan can only be to keep climbing to the top of the route.

▷ *Success is at hand, but what about getting back to the safety of the ground and rucksack?*

Adventure climbing

I t is the potential danger of adventure climbing and the total commitment it requires that attracts some and drives others away. Which of these camps you fall into is dependent on whether you are a risk-taker and thrive on retrospective enjoyment.

RISK ASSESSMENT

There is a big difference between making a bold dash for the glinting bolt and guaranteed safety, with the potential of retreat, and setting off up the rock ahead not knowing if any protection exists, or if it does, whether any of your diminishing rack will fit. The prospect of the perfect crack viewed from below turning out to be blind and flared, and the jug reducing to a sloper, awaits the adventure climber. Staying under control both physically and mentally in this setting is the key to successful ascents. Physical strength is obviously a great

△ *Loose rock, poor gear and no climbing down – total commitment!*

▷ *Can you get a hand off to get the gear in? The jugs usually appear when the protection is clipped.*

△ *Under control, with time to think and to get the protection right.*

attribute in a situation like this, but counts for little if it is not bolstered by clear foresight and a cool mind. You will notice that the placement of a good runner suddenly makes the footholds bigger and allows you to find the obvious jug around the corner — the whole thing suddenly becomes two grades easier. The trick is to create the same effect next time when the runner isn't there!

MOTIVATION

In climbing we often hear about people being "naturals". This is a nice idea, but most successful climbers emerge as a result of experience punctuated by failure, fright and constant learning. Anyone can develop the skills if they are determined enough. If there is no motivation, however, forget it. To succeed as a climber on committing crags you need to be a strange combination: selfish on one hand and a team worker on the other. The skill is to disguise the selfishness enough to avoid alienating your partner – not an easy task. It is hard to define the complex feelings that may course through your mind and body as you wind up to take on a big route. The most interesting feeling is the overpowering sense of inevitability: this climb is definitely going to happen. This should be countered by a healthy dollop of nervousness and a touch of self-doubt to balance the whole affair. Once you have set off up the rock, a sense of determination must take over. At this point the strangest things start to happen, depending on the day. They could range from one extreme to another – feeling as though you have never climbed before through to feeling as though you are on the easiest climb of your life.

SUCCESS AND RETREAT

It is important to respond to how you feel, but on a big climb you need to be able to push through the bad patches in the hope that a good one is on the way. Sometimes this just doesn't happen, so you have to either rely on your trusty partner or pack it in and go home. Backing off is an important skill for the adventure climber to develop. In Victorian times, armed with ropes that broke and no technical gear, the advice to the leader was to never climb anything that could not be reversed. Today we are blessed with equipment that allows us to abandon this approach, but we still need to be sure that the reading of the route and our forward planning allows us to bail out if need be or face the consequences. The real skill is to develop an awareness of when you have reached the point of no return, however you decide to proceed. There is a delicate and frustrating balance between recklessly hurling yourself at a problem and boldly climbing something right on the edge of your ability. If we always got it right, however, there would no adventure in adventure climbing.

▷ *Desperate moves and sustained climbing wait for you on mountain crags as well as on sport routes and roadside crags.*

▽ *Big, bold and desperate. Isolation as well as beauty in Ireland's Mountains of Mourne. The climb is Divided Years, possibly the hardest traditional mountain route in the world.*

Sea-cliff climbing

The crashing sea adds a very special and satisfying dimension to climbing. It provides a dynamic aspect to what is often a very static pastime. Sea cliffs are serious places. They are often big, under-cut, tidal and intimidating. Your option often is to climb or swim, unless you are prepared to face the embarrassment of the arrival of the lifeboat.

A SPECIAL PLACE WITH SPECIAL PROBLEMS

Never underestimate the sheer power and unpredictability of the sea. The fact that the tide tables are called tidal predictions should provide a good warning. Swell and wave patterns are often influenced by factors thousands of miles away, so the perfect weather and calm sea as you approach your route can be misleading. Tides rush in and take little account of the fact that you are finding the crux unclimbable. As you abseil (rappel) off, you may find that the sun-drenched beach you set off from is now deep ocean. Sea cliffs are not only the home of climbers; most have populations of sea birds in residence during the breeding season. Climbing through their nests can be very disturbing for the birds, but the birds can be very disturbing to you as well. Their defensive skills range from knocking you off your minute holds by dive bombing, through to regurgitating evil-smelling semi-digested fish all over your colourful climbing clothes. The breeding season usually lasts for about six months of the year, leaving plenty of time for you to climb in peace.

VARIABLE ROCK

The rock on sea cliffs varies dramatically from the wave-cleansed lower sections, a joy to behold, to overhanging, shattered blocks covered in lichen and interspersed with grass and mud, guarding your escape at the top. Belays can often be delightfully problematical or non-existent. All this adds to the excitement and satisfaction when you eventually complete your ascent.

◁ *Hard climbing in a very serious setting. A long abseil (rappel) to the start of the route and only one way out.*

△ Abseiling (rappelling) down sea cliffs can lead to a difficult escape. It pays to leave a rope in place just in case.

▷ Perfect rock, perfect weather – sea cliffs aren't always beasts. Small tidal ranges in the Mediterranean help to create paradise.

▽ A classic sea cliff scene. Not far left to go, but has the climber made other plans for escape should he not be able to make it to the top?

● ESCAPING FROM TROUBLE

If you have to abseil (rappel) down a sea cliff to the start of your intended route, consider carefully the consequences of not being able to finish your climb. Is there an easier route by which you could escape? Is your partner a better climber and able to take over? Is there an easy scramble out of danger? What effect will the tide have on your plan? Is there a problem leaving your belayer on a low stance if you take longer to lead the first pitch? Might they get wet feet – or worse?

Always consider leaving an abseil rope in place, so that you can, as a last resort, prussik back up the cliff.

A question of access

The restriction of access to crags will probably be the biggest threat to climbing in the twenty-first century. Climbers can be a selfish and self-righteous lot, who historically have cared little for who owned the mountains and crags so long as they could climb on them. This attitude may have to change if access is to remain open.

WHO OWNS THE LAND?

It should be remembered that all land is owned by someone and, with the massive increase in climbing and other outdoor sports, we can no longer expect the tolerance of the owners. It is your responsibility as a climber to know whether you are permitted to climb on a particular crag and to be aware of any special requirements associated with access. These special agreements range from those designed to preserve bird and plant life to military restrictions and safety considerations to protect tourists. Climbers are often their own worst enemies. Through their ill-considered behaviour, some crags have been closed to climbing after years of free access. This type of occurrence should be a warning to us all that we must consider our behaviour carefully and respect the rights and wishes of the owners of our play areas.

Climbers have no special rights beyond those of any other citizen, although to read some of our climbing magazines you may get a very different impression. If you climb in many different countries you would do well to familiarize yourself with any aspects of criminal or civil law that may affect you. In keeping with the anarchic facade we like to cultivate, most climbers are pleasantly ignorant of their legal responsibilities. This is a delightfully relaxing approach until something goes wrong.

CONSERVATION – THE BALANCE

Climbers want clean rock and clean cracks to climb and nice wide, dry paths leading to the crags. They want to walk along the tops of the crags and mill about the bottom to watch their friends. They want their dogs to watch them climb and their dog is never the one that chases

◁ *Climbing bans range from the flippant to the serious. Know your rights, but more importantly know your responsibilities.*

sheep. They want handy trees to belay on and to abseil (rappel) off. They want to climb all year round and they want to drive to and park as near to the crag as possible. They also want to conserve the pristine wilderness. Unfortunately, the balance does not hang level. All our "normal" behaviour has a dramatic effect on the country we climb on. It kills the ground cover and the trees, it chases off the birds and it jams the roads and clutters the verges. Small numbers of climbers do little harm; large numbers cause huge amounts of damage. It is always the other people who cause the damage and make up the crowds. This may sound cynical but it is very hard to pretend that climbing is good for the wilderness. We can't stop the damage but we can do a lot to minimize it through sensible, considered behaviour. The main thing to remember is that crowds are made up of individuals and your individual behaviour will contribute dramatically to a positive or negative outcome. So we must all try to bear in mind our own impact on the very environment we love to operate in.

◁ *Climbing can never be good for the wilderness. Dead trees caused by compacted earth and ring barking from abseil (rappel) ropes are commonly seen on crags.*

▽ *Footpath erosion is inevitable as the outdoors become more crowded. Repairs cost a fortune. Are we prepared to pay?*

Emergency procedures

The mountains are neither for nor against a climbing team, so they are not out to get you. From time to time however, climbers' interaction with the mountain can lead to an accident or injury. This can be caused by you hitting the mountain, by some of the mountain hitting you, or by the weather turning against you. If this happens, you can load the odds in your favour by knowing how to deal with an incident and how to preserve life.

FIRST AID
In the event of an accident, stop, think – think again. Then act decisively. This is more easily said than done. A lot will depend on your own experience with first aid. It is strongly recommended that you attend one of the many first aid courses to acquaint yourself with some of the basic knowledge for dealing with an accident victim.

△ Carefree and fun but let's hope your friends can cope if the holds run out.

◁ A good knowledge of how to deal with emergencies is vital in wild, isolated country.

● THE FIRST PRINCIPLES AND AIMS OF FIRST AID

① Your own safety is paramount – you are not only useless if you become a victim as well, you will also complicate the situation and put everyone at greater risk.

② Leave the patient no worse off than when you began. Only move an injured person if it is absolutely essential. Often the best first aid is to do nothing.

③ Reassure the patient. This will contribute to a feeling of well-being and will help fight medical shock.

④ Keep the patient warm. A major job in a mountain setting.

The aims of first aid:
• preserve life
• prevent deterioration
• promote recovery

You should arrange for help to be mobilized, and continue with the aims of first aid until the arrival of medical aid, which will most commonly be in the form of the Mountain Rescue team.

● VITAL SIGNS

Before you can tell whether someone is injured or ill, you must know the vital signs of a normal, healthy adult.

• Breathing – 10 to 15 breaths per minute. This will obviously be increased if they have just run up a hill or fallen off the crux of a climb.

• Pulse – 60 to 80 beats per minute. Again, this may be much higher if they have been through a traumatic experience or heavy exertion.

• Level of consciousness:
  Alert – capable of initiating a coherent conversation
  Vocal – may speak if spoken to, but incoherently

Responsive – responding to pain
Unresponsive – not responding to pain

The important thing for the first aider is to monitor whether the patient is remaining stable or becoming more or less conscious. Do this by recording breathing and pulse rate and level of response, every 10 minutes.

Colour – pink and oxygenated. The inside of the lips is the best place to check this, as it avoids confusion due to outside factors and difference in skin colour.

Temperature – core temperature of 37.5°C (98.6°F). Difficult to determine in the mountains with no equipment.

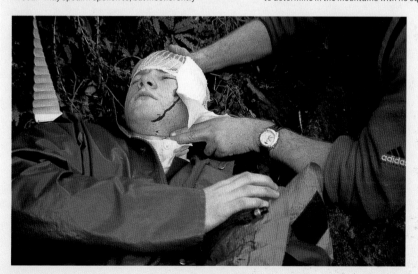

◁ Monitoring an injured person's vital signs is one of the main responsibilities of the first aider once you have stabilized the situation.

Dealing with an accident

An accident in a crag setting will unnerve you, so you must be sure to assess the situation accurately before acting. Establish whether the victim is conscious by introducing yourself and if necessary by gently squeezing the shoulders. Then carry out the A B C of survival:

A – AIRWAY. Check they have an airway that is open; if not open it. If someone is speaking or screaming their airway is open.

B – BREATHING. Check by looking, feeling and listening.

C – CIRCULATION. Do they have a pulse? Check the neck pulse for 15 seconds. Check for severe bleeding.

Unconsciousness

A person is unconscious if they cannot instigate a coherent conversation. One in four unconscious persons will die if they are left lying on their backs. They must be placed in the recovery (safe airway) position and monitored for A B C.

△ Dealing with bleeding – use direct pressure, elevation and then good padding and bandaging.

Shock

Medical shock is the reaction of the body to insufficient oxygen reaching the vital organs due to a drop in the effective circulating blood volume. The signs of shock are:

• a rapid weak pulse
• rapid breathing
• cold, pale, clammy skin and a feeling of anxiety

You are dealing with a life-threatening condition. Treat the injuries. Reassure the casualty. Raise the legs and keep the patient warm. Keep reassuring the casualty throughout this procedure. The psychological benefits of this are immeasurable.

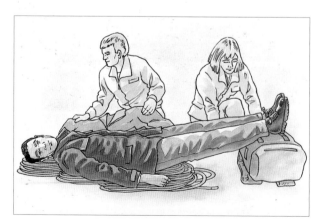

△ Head low, legs elevated, then warmth and reassurance all help a person suffering from medical shock.

◁ *To help stop bleeding, raise the injured limb. This will reduce the flow of blood to the wound.*

▷ *Bandage the wound, having put a pad on to the wound itself. Do not overtighten, or this will cut off the blood supply to the limb.*

SEVERE BLEEDING

Severe bleeding is controlled by direct pressure to the wound site, elevation of the wound above the heart, if possible, and then padding and firm bandaging. If the initial bandaging does not stop the bleeding, leave it in place and put further bandaging on top.

HYPOTHERMIA

The human body reacts badly if the core temperature (that of the vital organs) drops below 37.5°C (98.6°F). A 2°C (3.5°F) drop is a medical emergency, a 5°C (9°F) drop can kill. We lose heat in the mountains through convection, conduction, radiation and evaporation.

COMBATING THE ELEMENTS

WIND, WET and COLD together are the worst combination, often with a relatively high air temperature. Prevention is far more effective than having to treat someone in a mountain setting. The signs of hypothermia mirror drunkenness: stumbling, confusion, erratic behaviour and slurred speech. Below 32°C (90°F) unconsciousness will occur. Often the best you can achieve in a mountain setting is to prevent further cooling. Any re-warming undertaken must be *slow* and *gentle*. The availability of a nylon emergency shelter will dramatically improve the chances of saving a

victim of hypothermia by providing instant shelter as well as keeping a party in a contained setting that contributes greatly to communication and morale. Several people inside one of these shelters will raise the temperature considerably.

△ *Hat and gloves, good insulation from the cold ground and a group shelter will keep an injured person warm.*

Maintaining life

The most important thing to attempt to do is stabilize the situation. This may be done by arranging shelter and insulation for the casualty. It is very important to give reassurance and warmth. You should encourage other members of the party to help you with this. The morale of the victim can be crucial. You should also keep a constant monitoring of vital signs, such as heart rate, breathing, skin colour, consciousness and alertness, and response. Should their condition start to deteriorate, shown up in one or more of these vital signs, immediate appropri-

▽ Salvation from the air. When a helicopter arrives, make yourself visible, stay still and wait until you receive clear directions about what to do.

ate first aid action should be taken. This appropriate treatment will ensure a victim's best chance of survival.

HELICOPTERS

In many parts of the world, mountain rescues are primarily carried out by helicopter. In all cases the most important thing to do if a helicopter arrives on the scene is to make yourself visible, secure all loose or light equipment, and do nothing unless specifically directed by the pilot or crew. Never approach an aircraft on the ground unless a clear sign has been given

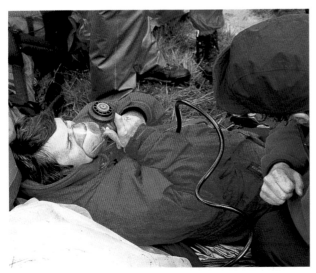

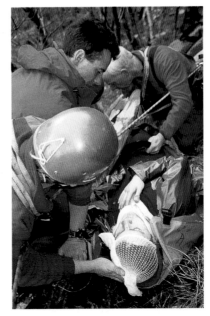

△▷ *With the arrival of experienced medical help, you will be asked to pass on all the information you have about the accident and the casualty's immediate and present condition.*

△ *A small but well-planned first-aid kit and some basic skills are all that is needed to save lives.*

to do so, then approach only in sight of the pilot and always from the front and downhill side of the aircraft.

EMERGENCY EQUIPMENT

When climbing on isolated mountain and sea cliffs you should always carry or at least leave at the bottom of the route an emergency shelter, first aid equipment suitable for controlling severe bleeding, warm clothes and head torches. This will ensure you are capable of stabilizing the situation in the event of an accident and of going for help in darkness, if this is the best course of action. Do you go for help or stay with the victim? The big dilemma. Textbook solutions are rarely of any help in making the right decision. The choice hinges around whether anyone knows where you are and if they are expecting you back at a particular time. If they are then the choice is easy; if not you must do a mental "profit and loss"

account before making your decision. Start with the fact that if the victim is unconscious, then the justification for leaving them alone must be overwhelming. Finally, you are the only one who can decide, so disregard what judgements might be made by others after the event and keep a clear mind.

▽ *A group shelter. These are light and cheap, and make all the difference in terms of warmth, shelter and morale when things go wrong.*

First principles

Everyone navigates continuously and at a very sophisticated level, far more complex and sophisticated than mountain navigation. We are not taught to navigate around our homes, workplaces, or our cities; we learn it instinctively. Drop us into the mountains however, and many of us panic and promptly abandon all the skills we have used for years. Navigation is mainly science with a touch of flair and art in the closing stages. To navigate successfully you need to know and monitor the following.

▽ Navigating along ridges is easy when the visibility is good. In poor conditions it is very easy to end up on the wrong spur.

YOUR DIRECTION OF TRAVEL

This is determined by following a line feature, such as a valley or a ridge for example, by using a distant object such as a peak as a goal, or by creating an imaginary line feature by following a compass bearing (a compass bearing is an angle made up of a line between two points and a line to the North Pole). The good old Boy Scout idea of using the sun should be treated with caution. You are unlikely to make it to the sun and it moves all the time! Clouds may also blot it out at a crucial moment.

TAKING A COMPASS BEARING

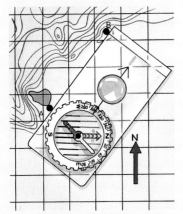

△ To get a bearing on the ground, simply point your direction of travel arrow on the compass at the feature you want to walk to. Then turn the compass housing until the compass needle lines up with the North sign. You will now have a bearing that you can read from the numbers around the outside of the compass housing. You will also have an imaginary line along which you can travel. Should the mist come down, you will still have a route to your goal. (See pages 184–7.)

GETTING IT WRONG

You may well think that you know where you are when visibility is good, or you may not be worried about being too precise. This is fine – as long as the weather remains so also. But don't forget in your desire to get to your mountain crag that weather is fickle. It changes quickly. Do not get caught out if the mist does come down. If you notice the weather deteriorating, establish precisely where you are so that you can use the map and compass to navigate from the point when the mist really does set in.

△ Cloud forms very quickly in the mountains and can turn a simple journey into a complex navigational problem. Here a compass is not much use as the rocks contain spectacular concentrations of magnetic iron.

MAKING THE LANDSCAPE FIT

Unless you have accidentally fallen out of the back of an aircraft at night, you will know where you are starting from and hopefully where you are going. However, a common mistake among mountaineers is that of making the landscape fit the conception of where they think they are on the map. For example, they may well be standing by a bridge over a stream in a deep valley, which fits with the map, but are prepared to overlook the fact that the stream is running the wrong way. This clue should tell them that it is the wrong bridge and stream! Neither map nor compass get things wrong (mostly, at least!). The trap of making what you see around you fit with where you think you are is convenient but may well be wrong. You must be rigorous with your navigation, especially when lost. Do not let clues as to your real whereabouts go unnoticed.

◁ Poring over the map won't help if you are determined to make the wrong landscape fit.

Time and distance

There are several principal methods of keeping track of distance travelled in the mountains. If you are working with reliable maps in country with obvious features then you can read the map and tick off the features as you pass them. This will enable you to know where you are all the time without necessarily knowing how far you have travelled. If you spend lots of time in the hills, you can build up a good picture of how far you travel over various terrain. Keep a mental track of distance during the day, filing the information in your head so you can recall it later in the day should it become necessary.

TIMING – NAISMITH'S RULE

To give you somewhere to start, there was a Scottish walking machine named Naismith who worked out he could pound through the hills at 5 km (3 miles) per hour plus 30 minutes for every 300 m (1000 ft) of ascent. Your job is to work out your own figures. If you have plenty of money, you can buy a reliable altimeter and when used correctly this can turn every contour line into a "tick off" point. All will be revealed later.

PACING

Another skill which is useful over short distances in poor visibility or darkness is pacing. You need to determine how many double paces (that is how many times one leg or the other touches the ground) you do in 100 m (330 ft). Do this over different types of terrain – a flat easy path, gentle incline, steep hill, rough broken ground and steeply down

◁ A perfect mountain scene, but it can all change very quickly. Keep track of where you are even in good visibility.

△ *Wild conditions with zero visibility and snow can occur in the mountains at any time of the year. Being ready for it is the key.*

△ *When things fall apart, change gear and accept that the journey home needs care and discipline. The more meticulous you are, the quicker you will reach safety.*

hill. Try to memorize your double paces for each of these, having tested them lots of times until you trust the figures and your ability to judge the terrain implicity. You can then count as you walk to measure the distance you have travelled. You will need to concentrate hard. This technique is not ideal if you have a mind that wanders!

THE PSYCHOLOGY

People fail to navigate accurately or get lost for two reasons, laziness or panic. Concentration, discipline and being meticulous overcome the first, and learning to be self-confident and developing the art of justified reassurance solve the second. Navigating in poor conditions is a lonely job if you are on your own with no one to bounce ideas off, or if you are the only member of a party who knows what to do. It is particularly testing if you are in a party surrounded by "doubting Thomases". An analytical and logical approach works wonders in helping you cope.

one double pace

shorter pace

one double pace

PACING

◁**1** *Make sure you know how many double paces you take to every 100 m (330 ft) of travel. This way, you can accurately determine your location over short distances if visibility is very poor.*

◁**2** *Bear in mind that your paces will be shorter going steeply up (and down) a hill. Therefore you will use more double paces for every 100 m (330 ft) covered.*

The map

Most navigation hinges around a map, which may range from a rough sketch map in a rock climbing guidebook through to a near-perfect national map series epitomized by the Swiss Carte Nationale or the British Ordnance Survey. You should familiarize yourself with all aspects of the maps that cover the areas in which you plan to climb. This will include magnetic variation (see page 187), the legend, contour intervals and scale.

A PICTURE OF THE LANDSCAPE

A map is a picture of the land. The good ones are brought alive by contour lines and clear, easily understood symbols. Most maps point roughly towards the North Pole; the only reason for this is that the early cartographers lived in the Northern Hemisphere. There is no up and down in space. It is important to grasp a few vital pieces of information from a map you are not familiar with before you start navigating.

△ *Maps vary the world over but have a reassuring similarity in most cases. Take care to become familiar with the map before you need it in difficult conditions.*

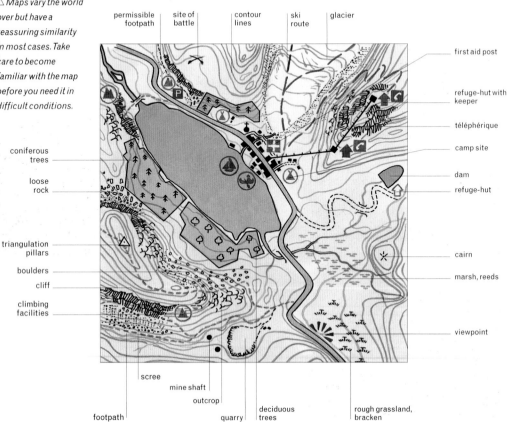

permissible footpath — site of battle — contour lines — ski route — glacier

first aid post

refuge-hut with keeper

téléphérique

camp site

dam

refuge-hut

coniferous trees

loose rock

triangulation pillars

boulders

cliff

climbing facilities

cairn

marsh, reeds

viewpoint

scree

mine shaft

outcrop

footpath

quarry

deciduous trees

rough grassland, bracken

SCALE

The first is the scale. This varies dramatically but the typical scale for mountain use is 1:50,000. This means that one unit of measurement on the map equals 50,000 of them on the ground. In practical terms, if using a metric scale, 2 cm on the map equals 1 km on the ground. The important thing is to be sure you know the scale and what that means to you.

CONTOURS AND GRIDS

Contour interval (lines of equal altitude) also varies a lot and can create embarrassing problems if you confuse it. Typically they are at 10 or 20 m (30 or 60 ft) intervals, get it wrong and your calculations will be 100 per cent out. Many maps have some form of grid or co-ordinate system which is unique to the country of origin. The good news is that in general they are made up of 1 km squares and the lines run pretty well north, south, east and west. The grid system is handy for estimating rough distances and makes taking a compass bearing easier and more accurate, but it is primarily used to positively identify a position that has a unique number reference that cannot be confused with any other.

Familiarity with the map and its symbols is vital and the more time you can spend pouring over it prior to going into the mountains the better. Trying to understand the map on a windblown col just as the unseasonable blizzard hits you is not the way forward.

● SCALES OF MAPS AND THEIR USES

Scale	Meaning	Use
1:15,000	1 cm=150 m	Orienteering
1:25,000	1 cm=250 m	Ideal for walking (very detailed)
1:40,000	1 cm=400 m	Mountain and orienteering maps
1:50,000	1 cm=500 m	Most common mountaineering map
1:100,000	1 cm=1,000 m	Cycling, holidays
1:250,000	1 cm=2,500 m	Motoring
1:1,000,000	1 cm=10 km	Map of country

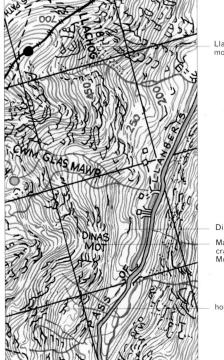

Llachog mountain top

Dinas Bach

Main climbing crag – Dinas Mot

house platform

◁ △ *The map represents the landscape in two dimensions. Contour lines are designed to give an accurate interpretation of the shape and height of the land. You can see this clearly in the map and accompanying photograph.*

The compass

After the map, the compass is the most important tool the mountain navigator has. Knowing how to use it is essential for accurate movement around the hills and mountains in poor visibility. This is not an easy skill to acquire. It is important to practise in a safe environment until you are thoroughly conversant with all the techniques involved with its correct use.

MANY TOOLS IN ONE

The modern compass used by mountain navigators is made up of several different components. There is the floating needle which points to magnetic north, a protractor, a ruler and the flat plate that holds the rest together. From early childhood we have been told that the compass points north. In reality an unmodified compass needle will point through the earth at a spot in northern Canada, and worse than that, this point

moves all the time, albeit very slowly indeed. Fortunately people with more skill than us keep it all under control by making the compass needle sit up and swing and by publishing the magnetic variation so that with an incredibly simple adjustment to the compass we can pretend it is pointing to the North Pole.

USES OF THE COMPASS

The compass can be used for many useful navigational tasks. These are as follows:

① taking bearings directly from the ground
② taking bearings from the map and applying them to the ground
③ measuring distances on your map
④ finding north (using the magnetic variation)
⑤ setting the map to the landscape
⑥ working out grid references

▽ The compass is a versatile tool: protractor, navigator and distance measurer all in one.

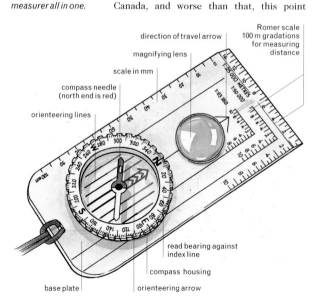

direction of travel arrow
Romer scale
100 m gradations for measuring distance
magnifying lens
scale in mm
compass needle (north end is red)
orienteering lines
read bearing against index line
compass housing
base plate
orienteering arrow

△ A direct bearing can be taken from the ground in the absence of a map, or the bearing can be applied back on to the map.

◁ *Most commonly in mountain navigation we take a bearing from the map (using grid north) and apply it to the ground (converting to magnetic north).*

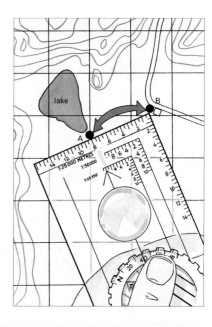

▷ *Make sure you are using the right scale on the compass when you are measuring distances off the map.*

BEWARE DISTRACTIONS

Tiredness and stress will work against you being able to work effectively in close navigation. Make sure that you give it all your attention when necessary. This may mean cutting yourself off from the rest of the party while taking your bearing and working out your timing and pacing.

● USING YOUR EYES, EARS AND BRAIN

These are almost certainly the most important tools in navigation. Things are not always as they seem, particularly when they are distorted by mist or darkness. So always look, listen and think. If you are trying to find a stream in the dark, then listening for the stream is obviously more important than looking for it.

● GETTING IT WRONG

One of the most common mistakes in navigation is to get your compass bearing 180 degrees out. This means that you will be heading off in exactly the opposite direction to that in which you want (or need) to go. It is the easiest thing in the world to place the compass wrongly on the map, in effect getting the map upside down. Try to guard against this by double-checking the bearing before setting off. You might also take a quick note of the landscape and special features from the map that you should see when turning to face your bearing – if you can see anything at all, that is!

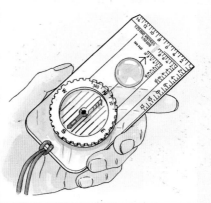

◁ *This compass is 180 degrees out – the red north-pointing arrow has been aligned to the south. This is a common mistake.*

The science

Is navigation a science or an art? It is probably a bit of both. It is certainly one of those skills that can be practised at home or other safe environment until you feel confident enough to trust your life to it.

THE MAP

Taking information of your route accurately from the map is the basis of good navigation. What direction do I need to travel in, how far do I need to travel, and what am I expecting to happen are the three questions you must ask.

The last is perhaps the most important, as this will reassure you that what you are doing is right or alert you to the fact that things are going wrong. You need to interpret the map to know whether you are about to go steeply downhill or that after a kilometre you will run into a very steep slope, at which point you must turn left. This is map-to-ground interpretation and in its most sophisticated form can be used alone to navigate extremely accurately. When combined with other techniques as well, your navigation will become bombproof.

▽ A featureless plateau can lead to massive cliffs, a big danger if your navigation is poor.

△ Keep your map safe and handy for reference. It is not much good to you at the bottom of your rucksack – worse still if it blows away.

◁ The top of this mountain ends in massive cliffs, a danger to any climber on a poor-visibility day.

THE COMPASS

Compass bearings become important in navigation if visibility is poor or you think it may become poor shortly. The most common bearing is taken off the map and then applied to the ground. Imagine you are at a stream junction having walked up a valley heading for your crag. The mist is down and the crag is nowhere to be seen.

Place the edge of the compass plate on the stream junction on the map and then on the crag. Make sure the direction of travel arrow is pointing from the junction to the crag otherwise your bearing will be 180 degrees wrong.

Turn the compass housing around until the lines on the base of it are parallel with either the grid lines or the vertical edge of the map. Make sure that the orienteering arrow on the base of the housing is pointing north.

You now have a grid bearing which must be adjusted to magnetic before you apply it to the ground. Magnetic variation is different depending on where you are on the globe, so you must look on the map to find what it is. It will be either east or west of grid north and it will be increasing or decreasing annually. In most cases the map will be dated and the annual change will be recorded. Having established the variation, adjust your grid bearing accordingly.

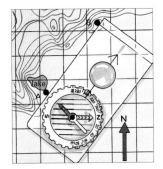

△ **1** *Place the edge of the compass on the point where you are (A) and the point you wish to reach (B). Make sure the direction of travel arrow is pointing to your destination.*

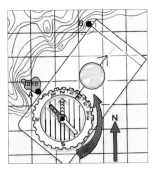

△ **2** *Turn the housing of the compass around until the lines on its base are in line with the grid lines on the map. Make sure the orienteering arrow is pointing to north on the map.*

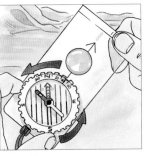

△ **3** *Add or subtract the magnetic variation (this will depend on which part of the world you are in).*

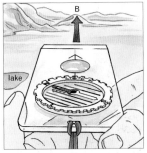

△ **4** *You now have a magnetic bearing to march on. Turn the compass until the north needle lines up.*

● MAGNETIC VARIATION

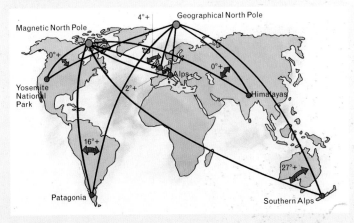

◁ *Magnetic variation is hard to visualize because we are dealing with a sphere – the earth. The important thing is to read your map to find the appropriate magnetic variation figure and the rate of annual change.*

Using an altimeter

Like most pieces of specialist equipment, the altimeter certainly has a place in the armoury of the modern climber. But it is as well to know when and where to use it.

THE ALTIMETER

An altimeter measures the change in air pressure, so if you remain in one place it acts as a barometer and lets you know if the atmospheric pressure is changing as weather systems pass over you. If you climb up or down, it tells you how far you have ascended or descended. However, if the atmospheric pressure is changing dramatically as you are moving up or down, it will act as a barometer and an altimeter at the same time and will therefore be very inaccurate. Properly used and with a knowledge of the problems outlined above, an altimeter is an invaluable navigational tool. Altimeters use an aneroid or vacuum vessel which expands or compresses

1000 m outer ring | km window

adjustment for 1000 m ring

△ Good-quality altimeters are expensive but very accurate if used properly.

▷ How much farther to the top of the climb? An altimeter will solve the problem.

as the surrounding air pressure varies. This movement is then transferred either mechanically or electronically to an analogue needle or an LED display which is calibrated to read in metres.

With the arrival of watch-based altimeters, the cost of owning one has dropped dramatically, but do remember that you tend to get what you pay for. Altimeters work best if they are used over short periods of time and can be regularly re-set at known altitudes. They are most useful for identifying obscure turn-off points in ascent or descent, so can be used for short periods using more obvious features as starting points. It is worth noting that every 1 milli-bar of atmospheric pressure change represents 8 m of altitude. Maintaining time and distance calculations in descent is notoriously difficult so this is really where they come into their own. They can be used either by setting them on a known altitude or they can be zeroed and then used in an absolute mode for however many vertical metres you wish to travel. This is often the best method in bad conditions as calculations are easier and less open to mistakes. Altimeters will never be a substitute for accurate navigation using more traditional methods, but as an extra tool to reassure and double-check in bad conditions they are invaluable.

◁ *Watch altimeters can be cheap and convenient but they are not always accurate. You get what you pay for.*

▽ *When the conditions are like this on the way home, an altimeter can make all the difference for safe and efficient navigation.*

The art

▽ Getting to the top of the climb is sometimes the easy bit. Now you have to get home again! This is often where the navigation starts.

To be a successful navigator you will need to be confident in your own skills. You will need to be able to juggle with lots of competing data, to sift through it and to prioritize it. You will also need to be flexible in your approach. No two situations are ever the same. Get in the habit of choosing your main skills that you will use for the situation you are in and call upon other data to back you up. For instance, you may choose to pace a short leg, walking on a bearing. But you might also work out how long it should take to reach your destination (probably only a matter of minutes in this instance), and use your watch to back up your pacing. This is where the flair and imagination comes in.

KEEP YOUR LEGS SHORT!

Navigation at this level will always be an inexact game but it is designed to keep the level of accumulated error to a manageable scale. Obviously, the shorter the navigational legs you undertake the smaller any error will be and you can relocate after each leg. So cut the journey up into small bits using the most obvious targets as way points.

USE COMMON SENSE

Keep a sense of scale. If what you are looking for is 500 m (550 yd) away from you to start with, then there is no point in crashing on looking for it for 2 km (2,000 yd). If when you have travelled the correct distance on the correct bearing and you can't find what you are looking for, stop and have a think about where it might be. There will be many things to think through. If you are walking up a stream looking for a junction and have not seen one when your distance calculation is up, then it is most likely it will be in front of you a short distance. Continue on for a further 10 per cent of the original distance and you should arrive at it. If

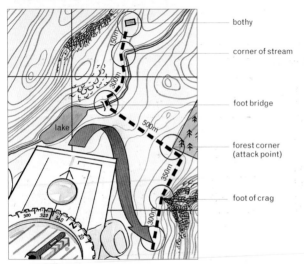

bothy

corner of stream

foot bridge

lake

forest corner
(attack point)

foot of crag

◁ Navigating via short legs in bad conditions reduces accumulative errors. Divide your journey up so that you find each point – foot of crag, edge of forest, foot bridge, stream and bothy – in turn.

you find a stream junction too early then you have more of a dilemma. It may be the wrong junction if it is very early or you may just be travelling faster than you thought. Check the angle at which it joins the main stream: does it fit? It would still pay to carry on to see if there is another junction, but again have a definite distance in mind.

There is an old saying in navigation, "The tent will not come to you no matter how long you wait for it." You must find it, it will not find you. So you must be quite aggressive when you have navigated yourself near to your target, but make sure your search is logical and controlled; running around like the proverbial headless chicken is of no value to anyone.

◁ *Taking a bearing in wet, cold and windy conditions can be very testing. It is often hard to achieve the accuracy you need in difficult conditions.*

● SEARCHES

In very poor visibility, it is essential to be totally accurate in pinpointing each stage of your navigation legs. You must find what you set out to arrive at. It is no good saying that the crag foot must be somewhere near, and then trying to continue on to the forest corner. Small errors at each leg may mean that you miss the bothy by hundreds of metres (yards), which in a storm could mean the difference between life and death. So, if you cannot find the foot of the crag after your pacing on a bearing, and timing, then organize a search to find it. You must assume that you are in the vicinity. Here are three examples of the type of search you might choose to use: the star search, sweep search and box search. Always make sure you know your way back to your starting point.

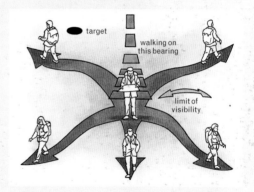

△ *You can adopt the star pattern with several people or alone, providing you return each time to your original spot.*

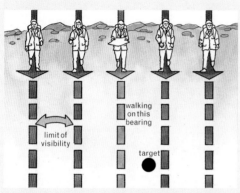

△ *Sweep search – useful for finding your tent or an injured person if you are travelling with several people.*

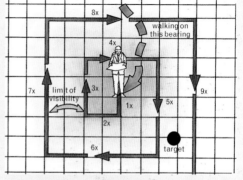

△ *Using the box search is a sure way of eventually finding your goal but it is tedious and very time-consuming.*

What do we mean by weather?

Weather is generally taken to mean the day-to-day effects of the humidity, precipitation, temperature, wind speed and direction, cloud cover and visibility at a specific place on earth. This is different to climate, which indicates the average conditions that weather produces over long periods of time in a specific place. It is the weather that we as climbers will be interested in – what is it going to do today?

Like navigation, weather forecasting is a mixture of science and art. It is important for climbers who venture farther afield to be able, through whatever means, to be able to make their own judgements about it.

A CHANGEABLE MEDIUM

Weather by its very definition is changeable – in some places at certain times this may be a constant factor, almost hourly; in other places the weather may be more stable and predictable. With the development of modern physics

theory, Seligman's statement appears to be more accurate than he imagined. This does little to reassure the humble rock climber wrestling with a weather forecast prior to committing themselves to a towering mountain route. However, despite the seeming chaos of the atmosphere, there is a lot we can do to up our odds against the weather. Armed with the best and most up-to-date forecast, a little knowledge, good observation and common sense, it is possible to win most of the time.

At various times all these can be good or bad for the rock climber, depending on circumstances. There is nothing like a bit of rain to allow you to rest!

THE GLOBAL PICTURE

The world's weather is driven by the sun. Because the earth is a sphere, various areas of it receive more or less radiation than others, creating dramatically differing temperatures, hot at the equator and cold at the poles. Hot air

▷ *A fine day in early summer and all is well in the mountains …*

rises at the equator and descends at the poles, creating an area of low pressure at the equator and an area of high pressure over the Arctic and Antarctic. If only it was that simple. As the warm air flows towards the poles, it gets obstructed by the stable high pressure and some of it descends in the subtropical regions to create a band of subtropical high pressure. The semi-permanent Azores High that creates the wonderful climate of the Mediterranean is part of this system. Mid-latitudes are dominated by low pressure, which explains to some extent the climate of Northern Europe and Patagonia. To complete the circulation, air flows back from the poles to the equator, spreading over the earth's surface. As a result of the spinning of the earth, this air is deflected. The direction in which it is deflected is determined by which direction it is flowing and whether it is in the Northern or Southern Hemisphere.

△ ... until minutes later a summer snow shower has raced through, changing the situation dramatically.

GLOBAL CIRCULATION

▽ The weather is a complex machine driven by the sun. It is complicated by the tilt and spin of the earth.

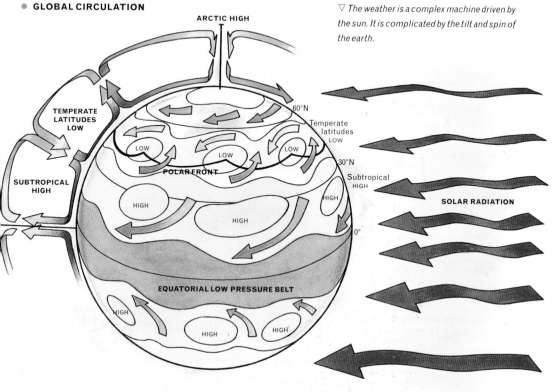

Major weather systems

Major prevailing weather systems provide clues to weather patterns in most parts of the world. These should be studied and absorbed for the place in which you plan to climb. These weather systems will contain air masses coming from particular directions, having travelled over certain landscapes or seascapes.

AIR MASSES

An air mass is a body of air in which the horizontal temperature and humidity gradients are relatively slight. Air masses develop the characteristics of the terrain they are in contact with or are travelling over. So, if a mass of air is travelling over a large area of warm sea it will warm up and become very moist; a mass of air that is stationary over very cold land will become very cold and dry. If two air masses of different temperatures run into each other, one will either bulldoze under or will ski-jump over the other, causing air to rise.

ANTICYCLONES

An anticyclone is an air mass where air is converging at high levels and descending. It is an area of high pressure relative to its surroundings. Because the air is descending it is compressing, warming and can therefore hold a higher percentage of water vapour, so cloud will be limited and precipitation unlikely. Winds blow clockwise around an anticyclone in the Northern Hemisphere and anticlockwise in the Southern Hemisphere, and are generally light.

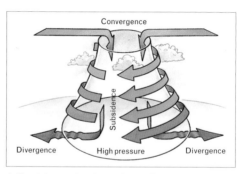

△ The air in an anticyclone is descending, compressing and warming. Cloud will tend to evaporate and winds will be generally light.

DEPRESSIONS (CYCLONES)

These are highly mobile air masses with divergence at high levels. Air rushes in the bottom and flows out of the top. This creates low pressure. The air is rising, expanding and cooling, therefore it can hold less water vapour so condensation results in cloud formation and precipitation in the form of rain or snow. Winds blow anticlockwise around a depression in the Northern Hemisphere and clockwise in the Southern Hemisphere.

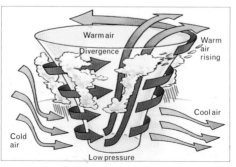

△ In a depression the air is rising, expanding and cooling. Water vapour will condense forming large amounts of cloud and shortly rain or snow will fall.

△ Sunny skies are associated with high pressure, but the wind is blowing hard. Low pressure is somewhere near, causing a steep pressure gradient.

FRONTS

These are the "battle areas" between diverse air masses. The name "front" was actually assigned to them in 1918 during World War I. They bring the wildest, wettest and most unsettled periods of bad weather.

COLD FRONT

A cold front occurs when a cold air mass runs into a warm air mass. The cold air moves along the ground surface pushing the warm air up. The rapid movement and steep slope of the leading edge causes strong lifting of the warm air, usually resulting in cloud formation, and precipitation associated with a cold front is usually confined to a narrow band of high intensity.

WARM FRONT

A warm front occurs when a warm air mass runs into a cooler air mass. A warm front usually moves more slowly than a cold front and the slope of the overriding front is very shallow. This ski-jump effect again creates cloud and precipitation which is spread over a broad area but is usually less intense than a cold front.

OCCLUDED FRONT

An occluded front develops when a rapidly moving cold front overruns a slower-moving warm front. The warmer air is lifted out of contact with the ground surface, cooling as it lifts. Cloud and precipitation result if there is sufficient moisture. The formation of an occluded front represents a breakdown of a frontal system. The weather associated with an occluded front may vary considerably in its intensity.

▷ An occluded front.

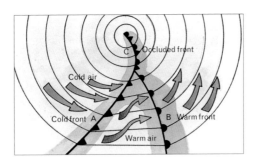

◁ A representation of a typical Northern Hemisphere mid-latitude depression.

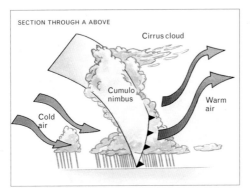

◁ A cold front.

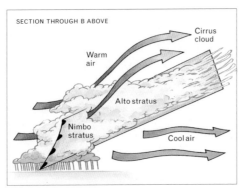

◁ A warm front.

▽ Racing cirrus clouds give warning of a warm front on its way. It is time to think about descent.

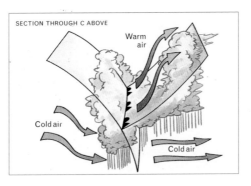

Interpreting weather charts

The weather charts we see in news-papers, on television, or coming out of fax machines are two-dimensional pictures of the atmospheric conditions at certain times. The chart is corrected to show sea level pressure despite the altitude of the terrain it covers. There are two types of chart commonly published for use by the general public. A synoptic chart is a picture of the actual weather situation at the place named on the chart. This is an exact statement of where each weather system was at the given time. The second type of chart is a forecast chart and is how the forecasters imagine the weather systems will look at a stated time in the future. If you cast back to Seligman at the start of the chapter you can see that these will be open to considerable error and therefore will require careful interpretation and conser-vative use. The newer the forecast chart or the more up-to-date the information you have to apply to it, the better.

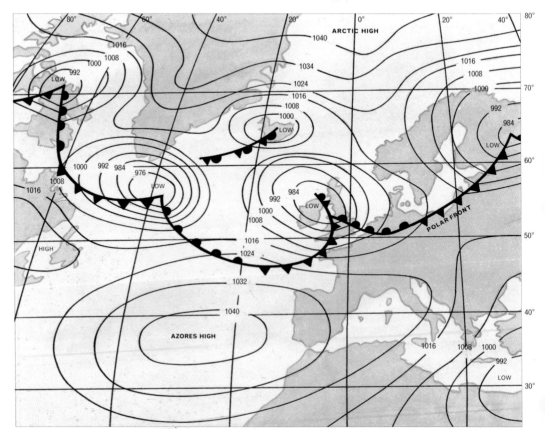

ISOBARS

The chart is dominated by isobars – lines of equal pressure. These define areas of high and low pressure, the wind direction and, depending on how close together they are, the wind speed. The other major piece of information on the chart is the position and type of front associated with the various weather systems. A single chart is of limited use to us unless it is accompanied by information as to how fast and in what direction the various systems are moving, and whether they are intensifying or decaying. A series of updated forecast charts will help bring the situation alive for you. The other piece of knowledge that is vital is where each weather system has come from and the nature of the terrain it has travelled over before it gets to you. This varies dramatically from season to season.

● GETTING TO KNOW THE WEATHER CHARTS

To make your own assessment of the weather, you will need to become familiar with these charts and the weather systems that they indicate. You will also need to know where you can get hold of accurate information in the area in which you plan to operate. This may not always be easy. You will need to be able to understand the symbols and other data, and be able to make a reasonable guess as to what this may mean for you over the next 10 hours, or whatever your timescale is. Be prepared to change your plans if foul weather comes in sooner than predicted and try not to get caught out high up on a multipitch route when the rain and wind drive in!

▽ *Climbing big walls in the Greenland summer. Here it is important to get a view on what the weather may be doing before setting off to climb.*

The effects of mountains

△ Cold temperatures high in the mountains mean snow will lie right through the summer, particularly on shaded slopes.

▷ This diagram shows the main effects that mountains have on weather in general. You can see how warm, moist air is forced to rise over the mountain barrier, causing it to cool and clouds to form. This may lead to rain or snow on the tops. Wind increases in speed and intensity as well.

Most weather forecasts are produced for the lowlands and to let people know if they should take an umbrella to work or not. Your job is to transfer this information into a mountain setting and to appreciate the differences. It will usually be colder and wetter, the wind will be stronger and there will be more cloud; or it may even be sunnier than the weather in the lowlands, in the instance of a temperature inversion.

TEMPERATURE

As you gain altitude the air becomes colder. This is because the pressure is less and so the air is less compressed. On a clear day the temperature will usually decrease by 1°C per 100 m (110 yd). If cloud is forming, this lapse rate is reduced to around 0.5°C as a result of heat being released into the atmosphere by the process of condensation.

TEMPERATURE INVERSION

This usually occurs after a beautiful clear night when the mountain tops have become very cold. This cools the air in contact with them. The air is now heavy and it rolls down the mountain side to pool in the valley floor, forcing the lighter, warmer air back up the mountain.

CLOUD AND PRECIPITATION

Mountains are cloudier and wetter than lowlands, because they force warm, moist air to rise, where it expands, cools and water vapour condenses.

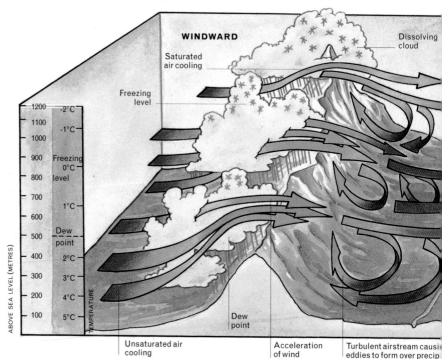

WINDWARD

Saturated air cooling

Dissolving cloud

Freezing level

ABOVE SEA LEVEL (METRES)	TEMPERATURE
1200	-2°C
1100	-1°C
1000	
900	Freezing 0°C level
800	
700	1°C
600	
500	Dew point
400	2°C
300	3°C
200	4°C
100	5°C

Dew point

Unsaturated air cooling

Acceleration of wind

Turbulent airstream causi eddies to form over precip

● WIND CHILL

Wind will have a dramatic effect on how warm or cold you feel. Even if the air temperature is a comfortable 10°C (50°F), a wind blowing at 32 kph (20 mph) will make it feel more like freezing or below. Any flesh exposed to this wind will go numb quickly. In the climbing context, this usually means your fingers.

WIND SPEED KPH/MPH						
64/40	-3/26	-12/10	-20/-5	-30/-22	-38/-36	-48/-54
56/35	-3/27	-11/11	-20/-4	-31/-20	-37/-35	-47/-52
48/30	-2/28	-10/13	-19/-2	-28/-18	-36/-33	-45/-49
40/25	-1/30	-9/16	-18/0	-26/-15	-34/-29	-43/-45
32/20	0/32	-8/18	-16/3	-23/-9	-31/-24	-40/-40
23/15	2/36	-5/22	-12/11	-21/-6	-28/-18	-36/-33
16/10	5/40	-2/28	-9/16	-17/2	-23/-9	-30/-22
	10°/50°	5°/40°	-1°/30°	-7°/20°	-12°/10°	-18°/0°
	AIR TEMPERATURE °C/°F					

△ Orographic cloud forming due to moist air rising, expanding and cooling, causing the water vapour to condense. As the air descends down the lee side the water vapour re-evaporates.

△ Perfect climbing weather above the low cloud and drizzle associated with a temperature inversion.

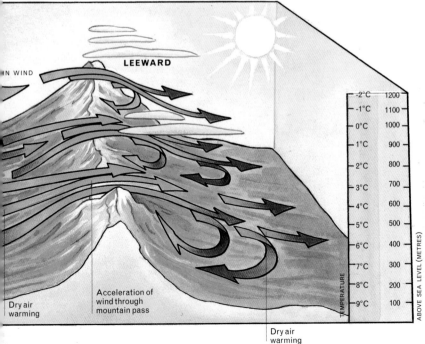

LEEWARD

IN WIND

-2°C	1200
-1°C	1100
0°C	1000
1°C	900
2°C	800
3°C	700
4°C	600
5°C	500
6°C	400
7°C	300
8°C	200
9°C	100

TEMPERATURE

ABOVE SEA LEVEL (METRES)

Dry air warming

Acceleration of wind through mountain pass

Dry air warming

△ The wind on top of mountains may be two or three times stronger than that felt 1,000 m (3,000 ft) lower down.

Special considerations

Certain conditions that might be experienced in the mountains can at first appear puzzling or perhaps so obvious as to pass unnoticed. However, they may become significant as the day wears on – such as the effect of sunshine over a period of time.

WIND TURBULANCE

As the wind blows over the land and sea, it is slowed to a greater or lesser extent by friction when it comes into contact with the features on the surface of the earth. An exposed mountain top will therefore be in the stronger air flow. There are no rules to determine how much windier it will be as we gain altitude, as there are so many variables, but you should always assume it is going to be windier as you gain height or approach an exposed ridge. The mountains act like boulders in a river and create unseen rapids in the air. This causes spectacular turbulence that can lead to gusts far in excess of the actual wind speed. Not nice if you are teetering up a delicate runnerless pitch!

△ *Clear skies can seem perfect, but hot sun brings disadvantages such as sunburn, dehydration and heat exhaustion.*

▷ *Wind in the mountains can dangerously cool you and can also be strong enough to knock you off your feet or blow you off your climb.*

SUNSHINE

High in the mountains the air is free of the dust, dirt and pollution that we experience at lower altitudes, so the effect of the sun is much stronger. This can greatly increase the problems of sunburn and dehydration.

ELECTRICAL STORMS

The complex mechanisms of thunderstorms are still not fully understood, but the dangers of them are very obvious. They are caused by extreme instability in the atmosphere either as a result of heat or very active cold fronts. Apart from the obvious danger of being struck by lightning, thunderstorms also produce very heavy rain and spectacular hail that can turn a pleasant, sunny rock climb into a survival nightmare in minutes. Good planning and finishing your route as early in the day as possible will reduce the risk of being zapped. Storms triggered by the heat tend to hit in the late afternoon or early evening. If you are caught, then try and avoid high points, exposed ridges, caves and chimneys. If you are going to sit it out then the place to be is 100–200 m (330–650 ft) down the side of a ridge or face.

◁ The ominous cumulo-nimbus and anvil cloud associated with electrical storms. Beware if you are downwind of it – it is coming your way!

● ANABATIC AND KATABATIC WINDS

Air that comes into contact with the ground is heated or cooled depending upon the temperature of the ground. When it is warmed, the surface air will move uphill. This is known as an anabatic wind. The reverse is true when the surface cools the air in contact with it. Wind will tumble down off the hillsides into the valleys, causing frost hollows and belts of fog. This wind is known as a katabatic wind, and it reaches high speeds around high mountains.

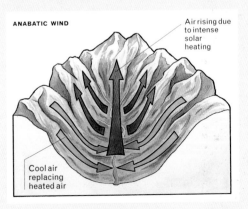

ANABATIC WIND
Air rising due to intense solar heating
Cool air replacing heated air

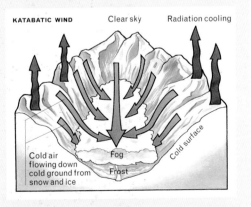

KATABATIC WIND   Clear sky   Radiation cooling
Cold air flowing down cold ground from snow and ice
Fog
Frost
Cold surface

Weather forecasts

There is no end to the availability of weather forecasts in this age of information. We can get them in newspapers, on radio and T.V., by fax and phone, on the Internet and by talking to the forecasters themselves in their offices and towers. Despite all this, we still spend most of our time moaning about how wrong they got it. You must remember that it is a forecast of what might happen and not a statement of fact. Armed with the forecast, you must put quite a bit of

work into interpreting it and applying it to the exact location you are in. Thought is also needed regarding the possible changes in the atmosphere that might have occurred since the forecast was issued.

THE ATMOSPHERE

An important thing to bear in mind is if the atmosphere is stable then forecasting is going to be very accurate; if it is unstable then the accuracy will be greatly reduced and the chance of local variability greatly enhanced. Unfortunately, it is when things are unstable that we need good forecasts most. Such is life.

UP-TO-DATE FORECASTS

To stay on top you need as recent a forecast as possible for as small an area as possible, and if you can get hold of several from different sources you will get a much broader picture of what is going on. Most forecasts are general in nature and you will have to apply some of the information above to get a picture of what is happening in the mountains. However, in many areas of the world where climbing is a major sport, specialist mountain forecasts are produced and are extremely useful. In most countries a 12-hour forecast will be broadly accurate to around 85 per cent, but this accuracy drops off dramatically as you extend the time scale. A 4-day forecast will drop to around 50 per cent. Watch the development – the key to your own short-term forecasting.

FORECASTS IN THE FIELD

In order to accurately forecast changes in the weather we need to be fed new information. This is not normally possible when you are on a climb, so we need to observe continuously and make our decisions on what we see. You

▽ *Perfect climbing weather associated with the semi-permanent high pressure that establishes itself over the Mediterranean in summer.*

◁ *Wild wave clouds provide a timely warning as a front approaches the Southern Alps of New Zealand. You have a few hours to finish your climb and find shelter.*

▽ *Thickening high cloud follows cirrus clouds as the front gets nearer.*

need to decide on a time-scale based on the seriousness of the situation. If you are on an easy rock climb with a straightforward descent, then it probably doesn't matter whether it rains or not. A very different situation would be if you are already ten pitches up and about to traverse three pitches across into an inescapable gully system that will turn into a cascade if it rains. In this situation, before you commit yourself, you need to look back to the start of the climb and decide if the weather has remained the same or has deteriorated in any way and if so how much. Has the wind increased, decreased or changed direction? Has the cloud built up or has it dissolved, and more importantly are the clouds growing vertically or all dying at a particular height? Clouds growing vertically indicate an unstable atmosphere with a lot of lift. This will often lead to storms and rain. Has the temperature risen or fallen? If there have been significant changes, then you must decide if you are happy to push on or not.

▷ *Turbulence in the mountains can be severe. Ridges act like boulders in a river and cause acceleration and eddy effects in the air.*

EMERGENCY ROPEWORK

The art of getting out of trouble is not to get into it in the first place. All experienced rock climbers would agree, but it is easier said than done! Even the best-laid plans can go wrong and problems have a nasty habit of appearing when they are least expected. Incidents will inevitably happen and the trick is to anticipate the incident and change plans if necessary to make sure it doesn't become an accident. In other words, have an awareness of what's going on around you. All climbers have a responsibility to themselves and others on the crag so a certain level of self-reliance, knowledge and skill must be reached to deal with a problem situation effectively.

Opposite: *High on a mountain crag, where problems can quickly accumulate and become serious. Do you know how to deal with them when they occur?*

Getting out of trouble

By following the standard proce-dures that have been taught throughout this book, many poten-tially dangerous situations can be easily solved. The ropework and belay methods has been taught for the very good reason that, should any problem arise, there will be a simple answer to deal with it. All the different skills involved in rescue can be learnt individually and then used as needed. Treat each situation as the occasion demands – look at the problem, don't rush and, above all, think clearly and decide what to do and when. If in doubt, get help.

LOCKING OFF A BELAY DEVICE

Locking off a belay device under load is the action to take in most incidents. It allows a breathing space and ensures nothing else can go wrong. Moreover, it leaves the belayer with both hands free . The belayer can either lower the casualty or hoist them to the stance, whichever is most appropriate. Always make sure that the rope is tied off against the back bar of the karabiner and not the gate.

△ **1** *Keeping the rope in the "locked" position – take a bight of rope through the karabiner.*

△ **2** *Take a second loop through the first loop and pull the rope tight.*

△ **3** *Now tie a couple of half-hitches back around the karabiner.*

GETTING IT WRONG

◁ *In this picture the rope has been locked off against the gate. Always lock off against the back bar of the karabiner.*

△ **4** *The belay device is now locked off and you can take both hands off the rope.*

△ **5** *To release the load take the half-hitches out and pull the tail, keeping the hand against the rope and the belay device.*

Prussik knots

Prussik knots consist of a 6 mm (¼ in) cord which is wound several times round the main climbing rope, tied and then locked off. All prussik knots have slightly different properties and it is important to be aware of them. For example, the French prussik (see page 143) can release under load. Therefore there are situations where the French prussik can be dangerous when climbing (prussiking) up a rope. If the French prussik is grabbed in the heat of the moment it could let you down.

THE ORIGINAL PRUSSIK

Advantages: Quick, easy to tie one-handed. Number of turns can be increased when using thicker ropes or to increase the amount of friction.

Disadvantages: Tendency to jam solid especially on wet ropes. Not recommended with tape/spectra – cannot be released under load.

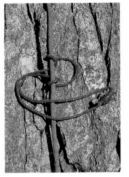

△ **1** *Take the prussik loop two or three times around the main rope and push the end through itself. Pull tight.*

△ **2** *The completed knot. It should be neat and tidy if it is to work efficiently on the rope.*

THE KLEMHEIST

Advantages: Any thickness of rope can be used – the number of turns is variable. It can be tied either with tape or spectra.

Disadvantages – Cannot be released easily when it is loaded.

△ **1** *Take the prussik loop three or four times around the main rope and push the lower end through the top end.*

△ **2** *The completed Klemheist. It can now be clipped directly on to the waist harness with a screwgate (locking) karabiner.*

Mechanical devices can be used instead of prussik knots; they do the job more efficiently but are relatively expensive. If rock climbing is to be attempted in serious situations, either in sea cliff or high mountain locations, their use may be worth considering. Ascenders, metal clamps which attach to the rope, come in a variety of guises, with or without handles and will slide one way (preferably upwards) and by means of a cam lock on the rope when downward pressure is applied. All are supplied with manufacturer's instructions which must be followed to the letter.

△ *The handled ascender (left) and ropeman have almost rendered prussik loops obsolete but are relatively expensive pieces of equipment for occasional use.*

Hoisting

There are situations in which you may need to help your second over a difficult move by giving them a quick hoist on the rope. Or you may need to help a climber knocked unconscious by a falling stone. These are but two of the many, though hopefully rare, situations in which you may need to set up a hoist. There are two basic kinds of hoist.

ASSISTED HOIST

This is a relatively simple method of giving someone a quick pull over a difficult move. Even so, it should only be tried when all other efforts have failed. The stages are:

① Lock off the belay device as described on page 206.
② Attach a French prussik or auto-block, (see page 143) to the rope immediately below the belay device and clip with a screwgate (locking) karabiner to the rope loop around the harness, making sure there are a few centimetres (inches) of slack in the prussik. If there is more the hoist will be inefficient.
③ Throw a loop of rope down to the second instructing them to clip it to the main load-bearing loop of their harness with a screwgate karabiner. The rope now goes from their harness, through the French prussik and belay device, back down to their harness and back up to you. Untie the belay device carefully, making sure the French prussik is gripping the main rope.
④ Get the second to pull on the rope running down to them while you pull on the rope coming back up.

△ **1** If your second is tiring and is faced with a difficult move, you can perform an assisted hoist. First, lock off the belay plate.

△ **2** Attach a French prussik below the plate and around the main climbing rope. Clip with a screwgate (locking) karabiner to the rope loop in your harness.

△ **3** Throw a loop of rope to your second so they can clip it to a load-bearing part of the harness with a screwgate. Untie the locked-off belay device and check that the French prussik is holding.

△ **4** Your second can then pull on the loop running down to them while you pull on the rope coming back up. Keep an eye on the French prussik; they can let you down.

MECHANICAL ADVANTAGE

In technical terms the assisted hoist gives a 3:1 mechanical advantage, and the advantage of both climbers pulling on the ropes. The French prussik gives a one-way braking system, so the leader and second can take a rest. Watch the prussik closely. If it is too tight it will jam in the system and if it is too loose it won't grip the main rope. In theory, the assisted hoist can be used where the second is less than 15 m (50 ft) below the leader, although in practice it can be difficult to get the rope in position and communicate effectively at this distance. When the system is established there are three lengths of rope between both climbers – and there is generally only 50 m (165 ft) available. If the climbers are more than 15 m (50 ft) apart, can't communicate or have difficulty in getting the rope in position, the unassisted hoist must be used.

UNASSISTED HOIST

The unassisted hoist would be used if you did not have enough rope to send down to the climber who needs a hoist. It would also be used if the climber in question could not assist you in any way (they are unconscious or have received an injury to the arm, for example). Be warned: this is a very tiring exercise to undertake, and you may find it easier to lower rather than to hoist.

① Lock off the belay device and attach the French prussik (or auto-block) as in the assisted hoist.
② Tie a further prussik on the main rope. Attach the loop of rope (which in the assisted hoist would have gone to the second climber) via two snaplink (back-to-back) or screwgate (locking) karabiners. This will give a greater radius for the rope to run round and reduce the friction.
③ Slide the second prussik down the rope as far as possible with the foot. Now untie the locked-off belay plate, again ensuring the prussik is working effectively and pull on the tail.

The Z system, or 3:1 ratio, is exactly the same as before but over a much shorter distance, so the autoblock (brake) will be needed after each pull while the lower prussik is pushed down ready for the next hoist. Always keep hold of the "tail" of the loop and keep a watchful eye on both prussiks.

△ **1** *Lock off the delay device and attach the French prussik (or autoblock) to the rope loop around the harness.*

△ **2** *Place the second prussik around the main climbing rope and clip in a loop with either a screwgate (locking) karabiner or two snaplinks to increase the radius and decrease the friction.*

△ **3** *Slide the second prussik down the rope with your foot until you can make an effective pull. The procedure may have to be repeated several times because the casualty can only be moved a short distance at a time.*

Escaping the system

You may need to get out of the belay and free yourself from the rope to go and get help in the event of an accident or abseil (rappel) down to your partner to render first aid. This is a serious situation, especially if the injured climber is hanging by their harness in free space and is unconscious. This is a worst case scenario, for in this situation you will have to act very quickly to prevent them from suffocating as they hang backwards.

ANCHOR WITHIN REACH

The use of the Italian hitch in this situation should allow you to either lower the casulty or set up a 3:1 hoist to pull them up to the stance, once their injuries have been dealt with. When you have escaped the system, you can either abseil (rappel) or prussik to your casualty, or get help.

△ **1** *If you decide that you need to escape the system, first stabilize the weight of the climber on the end of the rope.*

△ **2** *Lock off the belay plate and confirm that you can reach the anchor by touching it.*

△ **3** *Now put a French prussik just below the belay device and attach this to the anchor with a sling and screwgate (locking) karabiners, and weight this.*

△ **4** *Take the main rope, released from tension by the prussik and sling, and attach this to the anchor via an Italian hitch that is tied off to a screwgate (locking) karabiner.*

△ **5** *Release the French prussik and remove it. The weight will now be off your harness. Retrieve any gear not needed. Protect yourself with a cow's tail and escape from the system.*

Anchor out of reach

If the anchor point is out of reach, proceed as with the anchor in reach, but taking several extra steps as shown in the sequence here. If you are working with a single anchor point, it should be possible to transfer everything to the main anchor point and retrieve the rope. Otherwise, with one end of rope trapped in the system, you may have to prussik down the loaded rope to reach the casualty – unless, of course, you have some spare rope with you.

▷ **1** *Lock off the belay device and tie a French prussik on the load rope. Tie a Klemheist prussik with a tape sling around the main belay rope. Attach a screwgate (locking) karabiner and connect the two prussiks with a sling.*

△ **2** *Create an Italian hitch and clip this to the Klemheist with a separate screwgate karabiner. Release the belay plate (gently) and pull the spare rope through the Italian hitch.*

△ **3** *Lock off the Italian hitch in the Klemheist and make yourself safe with a cow's tail. You can now untie and escape the system. Leave a knot in the end of the rope, just in front of the Klemheist.*

△ **4** *Take the rope back to the main anchor and use a tied-off Italian hitch to secure it. Don't hesitate to back up the main anchor if there is any doubt.*

△ **5** *Both prussiks can now be released so the load is transferred to the Italian hitch on the main anchor. Where there are several belay points, tie a Klemheist around all the ropes.*

Accompanied abseil (rappel)

▽ *An accompanied abseil (rappel) in action. This can be a particularly useful technique where either minor injuries are concerned or the casualty is nervous of abseiling.*

This is not as difficult as it sounds and can be used to introduce beginners who are simply nervous of abseiling or situations where there is an injured person to assist down the crag. Accompanied abseils can be done on either single or double ropes but due consideration must be given to the combined weight of two people on the abseil device and extra friction may be required.

HOW TO GO ABOUT IT

Tie an overhand knot in the middle of a long 2.5 m (8 ft) sling and clip the abseil (rappel) device via a screwgate (locking) karabiner into both halves of the sling. One end of the sling is for each abseiler and the control rope is taken by the person in charge of the abseil. A French prussik on the leg loop is essential and if extra friction is required use an Italian hitch on the load-bearing loop of the harness. The position of the casualty can be adjusted by changing the position of the overhand knot in the sling. If the knot is in the middle they will be alongside. If the knot is moved 50–70 mm (2–2¾ in) one way with the controller on the longer end the casualty will be above (across the lap) of the controller. On steeper ground it should be possible to straddle the casualty and put them face outwards, which is particularly useful if they have sustained a lower leg injury. A quickdraw clipped between the load-bearing loops on the harnesses should ensure the casualty's back is clear of the rock. It is worth noting that a close eye can be kept on the casualty when using this method, which is a distinct advantage.

ABSEILING (RAPPELLING) PAST A KNOT

If it is known there is a knot or damaged area within the rope, attach a French prussik above the abseil device, ensuring that it stays within reach (you can use a quickdraw). Three hand-widths above the knot, lock the French prussik off and apply a second abseil device or Italian hitch to the harness and lock off before removing the first one. By releasing the French prussik it should be possible to continue with the abseil. Before you do so, make sure that you reposition the French prussik on the leg loop.

LOWERING PAST THE KNOT

For whatever reason you need to lower your partner off a crag, you can combine the length of two ropes tied together to get maximum distance. It will entail lowering past a knot. Equally, if your rope has been damaged and you want to lower someone, you will have a knot to pass. Tie a simple overhand knot at the damaged area, thus eliminating it. Lower the casualty until the knot is three hand-widths from the lowering device and apply a French prussik with a 1.2 m (4 ft) sling to the anchor. Thread a second lowering device or Italian hitch, locked off above the knot. Remove the first lowering device and release the French prussik temporarily to allow the knot to pass through. Then continue lowering.

△ **1** *Join the ropes with either a double fisherman's or an overhand knot. Lower the casualty down until the second rope, which is already tied on, appears.*

△ **2** *Apply a French prussik, using a 1.2 m (4 ft) sling to allow sufficient freedom of movement and lock the lowering device off.*

△ **3** *Thread a second lowering device or Italian hitch on to the second rope above the knot and lock this off.*

△ **4** *The first device can now be removed. This will introduce a little slack into the system but if the French prussik is released slowly the weight will eventually come on the second device.*

△ **5** *Remove the French prussik temporarily to allow the knot to go through the system and continue lowering as before.*

Dealing with traverses

Traverses present the leader with a variety of problems. They not only have to protect themselves, but they should also be thinking about how best to protect their second when they come to climb the pitch. If something goes wrong while the second is on the traverse, then these problems become considerable. For example, if a second is unable to make the moves on a straight up and down pitch, or is injured, then the leader can arrange to hoist them over the difficult move (see page 208) or right up to their stance if necessary. But in the case of a traverse the leader's belay is not directly above the second. A hoist becomes much more problematic. However, there are solutions.

● THE STAGES OF TRAVERSE RESCUE

These diagrams clearly show the main stages in performing a traverse rescue.

A – Leader's harness
B – Anchors

C – Clove hitch
D – Second's harness

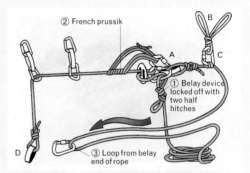

② French prussik
① Belay device locked off with two half hitches
③ Loop from belay end of rope

△ **1** *Tie the belay plate off and apply a French prussik to the load rope. Now take a loop of rope from the belay end, that is direct from the anchor, and throw it to the casualty.*

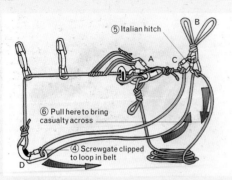

⑤ Italian hitch
⑥ Pull here to bring casualty across
④ Screwgate clipped to loop in belt

△ **2** *Instruct the casualty to clip this to the main load-bearing loop of the harness with a screwgate (locking) karabiner. The other end goes to an Italian hitch on the main anchor.*

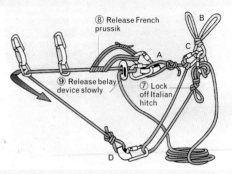

⑧ Release French prussik
⑨ Release belay device slowly
⑦ Lock off Italian hitch

△ **3** *Pull the loop as far as possible then lock off the Italian hitch. Now release the French prussik, allowing the tension in the rope loop to swing the casualty across.*

△ *Any route that contains a traverse can present both the leader and second with a problem. If a climber falls off while either above or below their partner it can be fairly easy to sort things out. If however the climber falls off on a traverse the situation will require a little more cunning.*

THE STAGES

Lock off the belay plate and apply a French prussik immediately behind the plate. If the casualty is relatively close, a couple of slings tied together is the answer. Simply throw one end and pull them aboard. It may be necessary to release the belay device a little and give enough slack rope for them to reach the stance. If the casualty is 7–10 m (20–30 ft) away, lock the plate off and apply a French prussik as above, and throw them a loop from the belay end of rope so the rope is going from the anchor to the casualty and back to the belayer. Make sure there are no twists in this loop and get them to clip this to the load-bearing loop on

their harness. Do not use the rope loop on the harness in this case. Create an Italian hitch in the rope that is running back to the belay and attach to the main anchor. The casualty can pull on the loop going towards them while the belayer pulls on the loop and ties off the Italian hitch when no more of the loop can be pulled in. The next step is to release the French prussik on the belay plate slowly so the tension in the loop swings the casualty towards the belayer. Lock off the belay plate and repeat the procedure, pulling on the loop, to bring the casualty to a point alongside or just below the belay.

IN EXTREMIS

In extreme cases where a loop will not reach the casualty, it may be necessary to escape the system and throw the end of rope to them and then proceed. A lateral strain will be applied to any running belays and, if they fail, the casualty could pendulum rapidly towards the anchor. Once the casualty is pulled in, the original end to which they were attached can be untied, the rope retrieved and an abseil (rappel) retreat undertaken.

PRUSSIKING UP A ROPE

△ **1** *Two prussiks are used to ascend the rope, one tied above the other. You can use Klemheist or original prussiks. The top one is connected to the harness and the bottom one, via a sling, to the foot.*

△ **2** *Sit back in your harness and weight the prussik connected to your waist. Move the foot prussik up the rope.*

△ **3** *Now weight the foot prussik by standing in it. Move the freed waist prussik up the rope and weight that in turn. Repeat the procedure to the top.*

6

ADVANCED TRAINING

Rock climbing is being swept away by training hysteria. You only have to listen to a conversation at your local climbing wall or open one of the many climbing magazines to see just how much technical jargon and hype surrounds this controversial and fashionable subject. Gone are the days of pints of beer and pull-ups; today's climber speaks of plyometrics, intervals and super-compensation. To the average climber who aspires to improve their performance, the amount of conflicting views and information on training can prove overwhelming and, indeed, most climbers will use this as an excuse simply not to bother and to continue climbing in the same manner. This chapter seeks to clarify matters.

Opposite: *Rock climbing can be a serious business. Hard training and hard moves are the order of the day.*

Putting more in

The majority of climbers will experience a steady and satisfying rate of progress through the lower grades and up into the middle grades, simply by putting the time in on the crags and then using the wall on a fairly random basis during the winter season. However, regardless of our own individual base level of talent, we will all eventually reach a point where it simply is not possible to improve our performance any further without adopting a slightly more organized and self-analytical approach. Training does not mean taking the enjoyment away from climbing; it enables you to get more out as a result of putting more in.

A SYSTEMATIC APPROACH

Climbing is a complex, multi-faceted sport consisting of many subcomponents which contribute to overall performance. In your new systematic approach, you must think of climbing performance as a chain whose weakest links will hinder you far more than the stronger links will assist you. For example, it is

△ *Steep bouldering develops strength and power and refines technique.*

▷ *For gaining mental control and crag skills, there's no substitute for sharp-end experience.*

irrelevant how strong your arms are if your fingers are too weak to connect you to the rock. It is equally irrelevant how good you are at bouldering indoors when it comes to completing a long, arduous multipitch route on a remote mountain crag.

PRIORITIZE YOUR GOALS

Having examined your strengths and weaknesses, you must then offset them against your overall aims in climbing. It may be that you have no desire to be good at slabs and are content to dangle on overhangs from your marsupial-like arms for the rest of your climbing career – in which case, so be it, but never lose sight of the fact that the gaps in your performance will only widen as you hone in on your strengths and ignore your weak points.

PLAN TO BE FLEXIBLE

Fitting climbing and training in with all the other factors in your life can be a difficult task at times. Having determined what you want to achieve, both in the short, mid- and long term, you must then identify the key areas of training and practise what you will need to focus on in order to achieve those goals. Your approach should then prioritize those areas on an overall basis but not concentrate on them exclusively. For example, if your aim is to improve your ability to do long routes by training stamina and focusing on your on-sighting technique, don't become so channelled that you miss out on that long weekend's bouldering holiday with your friends. A balanced approach to climbing should accommodate minor day-to-day variations and changes of plan. After all it is unlikely that these deviations will disrupt the overall momentum of your program. If you are forced to take a week off in the middle of an intensive training phase, either through work or illness, worry not – it is incredible how often an unexpected break can motivate you to put that much more effort into the final part of the phase.

▷ *Your ability to remain relaxed on long, sustained routes can be significantly enhanced by specific endurance training.*

Periodized training

Those who wish to obtain maximum benefit from systematic training may wish to organize their climbing year into a periodized cycle. Periodized training is the term given to the use of a series of planned training phases (or microcycles) to provide momentum and emphasis towards a final peak. These microcycles may be anything between 3 and 12 weeks in length and they may show a specific bias towards a particular area of climbing fitness. For example, a so-called "strength phase" may consist of three sessions (or units) per week of bouldering and one unit per week of stamina training. The idea is that strength is emphasized and improved while endurance is simply maintained. If the endurance sessions were to be excluded then losses in fitness could be expected. Similarly a year's training (which can be regarded as a macrocycle) may be organized to achieve a particular degree of training emphasis, just over a longer time period. If your aim is to achieve a "balanced" performance peak (with equal emphasis on strength and endurance) then your yearly macrocycle could consist of consist of four strength microcycles and four endurance microcycles. Alternatively, if your aim is to focus more on your strength and bouldering ability during the climbing year, then you may choose to conduct six strength microcycles and two endurance microcycles in order to prioritize the overall macrocycle towards a strength peak. Again, this may sound far too rigid and organized to those who are used to adopting a carefree, random approach to climbing, but remember that it does still allow you to simply go climbing and have fun!

◁ *A balanced climbing program could combine short power problems at the crag . . .*

▷ *. . . with longer endurance circuits on the indoor wall.*

Physical training principles

Climbing is not like weightlifting, and stored strength or endurance are useless unless you have the technical ability to utilize them. Gymnasts always incorporate a high skill element into their physical training and climbers are well advised to do the same. The age-old cliché that "the best training for climbing is climbing" still holds true up to a point.

PROGRESSIVE OVERLOAD

It is always tempting to start a new training phase by launching straight in and pulling as hard as you can on your hardest routes or boulder problems. Yet every prolonged period of training should start with a light foundation of easier climbing to prepare your body for the more intensive sessions that are to follow and to help you avoid injury. By increasing the overload (the term used to describe the level of healthy training stress) gradually and progressively, you will also avoid burning out prematurely and be able to stay at a peak for longer when the phase is complete.

UNDER-RESTING

Over-training has become a less popular term with sports coaches as it can act as a deterrent from hard training. The secret is to train hard but rest well. Ensure that you allow your body enough rest between training sessions; in doing this you must take into account not only the intensity of training but the type of climbing from which you are recovering (most climbers need to rest longer after strength training than endurance training). You must also take sufficient rest between longer training phases to allow complete mental and physical rejuvenation. A week of complete rest or light activity every two to four months will usually suffice.

◁ *Stay hydrated and energized both before and during climbing. Sports energy drinks and bars are a convenient solution.*

● LEVEL 4 SYSTEM

This system ranks training sessions according to their level of intensity or severity, level 1 being the easiest and level 4 being the hardest. A level 1 session barely allows you to break sweat and actually helps the body to recover by encouraging blood flow and gentle excitation of the muscles. A level 4 session would be an all-out fight, involving hours of gruelling training and climbing. The idea is that you use these rankings to assess what type of session you should have the next day, and in turn, how much recovery you need. You can also use this system to prevent yourself from going too hard in the early stages, and to allow you to attempt progressively harder sessions with correspondingly less recovery time as the phase progresses and you gain the fitness to cope. This process is known as progressive heightening.

Sample use of the level 4 system to achieve progressive heightening of a training phase (r = rest):

Week	Monday	Tuesday	Wednesday	Thursday	Friday	Saturday	Sunday
Week 1	3	1	2	r	3	2	r
Week 2	3	2	r	3	1	3	r
Week 3	4	r	2	3	1	3	1
Week 4	4	1	3	2	1	4	r

TRAINING LEVEL

Structuring your training

▷ *Dynamic moves on steep ground require a potent combination of arm power and finger strength.*

Another important training principle for climbing is to try as far as possible to structure your various different types of climbing workout in the correct chronological order so as to maximize their respective training benefits. For example, many climbers feel that it is both possible and worthwhile to have a quality stamina training session after a relatively hard bouldering session (whether it is in the same day or the following day), whereas to attempt to boulder after getting completely pumped on longer routes would be a waste of time and energy. The rule of thumb is to precede longer, less intense climbing with shorter, more intense climbing although you will need to experiment to see if this works for you.

PHYSICAL TRAINING

In this section of the chapter we will presume, hypothetically, that we have all developed perfect climbing technique and supreme mental control. The reality could not be more different, yet if this were the case then further improvements in our performance could only come from training our body's relevant energy systems which provide us with specific local muscular strength and endurance for climbing. That is to say, we will be focusing purely on gaining stronger and fitter muscles and tendons for climbing, with less regard to how we should actually use them most efficiently.

STRENGTH AND POWER TRAINING

Strength and power are the physical components of climbing performance which are required to execute short, hard crux moves or boulder problems. The predominant muscle and tendon groups affected are those of the fingers, forearms, upper arms, shoulders,

● PHYSICAL SUBCOMPONENTS OF CLIMBING PERFORMANCE

SUBCOMPONENT	VARIABLES
Finger strength	Finger angles / hold type
	Contact strength / hanging
Arm strength	Arm position / move type
	Isometric (static) or Isotonic
	(dynamic)
Anaerobic endurance	Move type / rock angle
Specific aerobic endurance	Move type / rock angle
	Rest availability

△ *In a campus board move, the arms work isotonically and the fingers work isometrically (see pages 226-7).*

◁ *Use strength and power training to help you tackle those hard crux moves.*

▽ *Finger strength is the most important aspect of overall climbing strength.*

upper back and, to varying extents, the lower torso. Although leg strength is of great importance for climbing on low-angled rock, most climbers find that their legs are sufficiently strong to attempt the majority of climbs in comparison to their fingers and upper body.

CLIMBING STRENGTH DEFINED

There are two main types of strength in climbing. Crudely defined these are: isotonic strength, which is the ability to make controlled movements against high resistance forces (for example when pulling up), and isometric strength, which is the ability to hold static positions (for example, in the fingers when holding a hold, or in the arms when "locking

off"). It must be made clear that finger strength is by far the most desirable type of climbing strength; after all, the fingers are the last connective link in the chain through which all other forms of bodily strength are channelled.

CLIMBING POWER DEFINED

Power in climbing is simply the ability to perform extreme dynamic moves at high speed when required. In these situations, sufficient upward momentum must be generated not only to gain sufficient height to reach the next hold, but in order to create a state of "split-second weightlessness" within which to latch on to it. This technique is sometimes known as deadpointing.

Strength and power (1)

Having outlined the basic definitions and concepts of strength and power for climbing, the rest of this section will deal with the most popular methods that are used by climbers to improve this vital aspect of physical performance.

BOULDERING

Bouldering is by far the climber's greatest weapon for developing strength and power in combination with climbing technique.

▽ *Variety is the spice of bouldering! Train at different angles and experiment with different holds and moves.*

However, to obtain maximum benefit from your boulder problems it is vital to be aware of the great number of training variables that can be incorporated. For example, if your aim is to improve finger strength then don't climb on a wall that is so steep that it only enables you to use huge jug handholds. Conversely, if your aim is to work your arms then make sure you use large but well-spaced handholds and the smallest possible footholds. The most important principle of bouldering is to use different training facilities with different types of holds and surface angles and to vary the types of problems that you try.

This can be achieved according to the following guidelines:

① **Vary the handholds**
Full crimp, half crimp, hang (open hand), sloper, pinch

② **Vary the type of moves**
Pull-down, undercut, side-pull, reverse side-pull

③ **Vary the number of moves**
2–4 moves – for maximum strength and muscle fibre recruitment
4–8 moves – for core mid-range strength work
8–16 moves – for the link between strength and anaerobic endurance

You can use a pyramidal structure with your bouldering, starting first with the shorter problems with harder moves and finishing with longer problems with easier moves in order to train in the correct order for optimum physiological adaptation. The most important thing is to take rests between attempts to maximize the quality of work.

SYSTEM TRAINING

Developed by legendary British training guru Matt "Smythe" Smith, system training is an advanced concept which enables you to apply systematic training principles to bouldering. It requires a specialized purpose-built training facility with the holds laid out in a uniform grid or ladder plan.

The idea is to be able to create boulder problems that enable you to repeat a series of identical moves in such a way that taxes a set sequence of climbing muscles repeatedly and to the point of absolute failure.

ISOLATION EXERCISES

For those climbers who find that they have a major deficit in either finger or arm strength, it may be worth performing some additional specific exercises that enable you to target your weak areas much more specifically than is possible with general bouldering. Note that these exercises should be used as a supplement (as opposed to a substitute) for bouldering.

① Finger isolation exercises

Deadhanging – This is simply a straight-armed static hang, performed most conveniently on a fingerboard with one or both arms (subject to ability) for a time duration of between 2–12 seconds. Select a hold that you can only hang from for 2–4 seconds and then work with it until you can hang from it for 8–12 seconds. When you have achieved this then move on to a poorer hold. It is important to experiment with different types of holds but beware of those that exert damaging "tweaks" on your joints or tendons.

② Arm isolation exercises

Pull-ups on a bar – The most basic exercise for building specific arm strength for climbing performed with one or two arms (and with additional weight if required) for between two and fourteen repetitions.

Travelling pull-ups – Perform as above, but move from one side to the other at the top of each pull-up.

△ *Footless bouldering is a superb high-intensity exercise for building specific strength and power.*

Bachar ladders – With this classic armblasting exercise, an overhanging rope ladder is tensioned off and climbed (with a foot for assistance, foot free or with additional weight subject to ability) for anything between two and fourteen repetitions.

Isometric locks – To train your ability to lock your arms statically, simply use a bar with one or two arms (and extra weight if required) and experiment by holding three positions (fully locked, 90 degrees and 140 degrees) using the same time guidelines as for deadhanging.

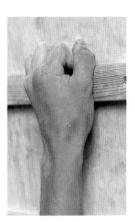

△ *A full crimp.*

△ *A half crimp.*

△ *An open-handed hang.*

Strength and power (2)

Note that those with a major overall weakness in upper body strength may benefit from a more general strengthening program. However it is important to seek appropriate advice and to avoid exercises or repetition structures which may cause you to gain excessive and unwanted muscle bulk.

ABDOMINAL AND LOWER BACK TRAINING

Climbing on steep rock requires a great deal of strength from the abdominal muscles, especially when attempting to lift your feet up to get them on to the rock. Certain extreme moves where you are stretched out a long way from your footholds also require what climbers sometimes refer to as body tension. This is the ability to keep your torso stable by using a combination of the abdominal and lower back muscles. Of course, this type of strength will be developed simply by climbing on steep rock but those who consider that they have a major weakness in this area may wish to perform the following additional exercises.

Abdominals

Crunch sit-ups – Lie flat on your back with knees bent and then curl your torso up to your knees.

Hanging knee raise – Hang from a bar and lift your knees up to your chest, keeping your legs bent.

Lower back

Hyper extensions – Lie flat on your stomach, hands behind head, and arch your spine upwards taking great care not to overstrain.

△ *A laddering sequence on the campus board.*

Advanced high-intensity strength and power training

For those who have already gained a good base level of strength and power, the following exercises can be used occasionally and cautiously to help you gain higher levels of strength and power than are possible with conventional bouldering. But be warned, it is vital to warm up thoroughly and to treat these exercises with extreme caution.

Footless bouldering

The first and most obvious high-intensity exercise is simply to climb boulder problems on a steep wall without using your feet. This is a superb way to hone your strength, power and neuromuscular co-ordination for hard climbing.

Campus boarding

The campus board is a gently overhanging wooden board which is climbed footless using fingertip rungs that are spaced at uniform intervals. Developed by the late legendary German climber Wolfgang Gullich, Campus boards are perhaps the most advanced and highly intensive training facilities that have

been used to date for developing extreme finger strength and upper body power. There are three main exercises:

① *Ladder climbs*

Simply start footless and climb to the top of the board, using the widest possible rung spacings and without matching hands on each rung.

② *Touches*

Start from the bottom rung, pull up as fast as possible, touch a high rung, drop back down and catch yourself on the low rung again. Repeat, leading with alternate arms until failure.

③ *Plyometrics (double dynos)*

A highly advanced and specialized exercise which was converted from training principles used for sprinting to develop the elastic response in relevant muscles to negative climbing movements. Start with both hands on a high rung, drop with both hands simultaneously and catch yourself on a lower rung (absorbing as much energy as possible with your whole body) and then explode back up again to catch yourself on the high rung with both hands.

Endurance training

Controlling and reducing the dreaded forearm pump is the cornerstone of climbing long sustained routes. You may well have the strength and technical ability to do hard bouldery moves, but if your arms are so full of lactic acid by the time you reach the crux that you can barely hold on to a huge jug then your skills will be entirely wasted. Developing endurance for climbing is as much an aspect of technique as physical fitness. Learning to spot rests and use them effectively is a learned skill, and sometimes even the fittest climbers are caught out by those who have a better eye for a place or a position in which to recover.

Most climbers find it useful for training purposes to split the broad category of "Endurance" into two distinct areas.

△ Endurance training can be developed at the wall by performing traversing circuits.

ANAEROBIC ENDURANCE

This applies to so called "middle-distance" routes which are sustained in difficulty and which are between approximately 15 and 30 moves in length. A typical anaerobic endurance route will have hard moves which will be less than your maximum bouldering capability but far too difficult to allow you to hang around and rest. Typically when you fail on an anaerobic endurance route you will not feel completely pumped with lactic acid; it is more likely that the sensation will be a combination of "pumping out" and "powering out"! Most routes at the average indoor climbing wall of 10–15 m (30–50 ft) in height will fall into this category.

△ Learning to rest takes skill as well as fitness.

△ Steep, sustained, middle-distance climbs demand high levels of anaerobic endurance.

Stamina and aerobic endurance

This is the type of fitness that will be required on long (20–60 m or 65–200 ft) single pitch or multipitch climbs with individual moves that are of a relatively low standard. By definition, it is important that it is possible for you to rest and recover intermittently on stamina climbs as the effort required must be sustained over a long time duration, that is anything in excess of 3–4 minutes. During an ascent of a stamina route you must consciously attempt to "shake out" and flush the accumulating lactic acid out of your forearms. This may be done mid-move with a quick flick of the arm or alternatively by stopping on a rest or good hold for as long as it takes for you to feel more recovered.

▷ *Longer climbs, in excess of 15 m (50 ft), require aerobic endurance – especially if traditional protection has to be arranged.*

● ANAEROBIC AND AEROBIC THRESHOLDS DEFINED

The terms "anaerobic" and "aerobic" refer to the ability of the body's energy systems to make use of oxygen to enable activity to be sustained during prolonged exercise. On longer stamina climbs, the body uses oxygen to take lactic acid (which is the bi-product of the energy production process) from the working muscles and transfer it into the blood stream in order for activity to be sustained. On the shorter, middle-distance climbs, the level of activity is too intense for this same system to be effective and energy must now be provided by a different, non-sustainable system which works in the absence of oxygen. In a process known as anaerobic glycolysis, a chemical called ATP is used and resynthesized within the muscles until such a point where lactic acid bi-products prevent the cycle from continuing. The inevitable result of this is that we fall off.

Anaerobic endurance

The best way to develop anaerobic endurance for climbing is simply to use routes or bouldering circuits of the appropriate length and difficulty in accordance with the criteria given above. However, it is important to gauge the difficulty of the routes so that you are able to complete them as opposed to burning out and falling off on every attempt. You must also allow yourself sufficient rest between climbs in order for you to complete a sufficient volume of quality work successfully.

TRAINING TO FAIL IS FAILING TO TRAIN

Forget the old and outdated cliché, "no pain, no gain". When it comes to anaerobic endurance training for any sport, there is an optimum level of training which must be sustained in order to tax and therefore extend the anaerobic threshold. If you climb until your fingers uncurl on every route, you will overtax your body and burn out before you are able to complete a sufficient volume of work. It is a simple equation: if the routes are too intense then you won't achieve sufficient volume; too much volume and the intensity is compromised.

INTERVAL TRAINING FOR ULTIMATE ANAEROBIC ENDURANCE

Achieving this balance between volume and intensity of climbing would be a nearly impossible task if it were left up to chance or guesswork. It is fortunate for us climbers that this

▽ *This classic 8a route requires anaerobic endurance.*

complex issue is well and truly understood in the more advanced world of mainstream sport. The French competition climbers were the first to realize that anaerobic endurance training can be summarized with one word: intervals. With interval training, you decide on a set route or grade of route, a set number of work intervals, a set recovery time (or rest interval) and then aim to compete all the work, but only just! – or perhaps to burn out only on the very last one. By definition, this means that the first few work intervals will feel relatively easy; but as the session progresses, you will start to feel under increasing pressure, until at the end it will be all you can do to squeeze out that final interval. Hence there is progression within the session and, ultmately, an intensity climax.

GUIDELINES FOR INTERVAL TRAINING FOR CLIMBING

The table below shows a sample interval training structure for combining the length and intensity of climbing work with the appropriate rest times for anaerobic endurance. The idea is to start by using the higher values for rest times and the lower values for the number of intervals, and to achieve the lower and higher values respectively as you gain fitness over time. Remember also to vary the types of routes you use and to use the crag for training as well as using indoor routes and bouldering walls.

△ *Anaerobic endurance also comes in handy for sustained sequences between rests on traditional climbs.*

● **INTERVAL TRAINING**

Suggested interval training layout for the development of anaerobic endurance:

Work time	40 seconds	60 seconds	90 seconds	2 minutes
Approx. no. of moves	10	18	26	34
Rest time	1–2 minutes	3–5 minutes	4–10 minutes	5–15 minutes
No. per session	6–16	5–15	4–12	4–10

Adapted from D.R. Lamb, *Physiology of Exercise*, 1984

Aerobic stamina

When it comes to developing endurance for much longer climbs with easier moves, the process which must be simulated in training is that of flushing out the burning cramp that is induced in fatiguing muscles by lactic acid. In this type of training you must maximize the volume of work at all costs, by using routes of a sufficiently low intensity to enable you to hang in there for as long as it takes. If you make the mistake of training on a route that is too difficult and which requires near-maximum effort, the local muscles are forced to contract so hard that the surrounding capillary network is literally squeezed shut and, hence, blood flow is temporarily restricted. The result is that the process of lactic acid uptake and transfer is hindered rather than encouraged. Stamina climbing is all about the ability to recover on easier ground. So by training at a reduced intensity for an increased duration we can actually increase the density of the capillary network that supplies the local climbing muscles, the result being more efficient use of oxygen and dispersal of lactic acid, a process known as capilliarity improvement.

▽ No situation will test stamina more than a long arduous and committing pitch on a mountain crag . . .

△ . . . except perhaps a long arduous and committing pitch on a sea cliff.

● RECOVERY

As said before, the ability to rest and recover on strenuous ground should be regarded as a technique in its own right. Any of the techniques given previously should be employed to reduce the strain on the arms when attempting to "shake out", though particular attention should be paid to making shifts in body positioning as you recover each arm. For example, if you have two evenly spaced footholds at shoulder-width and two equivalent high handholds, when you take your left hand off to shake it you should shift your body to the right to align your centre of gravity directly beneath your right arm. This will enable you to hang straight-armed beneath it and thus use less muscular force to hold on. You should then shift to the left when you change arms. Breathe slowly and deeply and hang your resting arm down as low as possible. It is vital not to shake the resting arm too vigorously in your attempts to get the blood back into it as this will only cause instability in your body and a resultant strain on the active arm. A gentle and relaxed flicking motion will more than suffice.

▷ *"Shaking out" on a steep sport climb.*

GUIDELINES FOR STAMINA TRAINING

With stamina training you should aim to climb for between 15 and 45 minutes at a time, on terrain which makes you feel moderately taxed, but in complete control. To make this possible, the climbing must be no harder than between approximately 30–50 per cent of your limit. For gauging intensity, a good rule of thumb is that you should be able to stop, chalk up and shake comfortably and hold a conversation at almost any point. You can also experiment by attempting some routes or circuits that have a fairly constant level of difficulty and others that have particular crux sections interspersed with good rests. Always aim to finish in a relatively well-recovered state, almost as if you could have kept going for an hour or two if boredom thresholds had allowed. With the shorter stamina routes or circuits that take between 15 and 25 minutes to complete, you may wish to repeat the efforts between four and ten times subject to your level of fitness or how hard you desire to train on that day. With the longer (25–45 minute) bursts, two to five repetitions will usually suffice. Note that one to three very light 15–20 minute stamina climbs can make an ideal active rest day to help you flush the toxins from your muscles and recover from previous hard sessions.

● STICK TRAINING

This popular method can be used when training stamina on a bouldering wall to help you simulate the effect of climbing on-sight on a route. The idea is for a partner to use a stick to point to the next hold or sequence of holds and for you to work out the most efficient way to climb between them. Obviously this requires good knowledge of your training partner's ability so you can set them a circuit of the appropriate standard.

ROCK AROUND THE WORLD

Rock climbing today is a world-wide passport to adventure. Low-cost air travel has made it easier than ever to be part of the international climbing scene. The experience of visiting far-flung and exotic destinations to climb can be as much, if not more, of an adventure than the sport itself. Exposed to new sights and sounds that threaten to overwhelm your senses, the climbing at times can almost seem like an excuse to be there. What follows is a brief tour around some of the world's most popular climbing playgrounds.

Opposite: *Rock climbing in Thailand – pure delight in a sun-drenched environment above a sparkling sea.*

Britain

▽ Lundy is a small island in the Bristol Channel. Around its granite coastline, it offers brilliant sea-cliff climbing of all grades. The island is approached only by boat or helicopter.

Although small in area Britain has a complex geology that offers a great variety of rock types and climbing venues, requiring a traditionally adventurous style of climbing using natural protection. Bolts are only used on a few crags, mainly featureless limestone. The unreliable weather is as much a feature of climbing in Britain as the wide choice and high quality of the routes.

THE SOUTH-WEST

Devon and Cornwall are home to marvellous sea-cliff climbing. Sennen and Bosigran are impeccable granite crags; the Culm coast offers plenty of excitement on less than perfect metamorphosed shale cliffs; and at Berry Head there are impressive limestone cliffs. Even with ideal tidal conditions, exercise caution if a heavy swell is running on any sea cliff. Most sea cliffs come into best condition from March through to autumn. Inland, Devon has granite climbing on the Dewerstone near Plymouth and the Dartmoor Tors, together with limestone at Chudleigh Rocks, a short distance from Exeter.

THE LAKE DISTICT

In the north-west of England is the Lake District National Park, where it is claimed rock climbing began as a sport in its own right with the ascent of Napes Needle in 1886. There are plenty of roadside crags in the accessible green valleys of Langdale, Borrowdale and Buttermere. Even the high mountain routes on Scafell, Great Gable and Bowfell take little more than an hour to reach from the road. Being a mountainous area, it is one of the wettest regions of England.

THE PEAK DISTRICT

Farther east, close to the cities of Manchester and Sheffield, is the Peak District – Britain's busiest national park. Climbing here is mostly on outcrops although some climbs reach 60 m (200 ft). Limestone crags can be found in sheltered dales and exposed gritstone edges stand stark against the otherwise featureless moorland. Gritstone gives the ultimate intense outcrop outing; jamming, balancy slabs and rounded breaks are all features of a day on grit.

▷ *The Dinorwig slate quarries in North Wales provide a post-industrial backdrop to some fine climbing on a unusual medium.*

NORTH WALES

North Wales has a variety of superb crags all within a short distance of one another, from rocky mountain bastions steeped in history to modern sport crags such as Pen Trwyn with desperately hard climbing. Gogarth is a world-famous sea cliff in the north-west corner of Holy Island just off Anglesey. Many of the routes are affected by the tide and since some parts are colonized by sea birds during the nesting season, a voluntary access restriction applies during this period. The weather on the island is substantially better than in the mountains of nearby Snowdonia. Clogwyn du'r Arddu on the flank of Snowdon is one of the great testing grounds. An outing to "The Black Cliff" is akin to a pilgrimage for some climbers. Its dark gothic grandeur is definitely best sampled in the summer. The Llanberis Pass and Ogwen Valley have classic, naturally protected routes of all grades with easy access.

SCOTLAND

There are plenty of mountain crags offering idyllic seclusion, such as Creag an Dubh Loch, 300 m (1,000 ft) high in the southern Cairngorms, which requires a 2½ hour walk-in. Carn Dearg on Ben Nevis, the highest mountain in Britain, the Shelter Stone Crag above lonely Loch Avon and the tiered sandstone of Torridon's Beinn Eighe will all give memorable outings. Glencoe in western Scotland and Buachaille Etive Mor standing at the entrance to the valley are popular Highland venues. Skye is a beautiful mountainous island out to the west with climbing on rough gabbro. To the north-east of Scotland lie the Orkney Islands and the famous 140 m (460 ft) sandstone sea stack known as The Old Man of Hoy. The sea cliffs around the Isle of Lewis in the Outer Hebrides have recently seen a great deal of climbing development. The best conditions for climbing are found in May and June; any earlier and snow may still be present.

△ *Strong natural lines on the imposing bulwark of Carn Dearg, Ben Nevis, are an obvious challenge to climbers.*

Europe

Continental Europe has some of the best climbing venues in the world. Most areas get warm, sunny summers that last for six months or more, so there is plenty of opportunity to spend long days on hot rock!

SPAIN

Think of climbing in Spain and sun-drenched bolted limestone comes to mind. There is no shortage of areas to choose from: Costa Blanca near Alicante and Benidorm with its holiday atmosphere; Costa Daurada, close to Barcelona; the atmospheric gorge of El Chorro, near Malaga; and the islands of Majorca and Tenerife are all popular destinations. Long adventurous limestone routes can be found in the Picos de Europa. For a radically different experience, try pulling on the pebbles protruding from the conglomerate walls and towers of Montserrat or yarding up the "vertical potatoes" of Riglos.

▽ The Sierra Bernia in the Costa Blanca region of Spain is a Mecca for climbers who enjoy hot rock.

FRANCE

France is the home of "clip and go" climbing. Although it may lack a variety of rock types, there is something for everyone on its endless, mostly limestone crags. The Verdon Gorge in Haute-Provence is one of Europe's premier climbing areas. Its immaculate white walls are set in a position of mind-blowing exposure, a fact you become immediately aware of since the approach to most routes is by abseiling from the rim hundreds of metres above the river that winds along the gorge floor. Routes vary in length from one pitch to over 300 m (1,000 ft). It can be very hot in July and August and too cold for climbing from December to March.

Buoux and Ceuse are also found in this south-east corner of France: two top-quality sport climbing cliffs that provide steep modern test-pieces. Further south, between Marseilles and Cassis, Les Calanques offers year-round sea-cliff adventures or cragging. The wooded sandstone area surrounding Fontainebleau, near Paris, is a Mecca for bouldering. Scattered throughout the beautiful forest are groups of fine grained sandstone boulders. Each area has individually numbered problems and colour-coded circuits representing certain levels of difficulty that lead you from one problem to the next on a grand tour.

ITALY

The Dolomites, a group of limestone mountains in north-east Italy, provide classic and modern routes on an alpine scale but with straightforward access. A unique feature of this region are the Via Ferratas – exposed walkways and ladders protected by cables. Arco, close to Lake Garda, has better weather than the neighbouring Dolomites and offers plenty of roadside crags.

△ *The mountainous Mediterranean island of Corsica is a spectacular climbing get-away. Strangely shaped granite crags, such as Roccapina on the coast, are a stark contrast to the cliffs of its rugged interior.*

◁ *La Chapelle is a good medium-grade route in the Mont Blanc, Chamonix region of France.*

Between Aosta and Turin, the Val Dell'Orco in the Gran Paradiso National Park gives excellent granite climbing. It can, however, suffer from mountain weather, which can restrict access. The Val di Mello in the rain shadow of the Bregaglia Alps is another granite venue and is best known for its poorly protected slabs. July, August and September are the best months to visit these two areas. The Mediterranean limestone of Finale di Ligura, less than 2 hours drive from Nice, allows climbing throughout the year.

SWITZERLAND

Switzerland has many big limestone and granite cliffs set against dramatic mountain backdrops. A high concentration of routes are based around the Furka, Grimsel and Susten Passes. As with the other alpine countries, a lot of excellent rock climbing is to be found that involves glacial approaches. Many of the routes to be found here offer both bolt and natural protection.

● ESOTERIC GEMS

The compact limestone of the Frankenjura, north of Nuremberg in Germany, gives mostly difficult but well-protected climbing. In stark contrast is the excitement guaranteed on the sandstone spires and walls found in the Elbesandstein and Rheinpfalz (below) regions of eastern Germany. Knotted slings are the only protection allowed between occasional widely spaced bolts. The Czech Republic's most well-developed area lies 110 km (70 miles) from Prague. The conglomerate cliffs of Meteora in Greece, with its perched monasteries, are a spectacular setting for climbing. Sport and traditional routes, up to 14 pitches long, can be found. Spring and autumn are the times to visit.

The United States

I t is difficult to grasp the scale and diversity of climbing in the United States. There is somewhere for every season and something to suit all tastes, from sport climbing at Wild Iris in Wyoming to big wall multi-day ascents in California.

YOSEMITE VALLEY

Yosemite Valley in California is the altar stone of American climbing and one of the world's best-known destinations. Famed for its big walls, it also offers good-quality cragging and bouldering. Walkers and tourists arrive in droves to view the glacier-carved features, such as the unlikely split mountain, Half Dome, together with the impressive 1,000 m (3,000 ft) sweep of granite known as El Capitan. This shield of rock has a mixture of

aid and difficult free climbs, inspiring climbers from both disciplines. Sometimes the speed of ascent is the most important consideration. In spring and autumn it is normal to see queues on the classic routes, such as The Nose and Salathé. To escape the heat and crowds, Tuolumne Meadows, less than 2 hours from Yosemite, provides a relaxing and scenic venue for shorter routes on granite domes dotted amongst pine forests, with views to the snowy Sierra Nevada.

In mid-summer the West Coast climbing areas provide cooler havens. Tahquitz, in the San Jacinto mountains, has a mixture of crack and face climbs on granite cliffs ranging between 60 m (200 ft) and 300 m (1,000 ft) in height. Neighbouring Suicide is a south-facing 120 m (390 ft) crag, ideal at the beginning or

▽ Half Dome in the Yosemite Valley is one of the most popular big-wall climbing venues in the world.

by the tree from which it takes its name. There are over 3,500 traditional and sport climbs on coarse granitic boulders between 6 m (20 ft) and 60 m (200 ft) high.

SMITH ROCK

Smith Rock in Central Oregon is a desert area with an unusual geology of soft volcanic tuff, forming complex multi-coloured towers and cliffs. It is best known for its single-pitch sport climbs. The mixture of crack, corners and face routes up to six pitches long rise above low-growing juniper scrub and sage brush. On the horizon, the snow-clad Cascade Mountain peaks can be seen. This venue is best visited in the spring and autumn.

◁ Superb hard crack climbing can be found in the Yosemite Valley. This route is Outer Limits.

▽ Fantastic climbing in a great setting – Smith Rock in Oregon.

end of summer. Set among coniferous forests in the southern Sierra Nevada, The Needles are a quiet summer venue. The climbing is focused on ten semi-independent summits. The characteristic bright yellow-green lichen-covered granite has routes on all aspects between three and twelve pitches long, giving some of California's finest crack climbing.

The steep airy granite of Lover's Leap near Lake Tahoe has a range of routes from moderate cracks to overhanging sport climbs up to 180 m (590 ft) high. Protruding quartz and feldspar dykes band the cliff forming small fingerholds to large ledges. Its north-west aspect offers welcome midsummer shade.

As Yosemite cools off at the end of autumn, many climbers head farther south to Joshua Tree National Monument in the Mojave Desert, where it is possible to boulder and climb through the winter and into spring. Many are attracted by its unique setting, characterized

△ Granite climbing at the City of Rocks National Reserve in Idaho.

RED ROCKS

Red Rocks in Nevada is a West Coast sandstone venue and is a complicated arrangement of crags and canyons cut into a 900 m (3,000 ft) escarpment rising out of the desert. The climbing ranges from short clip-ups to long free routes. The rock can be friable and some descents are complicated. Only a short distance from the gambling showtown of Las Vegas, Red Rocks is highly accessible and most popular in spring and autumn.

On the edge of the Sawtooth Mountains, the City of Rocks National Reserve is Idaho's number one climbing area. A multitude of granite domes and pinnacles give mostly one-pitch sport and traditional routes. At an elevation of around 2,300 m (7,500 ft) it is a place to visit in the summer.

BOULDER, COLORADO

Since the city of Boulder in Colorado has so much nearby rock to climb, it has unsurprisingly attracted a large climbing community. The solid sandstone of the 300 m (1,000 ft) Flatirons, Eldorado Canyon and the granite Boulder Canyon are all within an easy drive. An hour to the north lies Estes Park on the outskirts of the Rocky Mountain National Park. Bordering this runs Lumpy Ridge with its string of accessible granite crags for short excursions.

Within the National Park, mountain routes with long but straightforward marked trail approaches give a remote feel to the climbing here. Some bolted routes exist but most require a full rack of natural gear, route-finding skills and an awareness of mountain hazards. Although not glaciated, snow patches linger into the early summer and violent afternoon electrical storms are common. Much of the climbing is on an alpine scale at an elevation between 3,000 m (9,600 ft) and 4,000 m (12,800 ft), so acclimatization is necessary.

June to September are the best months for a memorable experience on the quality routes of Spearhead, Petit Grepon and the area's centrepiece, the impeccable granite of The Diamond on Long's Peak. Also accessible from Boulder are the long serious routes in the Black Canyon

of Gunnison. The harsh Utah desert is home to the sandstone towers of the Canyonlands and Zion National Parks, revered among climbers for their sustained crack climbs in some of the world's most incredible scenery.

△ *Unique climbing on a unique geological feature – Devil's Tower, Wyoming.*

EAST COAST

The north-east United States has a landscape of gentle slopes with crags set among dense forests, the most popular being the Shawangunks. They can be reached in a ½ hour drive north from New York City. The quartzite escarpment boasts over a thousand one-and two-pitch routes. Mostly naturally protected, they are characterized by steep juggy walls and roofs. Often hot and humid in summer, the Gunks are busiest during spring but perhaps best seen during the dramatic colours of autumn.

Recently very popular with East Coast climbers is the New River Gorge in West Virginia. Along the 24 km (15 mile) sandstone escarpment there is a mixture of more than a thousand single-pitch traditional and sport outings. Spring and autumn are the best seasons to visit.

▷ *Climbing near Boulder, Colorado – an area that has attracted a large climbing community.*

Australia

A ustralia is the flattest continent on earth. It also holds some of the best climbing crags to be found anywhere. Unlike many northern hemisphere venues, heat can be a major problem.

ARAPILES

Australia is home to one of the world's best-known climbing venues: Mt Arapiles in Victoria. Only a half day's drive from Melbourne, a line of brightly coloured quartzite-hard sandstone bluffs above a group of pine trees that shelter the campsite gives classic climbs at all grades. With easy access, good weather and plenty of routes to choose from, it is a deservedly popular destination on the international circuit. The climbs rely mostly on traditional gear with the odd bolt for protection. Spring and autumn are the most popular seasons while shade from the searing summer sun can be found on the walls rising out of the numerous gullies.

In recent years, the Arapiles has had to share the limelight with a group of newly developed crags close by known as the Grampians, offering a variety of climbing styles and settings. The rock is again sandstone although unlike the Arapiles extensive bouldering can be found here and the weather tends to be cooler.

Mt Buffalo Gorge about 300 km (185 miles) north-east of Melbourne in the Victoria Alps is an altogether different experience on coarse granite. The style of climbing can vary from big walls to run-out slabs and flesh-tearing cracks. At an altitude of 1,500 m (4,800 ft), it is an ideal summer cliff.

THE BLUE MOUNTAINS

The Blue Mountains on Sydney's doorstep is a fantastic national park! In the midst of eucalyptus forest a multitude of sandstone canyons and escarpments offer dozens of crags mainly known for their short sport climbs. If only a limited time is available in the "Blueys", then Cosmic County and Mount Piddington are an ideal introduction to the vast amount of high-quality rock to be found. It can be wet and cold here in the winter so best avoided; spring and autumn give the most pleasant conditions.

Australia's premier sport climbing venue is close to the town of Nowra. It is an ideal place in winter when you are feeling strong and the Blue Mountains are too cold. Short and steep, it has a high concentration of hard routes.

▽ Hanging out down under on one of the Arapiles best known routes, Kachoong, offering big holds and plenty of exposure.

Over the state border in Queensland, Girraween National Park is an idyllic venue and well worth a short visit. Set in prime bush-whacking country, the routes are mostly single-pitch with bolt protection on granite domes and curiously balanced huge blocks. At an altitude of 800 m (2,500 ft) the temperature can be below freezing at night.

About 1½ hours west of Brisbane is Frog Buttress, the ideal place to perfect your jamming and bridging techniques. Composed of rhyolitic columns up to 50 m (160 ft) tall, the crag is best-known for its continuous cracks and smooth grooves. There is very little fixed gear as most of the routes follow natural lines. Almost tropical in climate, it is definitely best to visit in the winter (June–September).

South Australia's finest climbing destination is Moonarie, about 400 km (250 miles) north of Adelaide, in the heart of the Flinders Range National Park. Situated on the crater rim of Wilpena Pound in an inspirational wilderness setting are routes of all grades up to 140 m (450 ft) long. Spring and autumn bring favourable conditions for climbing.

△ Mount Rosea in the Grampians offers long climbs high above lush eucalyptus forest.

◁ Cosmic County crag is one of the many sandstone cliffs and canyons found in the "Blueys".

Asia and the Middle East

A s well as being home to the highest mountains on earth, Asia offers great diversity to rock climbers, from the desert of the Middle East to the seaside crags of Thailand.

THAILAND

Thailand, the ancient kingdom of Siam, offers a paradise for climbers in which pocketed limestone walls draped with stalactites drop into the turquoise Andaman Sea. The main

▽ *Routes on the Ao-Nang tower, Thailand, can only be accessed by boat.*

△ *The aptly named Groove Tube is a gentle introduction to climbing on the Phra Nang peninsula, Thailand.*

destination for climbers is the Phra Nang peninsula, with around 300 sport routes within easy reach. Although the Phi Phi islands, a 1½ hour boat ride from Phra Nang, was the first area to be developed for climbing, the fixed protection has not been maintained and the poor condition of the bolts has meant a decrease in their popularity. Phra Nang's beaches can only be reached by boat, usually from Krabi or Ao Nang. Krabi is a 15 hour overland journey south from Bangkok or a 3 hour bus ride from Phuket. The peninsula has accommodation in bungalows across a wide price range; the cheapest bungalows can be found at Ton Sai Bay. In general the climate is a humid tropical one. Mid-November to the end of February is the best period for climbing. It can get very busy over Christmas and New Year.

▷ *In Hampi, India, there is a saying that every stone has a story to tell. For the climber it is like reading it in Braille.*

INDIA

Hampi, a holy village on the bare granite Deccan plateau of southern India, is one of the world's most unusual bouldering venues. It is an extraordinary landscape. Eroded into fantastic shapes, a confusion of huge stones sit piled up and precariously balanced in every direction you look. Many of them are strewn among the ruins that were once the capital of the Vijayanagar Hindu empire, destroyed in 1565. A sense of discovery and exploration still exists for the visiting climber.

CHINA

In southern China the area of limestone towers that rise out of the rice paddies around the town of Yangshuo have been tipped to become an important new climbing destination. A stunning limestone archway called Moon Hill is the main attraction for both climbers and tourists alike. At present the outcrop has 16 one- and two-pitch bolted lines. The middle of October to the end of February is the time to plan a climbing trip here.

JORDAN

The grandeur of the Wadi Rum desert in southern Jordan was first brought to the world's attention by Lawrence of Arabia. Prior to exploration beginning in 1984 to assess its potential for rock climbing, the region and its mountains were largely only familiar to the local bedouin. There are now some 300 routes of all grades on sandstone of variable quality. Original pioneers adopted a policy of using a minimum of fixed gear for protection to preserve the spirit of adventure. Recent excessive bolting has been seen as out of place in a wilderness area that has a timeless tranquillity about it.

▷ *Climbing the Vanishing Pillar in Jordan with the Wadi Rum Desert in the background.*

Africa

t is only recently that rock climbing in Africa has been brought to the attention of international climbers. South Africa and Morocco are already popular destinations; others are still awaiting discovery.

MALI

The Massif des Aiguilles de Garmi, in the Sahel region bordering the southern Sahara, has emerged as the biggest attraction for visiting climbers. This striking collection of five sandstone spires includes the formation known as The Hand of Fatima. The great West African classic, The North Pillar, follows the pinnacled edge of the east face of the tallest tower Kaga Tondo in around 15 pitches. Descents generally involve abseiling (rappelling) and are equipped for 60 m (200 ft) ropes. An incongruous strip of immaculate tarmac passes through the arid plain just below the cliffs, making

▽ *Base camp below The Hand of Fatima; taking advantage of what little shade is on offer.*

access easy. Camping is literally just off the road among boulders up to 15 m (50 ft) high, sporting numerous bolted lines. Hombori, the closest town, is 12 km (7½ miles) away dominated by the squat mass of Hombori Tondo, the highest point in Mali (1,155 m/3,789 ft). Some 140 routes have now been recorded. Many cliffs are under the stewardship of the local village and permission to climb should first be negotiated with the village chief. The Sahel can be ferociously hot so the best months to visit are December and January.

MOROCCO

Between the mountains of the High Atlas and the Sahara Desert in North Africa lies the Todra Gorge, a stunning natural feature of orange limestone standing some 300 m (1,000 ft) high and 30 km (20 miles) long. At its narrowest point it is only 10 m (32 ft) across. The gorge has hundreds of bolted single and multipitch routes with in situ belays. There is a regular bus service from Marrakech via Ouarzazate to Tinerhir (about 7 hours) and then a taxi from here covers the remaining 14 km (9 miles) to Todra. Two hotels close to the gorge entrance not only provide cheap rooms and dormitory-style accommodation but also details of routes. The best times to visit Todra are March to April and September through November. Further superb limestone climbing can be found in the Taghia Canyons of the Central Atlas, with climbs of all grades up to 700 m (2,250 ft) long.

NAMIBIA

The dramatic 600 m (2,000 ft) granite plug of Spitzkoppe is Namibia's big attraction for climbers. This national monument rises out of the Namib-Naukluft Desert to a 10 m (32 ft) wide summit with vast views. The classic route

▷ *The huge granite dome of Spitzkoppe in Namibia is a national monument and a big draw to climbers.*

begins with a meandering line and even a spot of caving before six pitches of mid-grade climbing takes you to the top in about 6 hours. It can be reached by car with a bit of off-road driving and camping is allowed at designated sites, for which a fee is paid to the local community. Bring your own water.

SOUTH AFRICA

Since the end of apartheid a steadily increasing number of climbers have visited South Africa, bringing back reports of world-class climbing on sun-hardened sandstone. Table Mountain with its cableway to the summit dominates the skyline above Cape Town and is home to some great mid-grade lines up to six pitches long. A half-day's drive from there, Rocklands in the Cederberg Nature Preserve has incredible rock formations with sport routes in an exquisite setting and superb bouldering. A couple of

hours drive south from here brings you to the overwhelming rock walls of Wolfberg and Tafelberg. The main face of Wolfberg, about an hour's walk from the campsite, is nearly 200 m (650 ft) high with many multipitch traditional routes on perfect orange rock.

◁ *The spectacular Todra Gorge in the Atlas Mountains of Morocco.*

▷ *South African climbing at its best – Rocklands in the Cederberg Nature Reserve.*

Glossary

Abseil – a method of descending the rope using friction from a belay device or a figure-of-eight descender. The word is of German origin and often shortened to "ab". The French word rappel, "rap", is more common in the USA.

Anchor – A secure point of attachment between the climber and the rock. This could be a wire, sling, nut, thread or cramming device with a karabiner to which the rope is attached.

Altimeter – An instrument used for measuring height above sea level. It works using the differences in atmospheric pressure as height is gained.

Bandolier (gear sling) – A rope or tape shoulder sling (often padded) to which climbing equipment can be attached and easily transferred between leader and second.

Bearing – The direction in which to walk to reach a certain point when navigating.

Belay – To belay: to hold the rope of the person climbing to prevent them going the full length of the rope should they fall. The belay: the location at which belaying takes place. A "good belay" denotes secure anchors for attaching the climber, a "poor belay" less so (see also Stance).

Belayer – The person belaying. The "inactive" climber acts as belayer for the "active" climber.

Belay device – A friction device fitted to the rope and used by the belayer. The device allows the belayer to control the energy generated by a falling climber and arrest their fall.

Bolt – A fixed metal eye through which a karabiner can be clipped for protection when leading, or as a secure anchor for attaching, bottom roping or abseiling. The eye is attached to a rod, which is glued or hammered into a hole specially drilled in the rock.

Bottom roping – A roped system in which the belayer stands at the bottom of the climb.

Bouldering – A general term for climbing without ropes on small boulders or pieces of rock a few metres (feet) off the ground.

Camming device – A mechanical device that can be placed in a crack for protection when leading, or as a secure anchor for belaying, top or bottom roping or abseiling.

Clove hitch – A special knot that is easy to tie and tightens when loaded, but is easily adjusted and untied.

Chock – An old collective word to describe wires and nuts. It comes from the word chockstone, which is a stone or boulder jammed in a crack or gully. A chock is a piece of protection.

Dynamic or dyno – A dynamic or dyno move will involve a directed lunge or jump for a hold. Climbing ropes are dynamic in their nature, absorbing the energy created by a falling climber by stretching.

Edging hold – A positive foothold on which the edge of the rock shoe can get purchase and support, no matter how slight.

Figure-of-eight descender – A friction device used for abseiling.

Figure-of-eight knot – The most commonly used and strongest knot for tying a climber to a belay anchor. However, the knot is difficult to adjust and can be difficult to undo after heavy loading.

Grade – A degree of relative difficulty given to a route. Grading systems vary around the world, but the principle remains the same: that of providing a means to compare difficulty between one climb and another.

Harness – Specially constructed and padded waist belt and leg loops worn by the climber and into which the climbing rope is tied. Massively strong, the harness helps to absorb the energy generated in a fall.

Hold – Anything which can be used by the feet, hands or any other part of the body to aid upward progress.

Jamming – A method of climbing in which any part of the body can be securely jammed into a crack or hole in the rock to aid upward progress. The most common jamming involves the hands and feet.

Karabiner – An aluminium alloy snaplink with a sprung gate most often used to connect the rope with protection when leading and with anchors when belaying. With screwgate (locking) karabiners a special sleeve covers the gate to lock it closed.

Lapse rate – The rate of change in temperature in terms of height above sea level. In most conditions, temperature drops as you walk or climb higher up a mountain. This rate of change will vary depending on weather conditions at the time.

Leading – The process of climbing whereby the first "active" climber on the rope places protection if traditional climbing, or clips bolts if sport climbing, while the second "inactive" climber belays.

Legs – In navigation, a leg is an intermediate stage in reaching an overall destination. For example, in trying to reach your campsite 8 km (5 miles) away, you may, in bad weather, break your journey down into eight legs, each of around a kilometre, going from specific points spotted on your map to the next until you reach your tents and safety.

Lower-off – Most sport climbs have bolts and chains at the top from which the lead climber can be lowered by the belayer.

Magnetic variation – The difference in degrees between magnetic north and grid north, as shown on most maps. This variation will change depending on where you are in the world.

Multipitch – A climb that is longer than one rope length. This implies creating belays as the climb is negotiated, with the leader moving up to the next belay until the top is finally reached.

Nut – A collective word to describe wires and roped nuts. A nut is a piece of protection.

Overhand knot – A knot formed by making a loop and then drawing one end through. It is frequently used to tie off spare rope.

Pacing – In navigation, a means of keeping in touch with how far you are walking when weather conditions provide little or no visibility. Pacing is only used over short distances, up to about 500 m (¼ mile).

Peg – A metal spike with an eye, a peg can be hammered into a crack and the eye clipped for protection when leading, or as a secure anchor for belaying, top roping or abseiling. In the UK pegs are rarely placed when rock climbing, although many remain in place. Corrosion is a problem and they should be carefully inspected before use. Also known as a piton.

Pitch – Climbs that are longer than the climbing rope have to be climbed in stages. Climbers call these stages "pitches".

Piton – See Peg.

Protection – A collective name to describe a bolt, peg, wire, sling, nut, thread or camming device that the leader can clip to the climbing rope for "protection". On traditional climbs protection has to be placed by the leader and removed by the second. On sport climbs the protection is fixed in place.

Prussik – A special knot used for ascending the rope. The knot jams when loaded, but can be moved up the rope when the load is released. They are usually used for self-rescue. Three types of prussik are described in this book: standard, French (autoblock) and Klemheist.

Quickdraw – A loop of nylon tape with a karabiner at each end, it is used for clipping the rope to protection and to facilitate easy movement of the rope through protection when climbing.

Rack – All the protection equipment necessary for two climbers on an average climb.

Rappel – See Abseil.

Rope drag – Unwanted friction created by the rope running over rock and through protection. This usually happens towards the end of a long pitch and can be quite alarming, as the effect is to pull the climber backwards and downwards.

Runner – Short for running belay, which is a technical term for any piece of protection clipped to the rope by the leader.

Seconding – When the leader is securely tied to the belay anchors he or she can belay the second up the climb. Seconding includes belaying the leader, climbing the route second and removing the protection placed by the leader so that it can be used on the next pitch or climb.

Searches – In navigation, a means by which an area of ground can be systematically covered when looking for a specific point or object. Searches are also used when looking for avalanche victims.

Shake out – With exertion, lactic acid builds up, especially in the arm muscles. Hanging each arm in turn and giving it a shake helps to restore blood flow and aids the removal of lactic acid. Anywhere this is possible is called a "shake out".

Shock-load – A sudden unwanted shock exerted on the anchors of a belay or abseil. Shock-loading can cause anchors to fail, which is why it is important to avoid it happening.

Single pitch – A climb that is less than a rope length. In other words, the top of the climb can be reached in one go, without the need to make intermediary belays.

Slack – Slack rope between the climber and belayer is to be avoided as it generates greater shock loads should a fall take place, as well as increasing the distance fallen. However, slack may be needed by the second to remove protection, or by the leader when clippping overhead protection. In this case shout "Slack!".

Sling – A loop of nylon tape, usually factory sewn but sometimes hand-knotted. Slings can be hung over spikes or threaded through holes in the rock and used as protection when leading, or as a secure anchor for belaying, top roping or abseiling.

Smearing – A method of using the foot to maximize friction between rubber and foothold when the hold isn't good enough to give positive edging support. You might also need to smear your hand on a sloper.

Sport climbing – Sport climbs originated in Europe and generally have fixed bolt protection. They have a different ethos and style of climbing than traditional climbs.

Stance – At the end of a pitch the belay may have a good stance or a poor one, regardless of how good the belay anchors are. There may be

excellent anchors, but the stance is a single foothold to stand on, or the anchors may be very poor, but the stance is an excellent, roomy ledge. Most often it is something between the two.

Tape – This is another term for nylon webbing used for quickdrawers, harnesses and slings. Zinc oxide tape is used by many climbers for securing sore finger tendons and for wrapping around the hands to prevent cuts when climbing, especially jamming.

Thread – A situation where a tape sling can be threaded through a feature in the rock and the two loops joined and used as protection when leading, or as a secure anchor for belaying, top roping or abseiling.

Top roping – A climbing system whereby the "active" climber is secured by a rope from above. The belayer may either be below or above the climber.

Traditional climbing – The form of climbing where protection is placed by the lead climber and removed by the second.

Traversing – Any situation where a climber moves horizontally or diagonally to the right or left for a number of moves, or even a full pitch.

Wire – Any aluminium wedge threaded on a wire. In general they are too small for threading on rope or tape. They are used as protection when leading, or as a secure anchor for belaying, top roping or abseiling. Also called nuts and chocks.

Contact Addresses

UNITED KINGDOM
British Mountaineering Council
177–179 Burton Road, West Didsbury,
Manchester M20 2BB

Association of Mountaineering Instructors
c/o MLTB, Capel Curig, Gwynedd LL24 0ET

British Mountain Guides
Capel Curig, Gwynedd LL24 0ET

AUSTRALIA
Australian School of Mountaineering
166B Katoomba Street, Katoomba, NSW 2780

Australian Sports Climbing Federation
GPO Box 3786, Sydney, NSW

CANADA
Alpine Club
PO Box 2040, Indian Flats Road, Canmore,
Alberta T0L 0N0

UNITED STATES
American Alpine Club
710 Tenth Street, Suite 100, Golden, CO 80401

Acknowledgements

No book would be complete without a strong team of writers who not only understand their subjects inside out, but have made decisions in everyday climbing and mountaineering situations based on that knowledge. To that end, the author has been extremely fortunate in having Nigel Shepherd, Nick Banks, Neil Gresham and Ray Wood as co-writers for this book. Thanks also go to Libby Peter for giving technical advice on many of the photographic shoots.

I would also like to thank all those who have either allowed me to trawl through their precious photographic libraries or assisted in providing specially commissioned photographs. These are Ray Wood, Mark Duncalf, Alex Gillespie, Nigel Shepherd, Chris Craggs, Tony Howard, Simon Carter, Graham Parkes, Nick White, David Simmonite and Nick Banks.

George Manley's clear and explicit diagrams have reached the parts that even these excellent photographers cannot reach.

I am grateful to the models Libby Peter, Sam Oliver, Edward Cartwright, Paul Houghoughi, Debbie Birch, Caroline and Simon Hale, Patrick (Patch) Hammond, W Perrin and Gavin Foster; and to Neil Adam and Roger Jones of Bethesda for the loan of historic climbing gear.

Finally, this section would not be complete without a word of thanks to Judith Simons at Anness Publishing and Neil Champion, who had the unenviable task of trying to tie up all the loose ends and deal with a crowd of itinerant climbers who insisted in disappearing to the four corners of the world at the drop of a hat!

The authors and publisher would like to thank the following companies and organizations for their generous help in providing clothing, equipment and facilities:

Troll
Spring Mill, Uppermill, Oldham,
Lancs OL3 6AA (for their harnesses)

Edelrid Safety Products
Shap Road, Industrial Estate, Kendal,
Cumbria LA9 6NZ (for their ropes)

DMM International Ltd
Y Glyn, Llanberis, Gwynedd LL55 4EL
(for their slings, karabiners, chocks, belay devices and rock shoes)

HB Climbing Equipment
24, Llandegai Industrial Estate, Bangor,
Gwynedd LL57 4YH (for their slings, karabiners, chocks and belay devices)

High Places
Globe Centre, Penistone Rd, Sheffield,
Yorks S6 3AE (for their T-shirts and sun hats)

Jagged Globe
45 Mowbray St, Sheffield, Yorks S3 8EN
(for their sweatshirts)

Regatta Ltd
Risol House, Mercury Way, Dumplington,
Urmston, Manchester M41 7RR
(for their fleece jackets and walking trousers)

Royal Robbins UK
16a Mill St, Oakham, Rutland LE15 6EA
(for their clothing)

Schoffel UK
16a Mill St, Oakham, Rutland LE15 6EA
(for their windshell and other waterproof garments)

Sprayway Ltd
16 Chester St, Manchester M1 5GE
(for their windshells, fleece jackets and other clothing)

Stone Monkey
Y Glyn, Llanberis, Gwynedd, LL55 4EL
(for their clothing)

Salomon Taylor Made Ltd
Annecy House, The Lodden Centre, Wade Rd,
Basingstoke, Hants RG248FL
(for their approach shoes)

Plas y Brenin
National Mountain Centre, Capel Currig,
Gwynedd LL24 0ET (for the use of their climbing wall and other facilities)

Index

Photo credits

© Simon Carter: pages 244 and 245 t b.
© Chris Craggs: pages 238, 239 b, 240,
241 t b, 242 and 253 t.
© Male Creasey: pages 5, 11 tl tr, 82 t,
114, 127 and 239.
© Alex Gillespie: pages 10, 100 b, 129 tl,
155, 160 br, 162 t bl, 164 l, 165 t, 171 b,
172 b, 173, 174, 177 tl tr, 179 t, 181 tl tr,
186 tl bl, 189 b, 190, 191, 198, 199 tr and
237 b.
© Neil Gresham: pages 15 tl, 28, 225 tl,
230 and 232 l r.
© Nomad: page 248 b.
© Graham Parkes: page 243 b.
© Nigel Shepherd: pages 11 bl, bc, br, 38 l,
51 l r, 52 t, 53 b, 131 b, 138 r, 156, 157 bl,
165 b, 170, 176, 177 b, 178, 179 b, 180,
182 tl, 184, 185, 186 r, 189, 192, 193,
194 b, 195, 197, 199 tl b, 200 bl, 201,
203 t c b, 236 and 249 t bl br.
© David Simmonite: pages 17 t b, 101 b,
167 b, 168, 219 and 231.
© Paul Twomey: page 16 t.
© Ray Wood: front jacket tl and br;
pages 2 t cl el b, 3, 4 t, 7, 9, 12, 13 tl tr b,
14 r, 16 b, 20 bl, 23 t cr, 35 b, 36 b, 38 r,
39 tl, 43 t, 54, 59 r, 64 l r, 66 br, 67 tl tc tr,
68 l c, 69 tl tc tr bl bc br, 71 tr b, 77 l r, 78,
80 l, 83 tl tr, 84, 85 r, 88 l, 103 t, 106 b,
112 tl, 116, 129 br, 132 l r, 134 r, 137 tr,
138 l, 144, 161 t, 163 t, 166 tl tr, 167 t,
169 tr b, 172 t, 188, 200 t, 202, 217, 218 l,
223 tl, 224, 235, 237 t, 239 tr, 246 bl tr,
247 t and 248.

NOTES

NOTES

N<small>OTES</small>

NOTES

NOTES

NOTES